101
EXTRAORDINARY GAA
OCCASIONS

101
EXTRAORDINARY GAA
OCCASIONS

JOHN SCALLY

Black&White

Black&White

First published in the UK in 2023
This edition first published in 2024 by
Black & White Publishing Ltd
Nautical House, 104 Commercial Street, Edinburgh, EH6 6NF

A division of Bonnier Books UK
4th Floor, Victoria House, Bloomsbury Square, London, WC1B 4DA
Owned by Bonnier Books
Sveavägen 56, Stockholm, Sweden

Cover images © Natasha Barton Photography (Marty Morrissey);
© INPHO/Bryan Keane (Katie Power); © Sportsfile/Brendan Moran
(John Mullane), Ray McManus (Joe Brolly), Barry Cregg (Shane Curran).

The publisher has made every reasonable effort to contact copyright holders
of images in the picture section. Any errors are inadvertent and anyone who
for any reason has not been contacted is invited to write to the publisher so
that a full acknowledgement can be made in subsequent editions of this work.

A CIP catalogue record for this book is available from the British Library.

ISBN: 978 1 78530 523 8

1 3 5 7 9 10 8 6 4 2

Typeset by Data Connection
Printed and bound in Great Britain by Clays Ltd, Elcograf S.p.A.

www.blackandwhitepublishing.com

Charlie Haughey: *Did you ever break any bones while you played?*
Páidí Ó Sé: *None of my own.*

Well I'd sure hate to be out there without one.
John Wayne when asked, on being introduced to hurling,
if he'd like to be out on the pitch himself with a stick

St Croans are coming from the well with a hole in the bucket.
The peerless Shannonside commentator, Willie Hegarty

Pat Flanagan has been in more places than Phileas Fogg.
Joe Brolly

*The referee is so cautious that he plays extra time before
the game starts in case of fog.*
Ger Loughnane

*Hurling and sex are the only two things you can enjoy
without being good at it.*
Jimmy Deane

To Keith Barr, who personifies the extraordinary characters who create the extraordinary occasions in the GAA because of his brilliance on the field and his personality off it.

As a young teacher just out of college, I found myself subbing briefly in Beneavin College, where Keith was doing his Leaving Cert at the time. I never taught him but I learned his name on my first day there because he was already a legend in the school.

I found myself supervising the mock Leaving Cert Irish exam. It was a very solemn occasion. All of a sudden, Keith, who was sitting at the back of the room, put up his hand and beckoned me over. I rushed over to him, expecting him to ask me to translate a difficult Irish word into English.

In a very grave tone, his query was of a very different nature: 'Sir. Have you a woman in your life?'

CONTENTS

FOREWORD

by Dermot Earley

My father was a great storyteller. His speciality was telling stories against himself. One of his party pieces was the one when he was coming out of a match. A man of mature years came over to him and shook his hand. He told Dad: 'You were a mighty footballer. You were the best I have ever seen. There has never been a footballer who could catch a high ball like you.'

Dad was feeling very good about himself and replied: 'Thanks very much. You are very kind.'

Then the man added: 'You kicked the best points I have ever seen.'

By now Dad was feeling twenty feet tall. The man headed back to his car after Dad had thanked him profusely for his generous compliments. Then he turned around and said to Dad: 'But Jaysus, you kicked some shockin' wides as well.'

Despite his intense love for Roscommon, Dad was not above poking some gentle fun at the Rossies. He liked to play the game: what country would a county be based on its GAA team? He said that Meath would be al Qaeda because they took no prisoners.

Roscommon would be Japan – their last great campaign was in the 1940s.

Dad was a fine public speaker and invariably told a joke against himself in each speech. The classic was about the night he was approaching Roscommon town when he saw a teenager thumbing a lift. As it was raining he picked him up. As they got close to the football pitch Dad asked the youngster if he had ever played in Dr Hyde Park. The young man replied: 'A couple of times.'

Dad said: 'I played a few good games here myself. In 1973 Roscommon were playing the All-Ireland champions of the time, Cork, here. The team were just a point ahead in the last minute when Cork mounted an attack and I made the saving clearance.'

The teenager replied: 'I know.'

Dad continued: 'In 1977 I played on with a broken finger and helped Roscommon beat Galway in the Connacht final.'

Again, the young man responded: 'I know.'

Undeterred, Dad persisted: 'I once kicked a 50 against a gale-force wind and landed it over the bar in a match against Down.'

Yet again the young man's reply was: 'I know.'

By now Dad was puzzled and asked his companion what age he was. When his guest replied that he was only sixteen, Dermot asked: 'All those matches were over twenty years ago, before you were even born. How could you possibly know about them?'

The teenager sighed deeply before saying: 'You gave me a lift two weeks ago and you told me the exact same stories then.'

My father would have enjoyed this book.

I hope you will too.

INTRODUCTION

The Throw-in

'Dominics are like a cocktail you get in Spain at three in the morning . . . LETHAL!'

WILLIE HEGARTY

I must begin by saying that it is the honour of my life that this book is endorsed by Barack Obama . . .

He just doesn't know it yet!

This book was conceived as I was suffering from withdrawal symptoms as Ireland became a hermit nation. The coronavirus that cut a swathe of dismay, despondency and despair through the world had a devastating impact on the GAA fixtures.

Then, as we went into lockdown, a new fear colonised me as a terrifying rumour enveloped the Emerald Isle: there was a real danger that we might run out of . . . potatoes.

The really important questions of life could finally be addressed: is The Cure's best song 'Just Like Heaven' or 'In Between Days'?

The pharmaceutical world was frantically seeking an antidote to the virus but I was seeking an antidote to my own existential crisis, which was manifesting itself in a myriad of ways, such as picking my top ten of Impact Subs in the GAA or my top ten of dirty corner-backs. Then I stumbled on one. Or, more accurately, I rediscovered one.

Gaelic games have a serious side. In 2023 the hurling fraternity united to support the Dillon Quirke Foundation, in memory of the Tipperary hurler who collapsed the previous year and died during a match for Clonoulty-Rossmore in Semple Stadium. The project shows the GAA at its very best and seeks to raise €1 million to help screen children from the age of twelve up for heart defects.

However, there are other sides to the GAA. Growing up on a small farm in rural Ireland at a time when we only had black and white television and just one channel, it was a very monochrome existence. We kept Friesian cattle, so even the cows were black and white. Gaelic games provided the colour to light up our often dull, grey lives.

I never thought I would be the sort of person who would get up early in the morning for hours of exercise.

I was right.

Given the severe limitations of my talents on the pitch, I acquired at a young age an enduring interest in the extraordinary side of Gaelic games. My own playing career was summed up by one of my teachers, a clever Christian Brother, who casually informed me: 'You are as useless as a chocolate teacup.' Morrissey would have described me as: 'One of the overly undertalented.'

Hurling is such a skillful game, we should be doing everything in our power to showcase it. I played a bit of hurling myself. I gave it up, though, when one of my teachers was watching me play a game with not great success and he said to me, 'Cut five inches off your hurley.'

'Do you think it is too big for me?' I asked.

He just turned away and said, 'No, but it will fit into the bin much easier.'

I promise I didn't cry afterwards. It was just that my eyes were sweating.

The Christian Brothers also gave me a deep love for maths, though I stopped studying the subject when I was sixteen. This year, Prime Minister Rishi Sunak announced that he wants all pupils to study maths until they are eighteen. For the life of me I can't see the need for them to study the subject for three years more than me.

Does this book serve a serious purpose? To quote that well-known authority on the GAA, the eighteenth-century Ulster philosopher and Presbyterian minister, Francis Hutcheson: 'Men have been laughed out of faults which a sermon could not reform.'

It is three years after 2020, so we enjoy perfect vision.

Nonetheless, I have taken a very elastic notion of 'occasions' for this book.

Discretion prevents me from naming the inter-county footballer who went to confession and said, 'Bless me Father for I have sinned. All day I hear a voice in my head telling me what to do. Am I possessed by the devil?'

The priest softly replied, 'No, my son. You're married.'

I will also take to my grave the name of the GAA legend of whom Páidí Ó Sé said to me: 'You can trust him with your life. But not with your money or your wife.'

Likewise, I will not disclose the current prominent inter-county hurler and big Beyoncé fan who agreed, in a drink-induced moment, to go on a date with a woman who, to put it kindly, did not look like Beyoncé. In panic, on the evening of the date he drove to the local hospital and took a selfie with an old woman who was a patient. He then sent the picture to his date, apologising profusely for having to cancel because he was visiting his sick grandmother in hospital.

Neither can I reveal the name of the hurling star who, when the cashier said, 'Strip down, facing me,' only discovered that she was talking about his credit card when it was too late.

Finally, a few words of warning. My memory is so good that I remember things that never even happened! There are books of truth. There are books of fact. This is not one of them. This will not be a publication for anoraks because my aim is neither veracity nor accuracy. I just want to entertain. Do not expect the truth, the whole truth and nothing but the truth. Instead be prepared for the truth where only the facts have been changed.

History is the enemy of good storytelling.

My basic rule for this book was that the facts should never be allowed to get in the way of a good story.

Welcome to the greatest show on grass.

1

MIGHTY MEATH

Seán Boylan Wins Four All-Irelands

'I wouldn't be surprised to hear that there are small boys in Dublin who believe that Mick Lyons is kept in a cage above in Summerhill and fed with raw meat.'

CON HOULIHAN

There has never been a team as teak-tough as Seán Boylan's Meath side. Seán is one of the nicest people you could meet. Yet he has an inner steel to him. This was something he had to work on after Padraig Lyons told him shortly after he became manager: 'Seán, if this Meath team is to progress, we need you to put your shyness in your arse pocket.'

It was a memorable experience for Boylan. 'I came home one evening and some of the senior players were in my house to work on a blueprint for success. I could hardly see them because our kitchen was covered in a cloud of my mother's cigarette smoke.'

It is said of Mick Lyons: 'Mick doesn't flush the toilet. He scares the sh*t out of it.'

Dermot Earley once joked: 'Death once had a near Mick Lyons experience.'

After Roscommon lost to Meath in the 1991 All-Ireland semi-final, Earley remarked: 'When the bogeyman goes to sleep at night, he checks his closet for Mick Lyons.'

In contrast, Dermot admired Seán Boylan for his intelligence. 'Seán is the only man to have counted to infinity – twice.'

ECONOMICAL

In 1987 Boylan sensationally resigned as Meath manager because he felt that the team needed to make a bigger effort in training. The players asked Joe Cassells to ring him and persuade him to return. The call was made, and a change of heart ensued. At the first training session afterwards, Boylan said, 'I believe I owe you ten pence for the phone call.'

To riotous laughter from the Meath squad, Cassells replied, 'Nah, it's okay, I reversed the charges.'

MY APOLOGIES

Liam Hayes tells the story of one of Meath's team meetings before a big game in Croke Park. It consisted solely of a video compilation of some of the team's biggest hits on opponents over previous years to the soundtrack of Queen's 'Another One Bites the Dust'. No words were necessary. Message received.

As Colm O'Rourke memorably put it: 'People thought of us as big thick f**kers. And with good reason.'

CLOSE MARKING

The Meath–Tyrone All-Ireland semi-final in 1996 was, to use a classic GAA euphemism, 'a robust affair'. The Meath team were criticised for their aggressive treatment of Peter Canavan and some of the Tyrone players. Discretion precludes me from naming the very earnest Meath legend who afterwards apologised in a team meeting for losing his man momentarily in the match. One of his colleagues had the dressing room in stitches – though not the player in question – when he quipped: 'Not to worry. The only reason you couldn't see him was that you had your boot on his throat at the time.'

UNTO US A CHILD IS BORN

Three days before the 1996 All-Ireland final against Mayo, Seán Boylan was on edge. His wife, Tina, was due to have their third child. Tina takes up the story:

'My doctor was a massive Meath fan and absolutely loved Seán. When Seán was visiting me in the hospital the conversation was forty minutes football and then two minutes baby followed by forty minutes football. The big fear we had was that the baby would not be born until the day of the All-Ireland. My doctor intervened and said: "We are going to induce the baby to make things easier . . . for Seán!"

'Every nurse in the ward was from Mayo, so when he was born they wrapped our baby in the Mayo colours. But I was out of the hospital with my new child in my arms for the final and the replay.'

Two Mayo fans marked the occasion with a banner in Croke Park saying: 'Boylan Rocks Baby. Maughan (the Mayo manager John Maughan) Rocks Sam.'

WISE WOMAN

Boylan says he learns something every day from his wife. 'Yesterday she told me: if a man says he'll do something, there's no need to remind him of it every six months.'

MONKISH

Seán Boylan has often spoken in public that as a young man he contemplated becoming a Cistercian monk. Despite his very happy marriage to Tina, he still feels it is a shame he never got the chants.

BREAKING THE ICE

Little things can break the tension for a team. In the strain of an All-Ireland final in 1996 against Mayo, Colm Coyle reduced his teammates to laughter when President Mary Robinson was being introduced to the Meath team before the match. He asked, with intimate familiarity, 'How are things at home?' For the rest of his colleagues, the pressure evaporated immediately.

THE BYPASS

Such was the tension in the 1996 replay, to quote Tommy Tiernan, there were women giving birth who weren't even pregnant.

Meath's win is best remembered for the brawl in the replay, but Seán Boylan's memories are more gentle:

'They were building a bypass on our normal route and I knew that would cause a problem for us, so we stayed in the Davenport Hotel in the City Centre for the game. That meant we had to find a new venue to have a training session and I got permission to have one in Trinity College. Who came to watch it but one of Ireland's favourite poets and one of Trinity's most famous lecturers, Brendan Kennelly, who himself had played for Kerry. He had a lovely chat with us after the session. When the match was a draw, I made the same arrangements for the replay. In the meantime, though, Brendan had a major coronary incident and of course was rushed to hospital.

8

While we were training, on the second day I got a message from Brendan: "Seán, sorry I had to miss your session today. Am on the bypass."'

A HOLY SHOW

For the week after the game there was a storm of controversy about the melee which saw most players on both teams engaging in a mass brawl. To get away from it all, Seán Boylan took his wife Tina to Howth for the weekend. There, they bumped into the former Dublin hurling and football legend, Lar Foley. He was not unduly bothered by the violence. He said to Boylan: 'You'd see more jostling going up to Holy Communion at Mass on a Sunday.'

PURE MAGIC

Seán Boylan is the personification of engaging company. The first time we met, he told me the story of an Englishman and an Irishman who go into a bakery. The Englishman steals three buns and hides them in his pocket. He boasts to the Irishman: 'That took great skill and guile, and the owner never saw me.' The Irish guy, though, is dismissive. 'That's just pure thievery. I'll show you an honest way to achieve the same result.'

He calls over the owner and tells him that he has a wonderful magic trick to show him. He takes three buns and eats them. The owner is puzzled and asks: 'Where is the magic in that?'

The Irish guy replies, 'Just look in the Englishman's pockets.'

Seán also enjoys Marty Whelan's jokes: 'I used to be a grave robber, but I don't like to talk about it. It's just digging up the past.'

SPUDS CRAZY

Seán joked to me that he insisted on eating potatoes for lunch every Sunday. When I asked him why, he answered: 'It's my mash of the day.'

IN SICKNESS AND IN DENIAL

In 2020 Seán was unusually trenchant in his criticism of the Dublin team for breaking lockdown rules during the first Covid lockdown. Other teams were also found to have done so.

With typical élan, Joe Brolly, tongue firmly in his cheek, claimed:

'Down County Board statement on recent events (as released to Joe Brolly):

"In light of recent misinformed speculation suggesting that the Down senior football squad held a training session in breach of the GAA embargo, we are happy to take this opportunity to set the record straight.

"In January, one of our senior players went for an evening walk in the grounds of Abbey Christian Brothers' School with Linden, his golden retriever. As he made his way around the perimeter of the pitches in darkness, he slipped on a water bottle. This in turn activated the floodlights, which are motion sensitive."'

THESE BOOTS WERE MADE FOR WALKING

Martin O'Connell was the one member of Boylan's team who was selected on the official GAA Team of the Millennium. His pride and joy was his football boots. There's many a woman that would have liked to have the kind of attention that O'Connell lavished on his boots. They were always immaculate. At one stage O'Connell's house was burgled while he was away. After his wife surveyed the damage when they returned, she came down the stairs distraught and sobbing, saying, 'My jewellery.

My jewellery.' Martin leaped off his chair. But not to offer comfort to her. Instead, he rushed to check if his boots were safe.

SECOND CHOICE

Another teak-tough defender on that Meath team was Liam Harnan. After his retirement from inter-county football, Harnan managed a club team. Legend has it that after a trial match he selected his first team and his second team. One player, though, was furious when he learned that he was relegated to the second team. He told Harnan how annoyed he was by his demotion and demanded to know why he was only picked for the second team. Harnan stared at him before calmly saying: 'Well it's like this. You're marginally too good to be playing for the third team.'

RAISING THE BARR

In 1991 during the famous four-game saga between Meath and Dublin, Keith Barr 'clashed' with Colm O'Rourke. Such was the damage that O'Rourke had to hobble off and was substituted but he returned to play later on. After the match the two met in the bar. Barr sheepishly said, 'I'm sorry for that challenge, Colm, but I know you would have done the same to me.'

'No, I wouldn't,' replied the Meath legend emphatically.

When Barr looked at him uncertainly, O'Rourke clarified: 'If I had gone for you, there's no way you would have come back.'

DOING THE DOUBLE

The GAA produced a stunning ceremony in 2020 to commemorate Bloody Sunday. In the game that followed, live on RTÉ television, Pat Spillane had confidently predicted: 'Meath, like last year, won't be beaten by sixteen points.' He was right; this time they lost by twenty-one points to Dublin.

NAVAN MAN

The most famous Navan celebrity is Tommy Tiernan. One of his guests on his television show in 2023 was his former geography teacher in St Pat's, Colm O'Rourke. As only he could, Tommy asked O'Rourke: 'All of the times you threw me out of class did you ever think the day would come when I would be interviewing you on my chat show?'

One of the spats of the 2023 Championship featured O'Rourke. He dismissed the criticism levelled at the Tailteann Cup by his former colleague on *The Sunday Game*, Dónal Óg Cusack. The Cork pundit described the competition as 'Gaelic football's Grand National for disappointed also-rans' in a radio interview.

O'Rourke hit back, declaring: 'The gentleman involved; I wouldn't pass the slightest remarks about what he would say about anything.'

The controversy spawned a full-blown shemozzle on RTÉ's *The Sunday Game* programme between Dónal Óg Cusack and Joanne Cantwell. One viewer was prompted to observe: 'In raising the topic, Ms Cantwell allowed Dónal Óg a glorious opportunity to dig himself gracefully out of a hole that he himself had dug. Instead, he chose to dig ever deeper by engaging in semantics that would make the most gimlet-eyed Vatican canon lawyer appear reasonable.'

Then Michael Duignan entered the fray claiming Dónal Óg Cusack's position as GPA (Gaelic Players Association) president was now 'untenable'. Duignan – who is, like Cusack, an RTÉ analyst – took exception to the 'Grand National for disappointed also-rans' comment. Duignan stated: 'The biggest problem I have with his comment is that it is coming from someone who is President of the GPA, one of their founding members. For the President of the GPA to say what he said about football's second tier All-Ireland competition – I think his position is completely untenable. I think he has to go. He clearly has no time for football, for so many of the GPA's own members and all the effort they are putting in.'

THE LIFE OF RYAN

Pat Shortt claimed in *Killinaskully* that, 'There's only one crowd worse than the Black and Tans and that's that shower in RTÉ.'

A young Ryan Tubridy learning his craft in radio was sent for a day to shadow Mícheál O'Muircheartaigh. The Kerry legend brought him to Croke Park, where he was commentating on a big Meath match. When he made his customary pre-match visit to the Meath dressing room, the players had rarely seen anyone as thin as Tubridy in Croke Park. Mick Lyons shouted at Mícheál as he stared at Tubidy: 'Where did you get Muscles from?'

2

THE MAN WHO GRABBED GER CUNNINGHAM'S BALLS

St Finbarr's v Glen Rovers

Tomás Mulcahy was the man of the match when Cork beat Galway in the 1990 All-Ireland final. He has another distinction. He once grabbed Ger Cunningham's balls. He was playing for Glen Rovers in a club match and he went in to shake Cunningham's hand. Ger was playing in goal for bitter rivals St Finbarr's and while he was there Mulcahy ran off with Cunningham's bag of sliotars to stop the Cork legend from taking his customary quick puck-outs.

GIVE A LITTLE RESPECT

According to Tommy Tiernan: 'Fans can be the harshest critics. A wife is often the harshest critic of her husband.'

It is a uniquely Cork tribute to Tomás Mulcahy that St Finbarr's fans told a story about his love life. In their version Mulcahy was very distressed one Saint Valentine's Day. He was quoted as saying: 'I'm very upset. For the last twenty years

14

I have received a Valentine's card every year from a secret admirer but this year I didn't get any. I'm devastated. First my granny died. Now this.'

DON'T LOOK BACK IN ANGER

Sometimes things get lost in translation. A few years ago, Joe Duffy got very animated about the story of a young man from Ireland who was very harshly imprisoned in a prison in Thailand. Joe spent an hour on *Liveline* fuming about human rights in 'a Thai prison'. Afterwards, there was a call from a very earnest woman from Kildare complaining that Joe was mistaken. There is no prison in Athy!

About the same time, St Finbarr's fans claimed Tomás Mulcahy went to the barber and asked to have his hair cut like Oasis's lead singer Liam Gallagher. One Barrs wit remarked: 'He went in for an Oasis haircut but came out with an "Oh Jaysus" one.'

Every time a friend succeeds, something inside me dies, wrote the US-born writer Gore Vidal. For their part, Glen Rovers fans told a story to emphasise the competitiveness of Mulcahy. They claimed that one day Tomás saw his neighbour put out her washing. He rushed out to the clothes line with his own washing. 'How are you getting on, Tomás?' his neighbour inquired.

'We are level pegging,' the Cork legend replied.

WORDS OF DISCOURAGEMENT

The rivalry between Glen Rovers and St Finbarr's did produce one great comic moment when, during a heavy defeat to the Barrs in the 1980s, a Rovers fan shouted out to one of their underperforming players: 'For Jaysus' sake, come off before the score is bigger than the attendance.'

RIGHT AS RAIN

The rivalry between the two teams was put on hold when Cork played. One time when Cork sustained a bad defeat to Tipperary during a downpour, the fans were united in sympathy:

Shocked St Finbarr's supporter: 'Jaysus, the Cork jerseys are so wet the red is running.'

Disgusted Glen Rovers fan: 'They are the only Cork things running in this match.'

LOVE ACTUALLY

Tomás Mulcahy was coached by the late Canon O'Brien to All-Ireland titles in 1984 and 1990. At one stage, the Canon was given charge of the First Holy Communion class in the local primary school where he was faced with a difficult student who was 'acting the maggot'.

He said to him, 'Martin Joe, I love you.'

Martin Joe, for once in his life, was absolutely speechless. Eventually he regained his composure. 'What do you mean, Father?'

'I love you because God says we must love everyone.'

'I see, Father,' says Martin Joe in an uncertain tone.

'I love you, but that doesn't mean I like you.'

Another challenging student was Ashling. The Canon asked her if he knew what her name meant. She told him that it meant *dream*. The canon's reply was: 'Your parents should have called you after a nightmare.'

When he visited a school called St Michael's to speak to the confirmation class, he gave them a passionate talk about the evils of consumerism. Then he asked the students what names they were taking for confirmation. His eyes lit up when Barry Walsh told him he was taking Michael as his confirmation name. 'That's brilliant, Barry,' said the Canon. 'Michael is God's greatest angel and St Michael's is the name of your school. That is the perfect name for you.'

Barry shook his head. 'That's not the reason I picked the name Michael. It's because I always wanted my initials to be BMW.'

The Canon was not overly interested in theology, but he did appreciate canon law: 'The Bible tells us what Jesus said. Canon law tells us what he meant.'

THE CULTURE CLUB

Such was his devotion to the Rebels, the joke was that when Canon O'Brien was performing baptisms it was said he blessed the new baby, 'In the name of the Father, the Son and Cork hurling.'

WET, WET, WET

I met the Canon on a particularly wet day. He quipped: 'Our God rains.'

He was still traumatised because a naked man had broken into his church. The gardai caught him by the organ.

SICK AS A PARROT

Once, Canon O'Brien was greeted at the end of the Sunday service with the frank appraisal of one worshipper: 'That was the worst sermon I ever heard. It was complete nonsense!'

Canon O'Brien, quite disturbed, informed the local bishop what the man had said. The bishop replied, 'That poor chap is not really responsible for what he says. He never has an original thought. He just goes around repeating what everybody else is saying!'

ARISE

Before their first Holy Communion, the canon was hearing children's confessions. He was puzzled to find child after child adding, after the recital of more familiar and intelligible sins, 'that of throwing peanuts into the river'.

Then, to his surprise, the very last boy did not confess that he had thrown peanuts into the river. So, the cleric asked the boy if he ever threw peanuts into the river.

The boy replied in a very puzzled tone, 'I don't understand, Canon. I am Peanuts.'

PROPER PREPARATION

The canon was preparing the pupils in the Ursuline school in Cork for the bishop's visit. A man of habit, the bishop famously asked one question on each school visit, but always the same question: 'Do you know what a pectoral cross is?' Canon O'Brien had the students word perfect on the answer. To his horror, though, the bishop broke the habit of a lifetime and asked the children: 'Do you know what a canon is?'

The pupils, though, only knew one answer so they replied in unison: 'It is the big heavy cross that hangs around a bishop's neck.'

CORK'S MOST FAMOUS RESIDENT

It is not that Cork people have a superiority complex. They just think they are better than everybody else. Hence the story that when Ireland went into lockdown during the coronavirus crisis, God was spotted walking around Cork. When someone asked Him what He was doing, He replied, 'I'm just walking from home.'

IS IT LEO?

At half-time in the 2021 Munster football final, the Cork goal-keeper Micheál Martin (son of the then Taoiseach of the same name) was substituted. Twitter went into overdrive as people in their droves asked: 'Is he to be replaced by Leo Varadkar?'

In May 2023 Leo, back as Taoiseach, found himself answering questions in the Dáil about a huge GAA controversy. A media frenzy began when former All-Ireland winning goalkeeper Dónal Óg Cusack criticised the decision not to transmit some big Munster hurling games free-to-air, alleging that the Munster SHC was being 'exploited' to get the GAAGO platform off the ground. In the GAA's five-year broadcast rights deal, announced the previous October, RTÉ retained thirty-one live championship matches, while streaming service GAAGO was granted rights to thirty-eight games: twenty-two football championship games, nine from the hurling championship and seven Tailteann Cup games. For a second weekend in a row, a major Munster championship clash was not broadcast free-to-air, with Cork and Tipperary broadcast on the GAAGO platform, a joint venture between the GAA and RTÉ. The previous weekend, Limerick were defeated by Clare in a classic in the Gaelic Grounds, also broadcast behind a paywall.

The day Leo was answering questions in the Dáil, Ireland again failed to qualify in the Eurovision song contest semi-final. One wit suggested that Ireland should show the Eurovision final on GAAGO instead of RTÉ as punishment.

MY BALL

During their 2021 All-Ireland final trouncing at the hands of Limerick, one of the Cork hurlers turned to one of the officials on the sideline and asked: 'Can you throw a sliotar onto the pitch?'

The puzzled official replied: 'You do realise that there is a sliotar there already?'

The Cork player replied: 'I know, but the Limerick lads are playing with that one.'

The following year a Cork fan watched Limerick win the All-Ireland again at a time when the country was enraged by the high prices charged by the hospitality sector. She paraphrased Marty Morrissey's famous quote after Clare won the 1992 Munster final: 'There won't be a cow milked in Clare tonight.' Her version was: 'There won't be a tourist not milked in Limerick tonight.'

Marty Morrissey is a big admirer of the toughness of the Shannonside hurlers:

'Mike Houlihan, the Limerick hurler, had his jaw broken by a kick from a bullock two months ago. He's back now. 'Twas some bullock that broke Mike Houlihan's jaw!'

SWIMMING AGAINST THE TIDE

Nine-time All-Star Tommy Walsh is one of the greatest hurlers of all time. Jackie Tyrrell gave a great window into the mindset of Walsh. During the winter following Clare's 2013 All-Ireland win, a group of players found themselves in Wexford for a stag do. Walsh was sharing his obsession with marking Tony Kelly – who was the reigning Hurler and Young Hurler of the Year – in the following year's championship.

The next morning Walsh was up at 8 a.m. He got one of the lads who was on the stag but wasn't drinking to drive him out to the beach in Wexford. He was 'tired and emotional' when he jumped into the freezing Irish Sea shouting, 'Tony Kelly isn't training in the sea in the middle of November. So, I'll be ready for him next year.'

LOVE STORY

The Cats got the cream.

The incredible summer of hurling in 2023 witnessed a first Leinster final appearance for Kilkenny without Brian Cody at the helm since 1998. Their opponents were Galway, managed by former Kilkenny icon Henry Shefflin. RTÉ cleverly in their coverage played Gotye's 'Somebody That I Used to Know' over their footage of King Henry in the build-up. Derek Lyng's side snatched a late victory over Galway at Croke Park to land Leinster title number seventy-five with Cillian Buckley's goal.

Before the 2006 All-Ireland final between Kilkenny and Cork, one Cats fan unfurled a huge banner of Derek Lyng in Urlingford which read: 'Our Lynger can beat 15 langers.'

PUT YOUR SWEET LIPS A LITTLE CLOSER TO THE PHONE

Another Kilkenny legend, Richie Hogan, had an embarrassing moment when he thought he was leaving three romantic voice messages singing to his girlfriend, but instead sent them to Colm Parkinson! Last February Richie explained to me:

'I actually am quite a good singer. I was doing a bit of work in the Middle East and my girlfriend kept ringing me at maybe eight or nine o'clock (Irish time) and the time difference was five hours so it was like one or two o'clock in the morning. So, I said I'd leave her a message when I get up. You know when you're kind of half-awake at five or six o'clock in the morning and when a message does come up on your WhatsApp, you click it just to see? I was trying to wake her up early but it kind of backfired because my three songs ended up on Colm's voicemail. I would love to have seen his face when he listened back to them!'

BOY GENIUS

Richie is a keen admirer of Joe Canning. Joe was a child prodigy and for that reason the cool Cat claims that a few days after Joe's mother gave birth to one of the giants of the ash, it was Joe himself who drove her home from the hospital.

JOHNNY COME LATELY

Diet is key to professional sport today. Roy Keane was invited in to speak to the Munster rugby team. He gave a passionate speech about the importance of eating healthily. Just as he was finishing, thirty pizzas were brought into the room for the Munster players!

Diet is a big thing in GAA teams, too, as it was for Joe Canning's Galway team. It was literally not to Johnny Glynn's taste. When a Galway manager of this era suggested that he eat pasta, Glynn bluntly rejected the idea: 'I eat spuds.'

RETUN OF THE MC

September began with the sad news of the retirement of Richie Hogan – one of the most skillful hurlers ever seen – even in Kilkenny! The big news this August was the second coming of Jim McGuinness as Donegal manager. He has a sharp sense of humour. The story is told that when he was consistently slagged off by an inebriated man, he turned around and said: 'I'll never forget the first time we met. But I'll keep trying.'

In his column in *The Examiner*, Tommy Martin captured the reaction. 'It is no exaggeration to say the rejoicing among Donegal GAA fans has been on a Biblical scale this week. Such is the aura that surrounds the Glenties man, he could not have generated more fervour among the Tír Chonaill faithful had he ridden into the Donegal GAA Centre of Excellence in Convoy on a donkey, followed by a trail of newly healed lepers (or as we in Donegal like to call them, Tyrone people).'

Joe Brolly was less upbeat: 'Just when you thought it was safe, he's back. Like Freddy Krueger appearing at the window. Or Jack Nicholson at the door with an axe, grinning, those dark eyes flashing. Heeeeere's Jimmy.'

3

THANK YOU FOR THE MUSIC

Pat Spillane Travels to Croke Park

He told me to duck off.

To be fair he was in a fowl mood.

Few counties have gifted the GAA with more great characters than Kerry. One of my favourites is Pat Spillane. I know he is not to everyone's taste. A friend of mine claims that if he'd had to listen to Spillane, van Gogh would have chopped off *both* ears. Another told me: 'My eyes were burning watching him, but I couldn't look away.'

Pat surprised me recently when he rang me to tell me he'd got a new job. Naturally, I asked him what it was and if it was a part-time one. He replied, 'I'm going to be a referee's assistant. I blow the whistle at the end of each game. It's full-time.'

I do worry about Pat. He once told me that his favourite novel was *Pride and Pre-juice*.

Mind you, I have contributed to Spillane's education. I told him that the Elvis Presley song is called 'In the Ghetto' not 'In the Gateau'.

23

In fairness to Pat, I admire him for not being a prisoner of history. Before England played Denmark in the semi-final of the Euros in 2021, he said, 'We all know about our history and the hundreds of years of oppression. It is time to forget about the past and forgive the Vikings and support Denmark.'

Spillane has a philosophical sensibility. He once asked me: 'Is Karl Marx's grave a communist plot?'

I can exclusively reveal that there is tension in Spillane's marriage. His long-suffering wife Rosarii is constantly telling him to put the toilet seat down. To be honest I can never understand why he carries it around with him.

Pat once asked me if I had signed up for the Self-deprecation Society yet.

I admitted that I had put myself down.

I did catch him on the hop before the 2022 World Cup when he said, 'I bet you can't name two Qatar players.'

I replied, 'Of course I can: Bruce Springsteen and Noel Gallagher.'

After England won their first game in the World Cup, featuring two goals from Bukayo Saka, Pat informed me that the Arsenal star was now set to star in a massive television advertising campaign for potatoes. The tagline would be 'Sak a Spuds'.

Spillane did make a confession to me: 'One of my pet hates is people who say the same word twice in the one sentence. Enough is enough.'

A BOUNCE

Recently Pat replaced his bed with a trampoline.

Unfortunately, he forgot to tell his wife.

She hit the roof.

CHRISTMAS IS CANCELLED

One of my favourite memories is seeing Roscommon win the Connacht final for the first time in 1977 by a single point. Brian Talty was on fire for Galway that day, scoring two goals. As the game proceeded, my dislike for him deepened by the second. Ten years later when I got my first job, I found myself teaching in the same school as Brian. The hostility immediately gave away to friendship.

Brian told me one of my favourite stories about his former famous teammate at Saint Thomond College: 'Galway were playing Kerry in December in a league game. There was a carpet of snow on the ground. Mike Judge was marking Pat Spillane and although Spillane was probably the greatest player in the country at the time, Mike was not taking any prisoners. Mike won every ball, but Pat was constantly complaining that Judge was not playing by the rules. At one stage the two of them tussled for a high ball and Pat went crashing onto the snow. Incredibly, the ref gave a free out to Galway. Pat went ballistic! But while he was bitching to the referee, Mike pushed him aside and said loud enough for us all to hear: "Stop whinging, Spillane, or Santy won't come to you this year."'

PRETTY MAN

Pat takes pride in his appearance. That is why he is pleased that not a single day goes by without someone calling him 'pretty'. As he always focuses on the positive, he blots out the fact that what they actually describe him as is 'pretty annoying'.

Pat has the capacity to fall out with people. He recently sacked the man who mowed his lawn.

He just wasn't cutting it.

WATCHING TIME FLY

When he retired from *The Sunday Game*, Spillane was invited to join the Templenoe Neighbourhood Watch.

He agreed to join – hoping he would get a Rolex.

The extra time has given Spillane the opportunity to muse on the big questions of life such as: is Joe Brolly's full name Joseph Umbrella?

MUSICAL LACK OF CHAIRS

Travelling on the DART can be a dangerous experience. Professor Luke O'Neill is the respected immunologist who became a regular commentator in the media throughout the Covid-19 lockdowns. Luke was subject to verbal and physical attacks as a result of his public profile. At one stage he was on the DART and he was working as he was very busy and a guy started shouting at Luke, across from him in the seat. Luke said, 'I beg your pardon, I'm working,' and left. His critic came after him into the next carriage, but this time was even louder and more insulting. A little old lady in her seventies came over and said, 'Leave Luke alone,' and he stopped. Luke claims: 'She is now my bodyguard.'

In recent years, as a response to the homeless crisis, it has become a tradition for a who's who of the Irish music to go busking on Grafton Street at Christmas Eve raising funds for charities like the Peter McVerry Trust and Focus Ireland. These luminaries include Glen Hansard, Gavin James and Kodaline. The massive draw is of course U2.

One year Bono got into the spirit of the occasion by commuting in from his Killiney home on the DART. The carriage was packed so he was standing near the door. A man of mature years was looking over at him and eventually said, 'I know who you are.'

Bono replied cautiously, 'Who am I then?'

'You're Bono.'

Bono replied in a tone of absolute incredulity, 'Bono? Bono? Bono? In the name of God, what would Bono be doing on the DART?'

Pat Spillane has some gaps in his musical knowledge. This was most evident when he named the singer of 'Bridge Over Troubled Waters' as Art Fartgunkel. Nonetheless, he was impressed when he heard about the way Bono had handled that situation on the DART.

It came to pass that Spillane was in Dublin last summer and had occasion to use the DART on his way to Croke Park. Outside, the sky had opened and the summer shower had come down in earnest, curtains of water soaking the already wet ground. As it was so wet, the carriage was packed and Pat found himself standing at the door. He studiously avoided the VIPS – the Very Intoxicated Persons. He noticed that a lady was staring at him. He told himself to play it cool and to just think of Bono.

Inevitably, the lady could contain herself no longer and said emphatically, 'I know who you are.'

'Bono. Bono. Bono,' Spillane whispered to himself before replying, 'Who am I then?'

'You're Pat Spillane.'

In a tone of absolute incredulity he answered, putting his hand over his mouth like a Mother Superior shocked at a glimpse of a bare breast: 'Pat Spillane? Pat Spillane? Pat Spillane?'

Dramatic pause.

'In the name of God, what would I be doing on the DART?'

TRAIN-ING RUN

When he played for Carlton in Australia, Cork star Colin Corkery also took the train. Corkery could not handle the brutal 10km training runs so he got around them by taking the tram.

Then one time he was spotted and his deception was reported to the coaching staff. The next day when he sneaked on to the tram his coach was waiting for him. Before the coach could say anything, Corkery reduced him to tears of laughter when he asked: 'Does this mean I can put in the price of the tram tickets on to my expenses claim form?'

ART OF THE POSSIBLE

Pat Spillane's finest hour was probably the 1986 All-Ireland final against Tyrone.

In August 2023, Tyrone football lost one of its great legends with the passing of Art McRory. He steered the county to All-Ireland final appearances in 1986 and 1995. He had a keen wit. In the late 1990s, he met two of his former players, both carrying some 'winter weight'. They claimed that 'training has improved'. Casting a cold eye on their waistlines, Art immediately replied: 'I see the grub has got better too.'

Another former player, Owen Mulligan, offered a revealing insight into McRory's personality:

'Art called me up in 2001 and gave me my championship debut. He also gave me probably the best advice I've ever received from a manager. After missing a Tuesday night training session, following a customary championship Monday night club rip, he called me over ahead of the Thursday night session. "Young Mulligan, you need to stop hanging about with your three best friends if you want to make it as a Tyrone senior football or get any sort of success."

'I asked him, "Who are they?" He replied, "The most popular ones. Arthur Guinness, John Jameson and Gerard Cavlan." He then pushed his glasses back up to his nose and smirked. "I miss nothing, ye bollix!"'

4

HERE'S TROUBLE

Clare v Tipperary

Clare people have a wildness in them.

TOMMY TIERNAN

If it wasn't for bad luck I would have no luck at all.

Yet I got a slice of luck when I got to know Ger Loughnane.

He is the man who encouraged me to surrender myself to the power of positive thinking.

I agreed.

Of course, I knew immediately it could never work.

When I asked him what age he was, he replied: 'Age is just a number and mine is . . . unlisted.'

Ger inherited his famed capacity for straight shooting in his genes. His granduncle was at Mass one day and he didn't think much of the sermon. He said to a man outside that he'd rather listen to a dog barking. His friend went off to tell the priest. The next Sunday, the priest got up on the altar and condemned him. Although at the time it caused a great scandal in the parish, Ger's granduncle didn't care.

I do want to mention one rumour that circulated about Ger when he managed Galway. The story is he was walking in Eyre Square and a tourist approached him and said, 'Excuse me, can you tell me the quickest way to the Regional Hospital?'

Legend has it Loughnane replied: 'Certainly. Just walk in front of that big lorry there.'

LOUGHNANE AND LOVE ISLAND

This is not a skit, but Tiger Woods admires Ger Loughnane. Tiger was making an advertisement in 2019 with Conor Moore of Conor Sketches. In preparation, Tiger checked out Conor's work on YouTube. When he met Conor he asked him about 'that man in the hat'. At first Conor did not know who he was talking about. After he discovered it was Loughnane, Tiger told him: 'He sounds like one tough dude.'

Conor claims that Loughnane's remaining ambition is to appear on *Love Island* because: 'I'd do exactly like I did in my hurling career. I'd pull like hell.'

ANOTHER BRICK IN THE WALL

In the 1990s the leading rugby coach in England was Bath's Brian Ashton. At the time, they had twenty-three internationals in their squad. Their standards were very high. Perhaps their biggest star was the English centre, Jeremy Guscott. At one training session he was unhappy with the quality of Ashton's session and said in front of everyone, 'Is that the best you can f**king do?' There was an awkward silence. Then Guscott walked off. It is not something that Clare players of the same era would have done to Ger Loughnane.

By profession Loughnane was a teacher. When an inspector from the Department of Education came to inspect his teaching, she remarked that he was 'a strong teacher'. Without blinking an eye, Loughnane replied: 'Yes I am. I can lift two chairs at a time.'

WE DON'T NEED NO EDUCATION

Loughnane's tongue can be so sharp and precise he could slice bacon with it. There were times when it was a diverting distraction like when he tried to teach poor Padraig to count:

'Padraig, you get two sliotars, a pair of sliotars, and a couple of sliotars. How many sliotars do you have?'

'Seven, sir.'

'Seven! You f— you infuriating boy. How could you possibly get seven? Let's do this one more time. You get two sliotars, a pair of sliotars, and a couple of sliotars. How many sliotars do you have?'

'Seven, sir.'

'Padraig, you would give an aspirin a headache. Let's try something else. You have two hurleys, a pair of hurleys, and a couple of hurleys. How many do you have?'

'Six, sir.'

'Padraig! You are a genius. But how could you get six that time and seven the first two times?'

'Ah sure, I have one sliotar at home already, sir.'

NEIGHBOURS

Rival fans like to put one over on each other. In 2023, when Liverpool beat Manchester United 7–0, former Liverpool player Jamie Carragher made a point on Sky Sports of holding up his drink for all United fans to wince at. It was a can of 7up.

By his own admission, there was no great welcome when Loughnane was initially appointed Clare hurling manager. During his time as Clare manager, Loughnane regularly hyped up the county's rivalry with Tipperary as a motivational ploy. Loughnane looks back on the time with affection:

'One time one of the women who taught in the school with me was in hospital. She was beside a lady from Cavan who asked her where she was from. When my colleague told her she was from Tipperary, her new friend said, "Ah, sure you don't get on with your neighbours down there."

'"What do you mean?"

'"Sure, with Clare. Do you hate Ger Loughnane as well?"

'She associated being from Tipperary with hating Ger Loughnane! That's all part of the rivalry and most of it is comical. People who take it too seriously are looking at it from the wrong angle. Without it you have nothing. It shouldn't be regarded as something to be afraid of. It is something to be embraced.'

TOUCHING TRIBUTE

In 1823 William Webb Ellis 'with a fine disregard for the rules of the game as played at the time' picked up the ball and ran with it in Rugby School in England, thus inventing the game of rugby. Little did he know that 200 years later there would be a World Cup in France where he is buried.

Loughnane would have loved his independent spirit. He did, though, find affirmation in unexpected places. He met the late Brian Lenihan when he was bringing kids from his school on a tour of the Dáil in the early noughties:

'Brian was passing and he recognised me and came over. He said, I have to tell you something about the day of the All-Ireland final in 1995. Himself and his wife, Patricia, were on the way back to Dublin from Galway and listening to the game on the radio. He had no interest in hurling, but they got caught up in the excitement of the game. They pulled in to listen. Brian said that he told Patricia that if Clare won and they had a baby girl, they'd call her Clare. And they did.'

EVERY LOVELY ROSE OF CLARE HAS ITS THORNS

Clare players understand how to combine hurling and partying. In April 2023, at TUS Gaelic Grounds, Clare beat Limerick by a score of 2–20 to 1–24. It was an historic evening for the Banner as they beat Limerick for the first time at the Gaelic Grounds in the Munster Championship and became the first side to beat the team in the Championship since July 2019, ending a streak that stood at sixteen games. John Conlon was awarded the Man of the Match award after the game, and revealed in his post-match interview that he left his brother's wedding at 4 p.m. to make throw-in. To add to the occasion, Conlon was his brother's best man!

STAR-GAZING

Anthony Daly once gave me an insight into what happens behind the scenes at an All-Stars banquet:

'It began with lunchtime flights from Shannon to Dublin. The women had hair and make-up appointments booked around the city not long after we landed, and a handful of us spotted the perfect window of opportunity to have the craic amongst ourselves before the night really kicked off.

'Back then, it was easy to lose yourself in the moment, to disconnect from everything else and just casually luxuriate in the company you were in. Mobile phones weren't exactly common in 1998. I had some kind of a yoke that resembled a brick and which you nearly had to roar into to be heard.

'We were sitting in a huddle in the Leeson Lounge when, next thing, the door opened and the late and great Páidí Ó Sé popped his head in the door. He hadn't a clue who we were but Páidí had an idea we were Clare hurlers; he had to, considering how often we were in the media during that crazy summer.

'He got our names fairly early in the conversation and he regaled us for the evening. He told us all the old classics. We were all cracking up. It was pure magic. The hours were flying by like minutes. Before we knew it, the bar was filling up with Friday evening work-crew. Eventually, one of the lads arrived in looking for us. "They're calling us for the dinner," he said in a panic. "Ye better get a move on."

'We literally only had five minutes to sprint out the door, and hare upstairs in the Burlington Hotel to get changed. I was lucky I had shaved myself that morning. I ducked in and out of the shower within about ten seconds. I fired on the monkey suit and tore downstairs like a lunatic, worse for wear.

'Ger Loughnane could see we were all over the place. "Jesus," he said, "ye'll fall and get killed going up on to the stage."

'That time, the All-Stars were called out before the dinner, so I knocked back two cups of coffee to try and straighten myself up before accepting my All-Star.

'I was nominated on six occasions – 1993, 1994, 1995, 1997, 1998 and 1999 – but that 1998 night was the standout memory. The craic was always deadly, especially when you could wind up in anyone's company.

'Gregory O'Kane from Antrim was nominated one year and it was obvious he felt kind of lost early on in the evening when he was the only hurler from the north at the awards. We made sure he wasn't on his own and the Clare crew looked after him all night, with "looked after" being a loosely termed phrase!'

SPIN DOCTOR

When necessary, Loughnane had a great capacity to put a positive spin on things. In 1997 his 'Captain Fantastic', Anthony Daly, was debating whether to attend the All-Stars. He was caught in two minds as he recalled for me on a wet evening in Ennis:

'I always really looked forward to the event. The one time I didn't go, in 1997, I had a solid excuse; Clarecastle were playing Patrickswell in the Munster club final two days later.

'I rang Loughnane and asked him if he could find out if I had won an award. If I hadn't, I didn't see how I could justify going up to Dublin, especially when I wouldn't have been able to fully switch off and enjoy the evening.

'I knew Ger "Sparrow" O'Loughlin was receiving an award, so I didn't see any point in two of us missing training before one of the biggest games in the club's history.

'On the Wednesday, Loughnane rang. "Dalo, I've good and bad news," he said. "I'll give you the good news first — you can train with the club on Friday."'

TEARS OF A CLOWN

Two of Loughnane's star players from the 1990s came up against each other in the 2023 Munster Championship. Brian Lohan's Clare beat Davy Fitzgerald's Waterford by twelve points. Davy spoke of Waterford having 'issues' after the game but declined to say what they were. Fitzgerald professed not to take the criticism afterwards personally but said he had no time for 'one of the clowns from Clare' who he said was laughing down at him on the sideline.

5

BORN TO SWIM

Meath v Dublin

Being sensible can't kill you but why take the chance?

In the final match of the epic four-game contests between Meath and Dublin in 1991, a Dublin fan looked at his watch. The fan beside him said, 'It is not a watch we need; it is a calendar to keep track of this saga.'

BONNY SCOTLAND

You do not have a twenty-two-year career as Meath manager and win four All-Irelands with essentially three different teams without paying attention to detail. Seán Boylan was not a man to leave things to chance and his reward was a final, dizzying twist to a four-game thriller:

'I suppose one of the things people remember most is the four-game saga against Dublin in 1991 and, of course, nobody will ever forget Kevin Foley's goal in the last game. I decided that we needed a break after the third match and I thought about taking the team for a break in a beautiful, quiet spot in Scotland. Before I made the arrangements, though, I rang all the wives and girlfriends of the players and asked them if they were okay with me doing it. Pretty much to a woman they all said, "Seán, whatever it takes to beat the Dubs."'

A HOLY SHOW

Boylan lights up at one memory from the trip. 'On the Sunday morning we went to Mass in the local church, which was a tiny, tiny chapel. We had seventy-six people in the group, including wives and girlfriends. The priest nearly wept for joy because he never got such a big collection!

'We did very little physical training but the only thing we did was to practise that move again and again which was replicated with Kevin Foley's goal. The only thing was that I had not expected it would be Kevin who finished the move.'

ANSWER THE QUESTION

There was an interesting postscript to the game: 'My abiding memory of the dressing room was of the journalist Donal Healy interviewing Kevin. He basically asked him ten thousand different ways if he had ever scored a goal before and Kevin kept answering that he had never, ever scored a goal before in any match he ever played. Eventually he got so frustrated he said to Donal, "Look, you are standing on my towel, and I need my shower," and he walked away.'

Given his refusal to capitulate, one Meath fan claims: 'Boylan can never fill out an online form because he will never submit.'

SWIM WEAR

Critics can be very cruel. In 2023, after a series of shocking errors, they rechristened Manchester United goalkeeper David de Gea 'David de Howler'.

Most people do not respond well to criticism. An exception is singer James Blunt. When a 'critic' commented: 'James Blunt has an irritating face and an annoying voice,' he countered immediately: 'And no mortgage.'

Seán Boylan is not unduly bothered by criticism. Everyone has a plan until they get a punch in the mouth. Boylan came up with an unusual strategy when his team needed refreshing – knowing he would get stick for it:

'The boys had a lot of miles on the clock by 1991 and I knew they would not be able for the wear and tear of brutal physical training again. Gerry McEntee is a top surgeon and was working abroad so I met him for training one night at the start of the year and I told him we were going to train in the pool. I had got the county board to splash out three and a half grand for buoyancy aids for the lads. I told the squad that we would be training for most of that year in the pool but, after that first session when I was giving Gerry a lift home, he turned to me and said: "Seán, what are you going to tell everyone when we lose the first round of the Leinster Championship?"

'In 2000, after Sonia O'Sullivan won the Olympic silver medal, she was paraded around Croke Park at the All-Ireland final. I hesitated before going up to congratulate her because I wasn't sure she would recognise me but as soon as she saw me coming, she said, "Ah, Seán. Do you remember when you got those buoyancy aids?"'

AROMATHERAPY

By profession, Boylan is a herbalist. In 1991, after Meath finally beat Dublin in the epic tussle which needed four games to decide the outcome, Seán was walking off the pitch when some Dublin fans poked fun at his vocation by saying, 'Get away, ya bleedin' witch doctor.'

6

WASPISH

Paídí Ó Sé Makes Friends

The first time we met, Paídí Ó Sé explained the essential difference between himself and Pat Spillane: 'I'm infallible but Pat is
inflatable. He is full of hot air.'

He was not impressed when I told him both sides of my family
were blacksmiths. His response was: 'I don't trust blacksmiths.
Everything about them is forged.'

Paídí enjoyed seeing fellow GAA pundits humbled. He
loved Anthony Tohill's story of when, less than two years after
winning an All-Ireland, the Derry midfielder played in two
reserve team games with Manchester United. His teammates
included the Neville brothers, Mark Hughes, Nicky Butt, David
May, Gary Walsh and David Beckham. Tohill even scored a
goal. He had the honesty to later confess to the *Derry Journal*
that when his friends asked him who would or would not make
it, he assured them that Beckham had absolutely no chance.

FRUITY

There was a particular pundit Paídí did not like because of his self-
importance: 'Sure, if he was a f**king banana, he'd peel himself.'

A PREGNANT PAUSE

A semi-regular customer walked into Páidí's pub and told him: 'My wife is about to give birth in the hospital any second now.'

Páidí replied: 'That's very exciting. Do you know what you're having?'

The man paused pensively before clarifying: 'A pint of Guinness, please.'

EARTH-SHATTERING

Páidí rejoiced in his image of being a hard man. He once joked to me: 'When I do push-ups I'm not lifting myself up. I'm pushing the earth down.'

For his part, Pat Spillane is convinced that Páidí's keen intelligence was greatly underestimated: 'Páidí once swallowed a Rubik's Cube and pooped it out solved.'

THE CIRCLE OF LIFE

One of Páidí Ó Sé's teammates in the glory days of the 1970s was Jimmy Deenihan. A bad injury caused Deenihan to retire prematurely but he went on to make a new career in politics. It was a bit of a cultural shock for him, particularly as he got some weird requests from his constituents. The strangest was the woman who asked him to see if he could arrange 'infidelity benefit' for herself and her husband.

MONEY, MONEY, MONEY

Many Kerry folk believed there were cast-iron certainties to win the 1982 All-Ireland. A song to celebrate the victory had already been written. Then Offaly's super sub, Seamus Darby, intervened with the winning goal and the Kingdom were deprived of history. Before the game a Kerry entrepreneur had invested a small fortune in making a large number of Kerry five-in-a-row

T-shirts. His money would surely go to waste. Not a bit of it. With exceptional cunning, even by Kerry standards, he made an even bigger fortune by writing 'RIP' on each of them and selling them all in Offaly.

FAIR TRADE

Sometimes people get confused. Brian O'Driscoll brought a stranger's dog home from the groomers instead of his own. In September 2022 he told his social media followers that his dog was 'a bit quiet with me because she hates getting her hair cut. When you take the wrong dog all the way home from the groomers . . . I just thought all the black had been sheared off her face.'

Brian's wife, Amy Huberman, explained:

'Brian going to the groomers to collect the dog and . . . taking home the wrong dog! Thought perhaps she had needed a serious groom and had taken off the darker fluff. Off they skipped. I cannot! He may defo need an ould top up on the laser eye surgery.

'Thank you to our ledge groomers for being so understanding, and hope that the other lovely dog enjoyed her forty-eight seconds in our gaff before going home.

'Also, I think I'll collect the kids from school this week. Also, I'm not sure I'll ask him to give me a lift home from the hairdresser's next time in case he heads off with someone else's wife.'

Páidí Ó Sé was discussing what they had bought the family for Christmas with a customer in his pub. 'I just got a bottle of whiskey for the mother-in-law,' said the man.

'Sounds like a fair swap,' quipped Páidí.

HOSPITALITY

One Christmas, Páidí was feeling particularly generous. He announced: 'This will be the seventh year in a row that my

41

in-laws will have called over Christmas. I think this year we will let them in.'

GIFTED

Páidí was talking to his young nephew, Tomás: 'What are you getting your younger brother Marc for Christmas?'

Tomás: 'I haven't decided yet.'

Páidí: 'What did you give him last year?'

Tomás: 'The measles.'

BULLISH

Before the Christmas holidays, the Kerry icon was interviewing a young man for a job in his pub. 'You'll need to be fit to work here over Christmas. It's mad busy,' said Páidí. 'Did you ever have any illness or accidents?'

'No, sir,' replied the young man confidently.

'But you're on crutches.'

'A bull tossed me last week. But that was no accident. The f**ker did it on purpose.'

DISQUALIFICATION

A lady once asked Páidí why is it that Santa Claus is not a woman. Páidí replied that a woman would not be happy to wear the same suit for years and years.

THE WEST WING

Staff member: 'Martin Sheen is in the pub.'

Páidí: 'Who the f**k is Martin Sheen?'

'Hollywood, Jesus. *The West Wing*, Páidí.'

'Oh, Jesus Christ, I'll be down in five minutes.'

Páidí introduced himself, pointing to the wall of his pub where there were photos of him with Dolly Parton and Tom Cruise. 'Martin, how are you doing? Nice to meet you, you're welcome.'

'You know Tom?' Sheen asked.

'Oh yeah, Tom and myself are personal friends,' said Páidí, who'd met Cruise only once.

He asked Sheen if he'd like a drink.

'No, thank you.'

'Ah, sure, look, it is not every day we have a Hollywood celebrity into the bar, look, you'll have a drink.'

'No, thank you, I'm an alcoholic.'

Páidí: 'No problem, no problem . . . Yerra Christ you'll have one!'

LAUNCH

Páidí was invited to launch a book of a club stalwart. The event was preceded by a 'session'. This may explain why instead of finishing his speech with the intended words: 'This is one of those books that once you pick it up, you will find it very difficult to put down,' he actually said: 'This is one of those books that once you put it down, you will find it very difficult to pick up again.'

HISTORY MAKER

Páidí was a big fan of a unique Cork star. In June 2023, the GAA was shocked by the death of Teddy McCarthy. Fourteen players have won All-Ireland medals in hurling and football on the field of play. Eight of them are from Cork: Billy Mackessy, Jack Lynch, Brian Murphy, Ray Cummins, Denis Coughlan, Jimmy Barry-Murphy, Denis Walsh and McCarthy. Teddy remains the only player in the history of the GAA to win All-Ireland titles in hurling and football in the same year, when Cork won the double in 1990.

The ultimate Teddy tribute came from Anthony Daly. He recalls going into a pub in Blackpool one night and having a fuss made of him when an unimpressed regular at the bar said, 'And how many All-Irelands did ye win?'

'Two,' answered Dalo.

The customer took a sip and said, 'We'd a fella did that in a fortnight.'

The Sarsfields and Glanmire club man had an eleven-year inter-county career with the Rebels. He split four All-Irelands evenly between both codes, as well as the Texaco Footballer of the Year in 1989. He was famous for his ability to soar into the air to catch the ball. In Ted Walsh parlance he was 'a great lepper'.

I once spent a memorable wet Thursday evening in Teddy's company. He told me that the sweetest victory for him was the 1990 All-Ireland final because: 'We had finally put the Meath thing to bed.'

He humoured me by picking his dream football and hurling teams. His dream hurling team was the Cork three-in-a-row team of the 1970s. For the first time, I publish his dream football team as an homage to a fallen hero:

1. Billy Morgan
(Cork)

2. Robbie O'Malley (Meath) 3. Mick Lyons (Meath) 4. Niall Cahalane (Cork)

5. Páidí Ó Sé (Kerry) 6. Conor Counihan (Cork) 7. Tony Davis (Cork)

8. Jack O'Shea (Kerry) 9. Brian Mullins (Dublin)

10. Matt Connor (Offaly) 11. Larry Tompkins (Cork) 12. Pat Spillane (Kerry)

13. Jimmy Barry-Murphy (Cork) 14. Eoin Liston (Kerry) 15. Mikey Sheehy (Kerry)

7

CHICKEN RUN

Dubs Fans Unimpressed in Croke Park

In April 2023, on a visit to Ireland, President Joe Biden congratulated his cousin Rob Kearney for beating 'the hell out of the Black and Tans' instead of the All Blacks. Kearney is clearly a misunderstood man.

It wasn't for the first or last time that the former Minister for Sport, Shane Ross, showcased the major gaps in his sporting knowledge when he mistakenly congratulated Dave Kearney following Ireland's Grand Slam success in 2018. The only problem was that it was Dave's brother Rob who had starred in the team that season.

In May 2019, Katie Taylor became world boxing champion. At the official homecoming the then Minister for Sport, Shane Ross, attracted ridicule on social media for the way he inserted himself into every photo taken of Katie. It seemed as if he was almost an extension of her shoulder. The *Irish Star*'s Kieran Cunningham had the line of the saga when he said, 'Not since Lar Corbett marked Tommy Walsh has there been a closer marking in Irish sport.'

NOT FRANK-LY SPEAKING

Managers do things differently. Mauricio Pochettino likes to keep a tray of lemons in his office, after an Argentine friend told him they absorb negative energy, and he believes he has the ability to see an aura around people.

Arsenal manager Mikel Arteta revealed he brought an olive tree into team meetings so as to show that growth only comes when roots are nurtured. 'It is very strong but needs a lot of care,' Arteta said. 'We have to look after the roots every single day, make sure they don't get poisoned, don't get damaged and remain in the right condition.'

Arteta also revealed that he brought a dog called Win into the club. 'The reaction of the players has been incredible,' Arteta said. 'She is one of us and will be on our journey. She changes your mood. You come in the building and she gives all her love. Suddenly you just feel the energy and the players start hugging her, it is beautiful to watch. Those things are very important. There are things at the club that can be done to connect with people, to show love, and I found this dog was the perfect representative of who we are now. We all love winning and Win needs a lot of love.'

In Pillar Caffrey's last year as Dublin manager in 2008 he famously issued *The Blue Book* to the Dublin panel. Each page had 'DUBLIN ALL-IRELAND CHAMPIONS 2008' emblazoned on top.

If Dublin won the 2008 All-Ireland, *The Blue Book* would have been regarded as a managerial masterclass.

Instead, Tyrone beat them by 3–14 to 1–8 in the All-Ireland quarter-final and Pillar got his P45. One bitter Dublin fan was not impressed by his literary output and asked him: 'Who do you think you are? Anne Frank?'

WEIGHTY MATTERS

GAA personalities tend to be cut from a different cloth. Although he did play for Waterford, Derek McGrath has a nice sense of self-deprecation when explaining why his inter-county career was not as distinguished as it might have been. 'I was too fond of snack-boxes.'

Dublin star Michael Darragh Macauley follows the advice of Oscar Wilde: 'Be yourself. Everyone else is taken.'

Earlier in his career he was told to retire at twenty due to an injury which led to a two-year break from football. In those two years he took an insurance job which taught him that he would never like to work a nine-to-five desk job again. He always got along with kids and wished to be a primary school teacher. His own primary school teacher was somebody who changed the course of his career 'for the better'. So, he went back to college at twenty-one to study Irish, while at the same time he won the All-Ireland. Sadly, his dad passed away during his first year of teacher training. He worked in a school in Tallaght filled with ideologies and 'hoping to change the world'.

'It's easy to be a bad teacher,' he muses, 'but it takes effort and enthusiasm to be a good one.'

There, he got some radical insights into theology from some of his students:

'The bishop wears a meter on his head to increase his offerings.'

'When a woman is married to just one man that's what's called monotony.'

'Insects is burned in some churches.'

'An epistle is the wife of an apostle.'

'A fast day is when you have to eat in a hurry.'

'The *Agnus Dei* is a lady composer of music.'

'Who was Joan of Arc? Noah's wife.'

NO THANKS

At the time, Michael Darragh was offered much higher paying jobs because of his status as a footballer, but these jobs did not appeal to him. He wished to leave a legacy off the pitch as well as on it. It is clear that he most certainly has.

During his time as a teacher he went to a lot of trouble to get tickets for two female students in his fourth class for a big match in Croke Park. He came on as a sub with just ten minutes to go and helped Dublin to a big win. He might have expected gratitude. When he went into school the next day he was greeted by the principal, who shook his head and said, 'You are in trouble.'

When he went into his classroom one of the girls was irate. 'I waited for nearly the whole match for you to come on. When you did, your hair looked stupid and your legs were bandy. You ran like a chicken.'

LET'S GET PHYSICAL

Michael Darragh played midfield in the 2019 All-Ireland final. His teammate, Jonny Cooper, was sent off for his tackling of David Clifford. The next day Today FM's 'Gift Grub' had a sketch which claimed that: 'Jonny Cooper was handling David Clifford so closely I am surprised the boy isn't pregnant.'

Such is David Clifford's genius that one Kerry fan said: 'Jesus can walk on water, David Clifford can swim through land.'

Joe Brolly's praise is more oblique: 'The only thing worse than being asked to lead the DUP is being asked to mark David Clifford.'

In 2022 David Clifford scored 1–6 from play in the league final as Kerry strolled past Mayo. During the match there were a record number of 999 calls for a fire brigade. Why? David Clifford was on fire.

EXIT STRATEGY

There was no place for sentiment in the Dublin ethos. Four-time All-Star Paul Flynn was very upset when he retired from the Dublin team because he had to leave the players' WhatsApp group. Within three minutes, though, he was invited to join another group for Dublin rejects.

Another legend to step away from the Dublin backroom team after Jim Gavin stepped down as team manager was Jason Sherlock. Jayo, though, still has star power as was very evident in the 2023 New York St Patrick's Day parade. Sherlock was in New York for the parade and was front and centre as the parade made its way down 5th Avenue. A huge group of gardai were marching in the parade but while they moved down the street the boys in blue spotted an icon in blue. Some gardai stopped to chat to Jayo – and take a photo – but some got so excited they hoisted him over the barrier so he could join their march in the parade. They held him aloft like the Sam Maguire Cup and chanted 'Jayo' as they continued down past the thousands of spectators in attendance. One local man said: 'I've been coming to the parade for years and I've never seen anything like that. That was awesome.'

Back home, An Garda Síochána shared the fun with a clip on Twitter stating: 'Our members are never off duty! An Garda Síochána's contingent that travelled to NYC to proudly take part in today's parade scoped out well-known @officialgaa star, @boomjayo in the crowd. He's now been taken in for questioning on his crimes against football!'

BIRDSONG

Michael Darragh Macauley was part of the Dublin team that won a historic five-in-a-row in 2019. After the game he met a fan who told him, 'I have a parrot who sings 'Molly Malone' every time Dublin wins in the Championship.'

'Really,' said Michael Darragh. 'What does he sing when Dublin lose?'

'I don't know. I've only had him for five years.'

It was suggested that the parrot should be called 'Mother Superior' after the substance abuser in *Trainspotting*, who earned his nickname because he had the longest habit.

GONE AND FORGOTTEN

Macauley has been the subject of a number of glowing endorsements from Joe Brolly. I was sad to hear recently that Joe was in hospital. He needed an operation on his funny bone. Doctors say he will be in stiches for weeks.

NOT LEAVING ON A JET PLANE

Joe and his wife Laurita (a cousin of Joe Biden) were to receive a very different invitation during Joe Biden's visit to Ireland in April 2023. At the state banquet in Dublin castle the American president invited them to fly with him on Air Force One the following day from Dublin to Knock airport. The request was politely declined. Why? Laurita had an early appointment with her hairdresser in Foxford the following morning. As Brolly explained, when you present a woman with the choice between flying with the American president on Air Force One or having their hair done there is only going to be one winner!

8

A MATCH NOT MADE IN HEAVEN

Garret FitzGerald and the GAA

At the time I thought he must be joking.

Now I believe he was deadly serious.

Outside, the sun was pale and hard-looking, like marble, as I asked the former Taoiseach Garret FitzGerald if he ever played Gaelic football. He shook his head forcibly. He told me that as a schoolboy he played football only twice until he discovered that the ball didn't stop where he was. He had to chase it, so he gave it up!

He happily confessed to me, with eyes dancing in merriment, that instead, when he was a youngster, one of his favourite books was a girl's school story called *Bashful Fifteen*. I wondered if he ever felt a compunction to present himself as a man's man – in particular when he was jousting with either Jack Lynch or Charlie Haughey. He admitted that his media advisers had suggested that he work a little on that.

He recalled that when there was grumbling about his leadership among his parliamentary colleagues in Fine Gael, he was told he should turn up more often in the Dáil bar, in an effort to alter the perception he was too remote. The only problem was that the evening he decided to go to the bar to buy a round of drinks for his party members was Ash Wednesday. Given the much more Catholic mores that prevailed at the time in Ireland, nobody was drinking alcohol on one of the two fast days in the year. He expelled a martyr's sigh as he explained that he ended up buying everyone an orange juice! This did not engender all the goodwill he had hoped to harvest so plans for regular visits to the bar were quietly shelved.

He conceded he suffered from memory lapses. This was particularly problematic when he put his suits into the dry cleaner's and then forgot which dry cleaners he went to!

Famously, in order not to disturb his wife Joan, one morning he got dressed in the dark and put on two odd shoes. The press turned it into a big story. Garret couldn't see why it was a big deal.

We spoke in the run-up to the Good Friday agreement. The North formed a huge part of his political career:

'There are two preconditions for a solution to the Northern situation. The first is that the minority there face the fact that North Ireland was going to remain in existence for the foreseeable future and that they must demand their rights within that state and accept the responsibilities of citizenship within it. This was achieved by the civil rights movement and the SDLP.

'The second condition has been that the Republic should cease to seem to be a threat to Northern Unionists, so that they be freed from their fears and allowed to work out a just governmental system with the minority. This objective we substantially achieved while in power, by the stand we took on the re-unification issue and in the quality and quantity of contacts we made with all shades of opinion in the North.'

On his infamous comment about Charlie Haughey having a 'flawed pedigree' he was remorseful because of its hurtful impact on the Haughey family. He told me that there is no space in this life for hate or resentment. When I observed that Don Henley wisely called such feelings 'Wasted Time' he looked at me in bewilderment. He had no idea who the lead singer of the Eagles was.

Our conversation took a more serious turn as he swam in ethical awareness. He was an optimist but he had concerns about trends he saw emerging in politics especially when politicians avoided responsibility, then avoided taking responsibility for taking responsibility. The problem was not that some of them lied but that they saw the truth not as a moral category but only a strategic factor. This reduced those politicians to juggling different narratives to find one that would stick. The line between plausibility and veracity simply shattered. Perception became everything. Public debate descended into popular opinion. Politicians did the right thing up to a point. However, when media attention was averted, or if they looked like getting into trouble, it was immediately discarded. Principle was condemned to the margins. While he saw politics as a vocation, he despaired of those whose every move was about obtaining or retaining power rather than about making sure that nobody got left behind.

NO HURLING HERO
I told him that during the civil war two former teammates in Kerry found themselves on opposing sides and one was killed in the line of fire. His wife spat at the man responsible – his former teammate. The volunteers under his command demanded he retaliate by killing the woman's son. He shook his head and replied: 'I can't have the death of the son of my full-back on

my conscience.' Garret was impressed, even moved, by this anecdote. While he believed deeply in the power of community it was clear that his appreciation of the GAA was more at the level of theory rather than practice.

It will probably come as a surprise to many people that Garret produced two memorable GAA moments – albeit for the wrong reasons. On the canvas trail in 1981, which would see him become Taoiseach for the first time, he posed for a photo opportunity swinging a hurley in the hurling stronghold of Birr. One of his media handlers thought it would be a masterstroke to set up a photoshoot involving Garret swinging a hurley and sending the sliotar into outer space. The only problem was, despite multiple attempts, Garret completely failed to connect the hurley with the sliotar. There was no Christy Ring moment.

In an effort to salvage something from the public relations catastrophe, the same media handler arranged an interview with Garret and a sympathetic journalist. The interview turned a disaster into a calamity as it unfolded as follows:

Interviewer: 'What prompted you to try hurling?'

Garret: 'I've always wanted to play hurling, so I thought it would be a good thing to learn the rudiments of the game.'

Interviewer: 'So, have you learned much?'

Garret: 'Yes, I have. How to swing a cue.'

BY THE BANKS

That same year in Poland, Solidarity was becoming the first independent labour union in a country belonging to the Soviet bloc. Solidarity was founded by Lech Wałęsa. In 1978 he started to organise free non-communist trade unions and took part in many actions on the sea coast. He was kept under surveillance by the state security service and often detained. In August 1980 he led the Gdańsk shipyard strike, which gave rise to a wave of strikes over much of the country. They were seeking workers' rights. The authorities were forced to negotiate with Wałęsa in the Gdańsk Agreement of August 1980, which gave the workers the right to strike and to organise their own independent union. The Catholic Church supported the movement, and, in January 1981, Wałęsa was received by Pope John Paul II in the Vatican with much fanfare in the international media. He would go on to win the Nobel Prize. Solidarity had a huge profile internationally, including in Ireland. Their colours were red and white and they became famous all over the world.

In 1981, while electioneering, Garret arrived in Cork on a Sunday and saw hordes of people swathed in red and white, at a time when the Solidarity movement in Poland was at its zenith, not realizing his arrival coincided with a Munster Championship hurling match. He leaned over to Cork's leading Fine Gael politician at the time, Peter Barry, and remarked: 'I never knew Solidarity had such popular support in Cork.'

9

KISS MY ASH

The Fierce Hurling Man

That most revered figure in GAA circles, the 'fierce hurling man', never misses an opportunity to trumpet the glories of hurling with slogans like 'Kiss My Ash'. Some have been known to overstate its importance like comedian P.J. Gallagher. 'I always thought hockey was hurling for Protestants.'

Nothing is more loved by fierce hurling fans than a big shock. In 2023 Westmeath produced one of the most stunning comebacks in hurling history to beat Wexford in Wexford Park in the Leinster Championship. Trailing by seventeen points, Joe Fortune's side turned things around against all odds to win 4–18 to 2–22.

IMAGINE

Most fans like to show off their wit. Witness a banner in Croke Park: 'Dean Rock strikes faster than Bus Éireann.'

Joe Wall, the lead singer with The Stunning, gave an unexpected answer when asked: 'Who is the first person you would ask to a dinner party and why?' He replied, 'I'd invite John Lennon, the hurler from Laois. I could then boast that the great John Lennon once came to dinner in my house.'

TOMMY TIERNAN'S PRESIDENTIAL CAMPAIGN
Tommy Tiernan has drawn on his love of the GAA to make his pitch to succeed Michael D. Higgins as Irish President: 'Nothing would suit me more than taking the king of Burundi to camogie matches.' However, his chance of topping the poll with female GAA fans may be affected by his description of Cavan women as 'half crow'.

THE LESS THAN FIERCE HURLING MAN
For a brief time, all of three days, I found myself working with one of Ireland's most 'distinctive' broadcasters, Vincent Browne. As part of my duties, I arranged for him to interview camogie's most iconic star, Angela Downey, on RTÉ radio. The interview was going well for all of three seconds when Vincent introduced her as 'a star of ladies' hurling'.

THE WICKLOW WAY
Oftentimes, Irish people emigrating to foreign shores bring their love of Gaelic games with them, such as the Wicklow comedian Dara Ó Briain. This led to a memorable interview on RTÉ.

Des Cahill: 'Do you have to explain to the English what hurling is about?'

Dara Ó Briain: 'No, but I have to explain it to the people of Wicklow.'

MOURNING DIANA
My favourite fan story, though, goes back to the day when Princess Diana died and a wag rang up the then PRO of the

GAA, Danny Lynch, to reverently inquire if the GAA would be cancelling all its games as a mark of respect.

Suffice to say they did not.

Lynch is a man who can see the funny side of Gaelic games. Reacting to the ever-growing size of back-room teams in county squads, he remarked, 'It seems that every inter-county team has every "ologist" except a gynaecologist.'

GO JOHNNY GO

Over 200,000 people have watched footage from the 2012 Galway County Hurling final on YouTube. Six points down with just a few minutes to go, Loughrea's full-forward Johnny Maher is fouled. Although he is given a penalty, Johnny reacts by striking two of his St Thomas' opponents with his hurl – one in a very tender part of his anatomy. He then scores the penalty and after the goal he reacts by kicking another opponent. The referee does not even book him.

ROBUST

The Munster Final replay in 1998 between Waterford and Clare had probably the most 'physically robust' opening to a game in GAA history. There's a story told about the two grasshoppers who came onto the field before the game as the pulling started between the players on both teams:

One said to the other, 'We're going to be killed here today. Do you feel the tension?'

The other replied, 'I do. Hop up here on the sliotar. It's the only place we'll be safe!'

One Clare fan marvelled at the manliness of Brian Lohan: 'He's so tough that his cowboy boots are made out of real cowboys.'

A GOOD WALK SPOILED

Michelle Obama claims that golf is a game to be played by men like her husband when they want to avoid their wives.

After retirement, many former GAA stars turn to golf. Waterford's erstwhile hurling All-Star, Paul Flynn, went so far as to compete in the West of Ireland Amateur Championship at Rosses Point when Ireland had a white Easter in 2013. In the Arctic conditions, Flynn struggled and scored an opening round of eighty-three. When asked if the experience was tougher than facing Kilkenny in an All-Ireland final, the former sharpshooter stoically replied, 'It was a slower death anyway.'

THE CLASH OF THE ASH

Disappointingly, Flynn found himself on the subs bench when Waterford reached the 2008 All-Ireland final only for the Déise to be humiliated in a twenty-three-points defeat. Before the match, Kilkenny's Christy Heffernan was asked if he thought the Waterford players would be fit enough. He replied, 'They should be fit enough, they've been training for forty-five years!'

After his retirement in 2008, Flynn became a pundit on *The Sunday Game*. As a pundit, Flynn raised eyebrows himself when he was critical of Davy Fitzgerald's management of the Waterford team, particularly of the type of drills done in training. While acknowledging that Flynn was one of the greatest hurlers of modern times, Davy's riposte was that while the training was 'up to speed, I am not sure Paul Flynn was'.

DAN THE MAN

Flynn left the game with many happy memories of his former teammates. A case in point is of Dan Shanahan, an employee for Top Oil, who went into a shop one day in 2007. At that stage, he had become hurling's supreme goal machine – he had starred in Waterford's triumph over Cork in the All-Ireland hurling quarter-final and had scored eight goals and eight points in his four games that year, bringing his championship score to an incredible nineteen goals and thirty-six points.

A little lady eyed him up slowly. Suddenly, a smile of triumph came over her face. 'I know who you are now,' said the woman.

'That's good,' said Big Dan politely.

'You're the oil man!' the woman replied with a flourish.

CRAZY HORSE

Ace Leitrim forward, Emlyn Mulligan, retired in the spring of 2023. He too has been the victim of a misunderstanding. He played club football for St Brigid's in Dublin. He was man of the match once in a club game. One of the reporters gave him a glowing report. There was one problem, though. The Leitrim star was described as Emlyn HUGHES, the Liverpool FC legend nicknamed 'Crazy Horse' who was also famous from his years as a captain on *A Question of Sport*.

10

THE BERRY VEST OF JACKIE TYRELL

The GAA's Style Icons

Passion runs through the Gaelic-games world. A humorous illustration of this was John Mullane's pledge in 2017 to ride through the streets of Waterford naked if the county won the All-Ireland.

THE CLOTHES SHOW

Historically, Irish sport has produced some stars who took a keen interest in their appearance. A case in point was former Irish rugby international Freddie McLennan.

Once, when Ireland played England, Freddie and John Carleton and were having a real jousting match. At one stage, John sent Freddie crashing to the ground in a tackle. As he was going back to his position, Freddie shouted at him, 'John, John! Is my hair all right?' If you watch the video of the game, you'll see John cracking up with laughter and Freddie straightening his hair.

In the past, such sensibilities were alien to the GAA. Myself, Jackie Tyrell and Paul Galvin have changed all that: Jackie and Paul as style icons. My own fashion sense has attracted considerable attention too. I have been officially sanctioned under the Geneva Convention for serious crimes against fashion.

However, the GAA landscape is changing. Christy Ring could never have imagined that a top Kilkenny hurler like Jackie Tyrell would become a fashionista. Ring would have appreciated that Jackie played on the edge. He would have been horrified that Jackie dressed on the edge too.

Pat Spillane is not bothered by the new fashion sensibilities in the GAA: 'We got a lot of criticism into *The Sunday Game* after Joe Brolly and Colm O'Rourke's repeated comments about the Mortimer brothers' and Ciarán McDonald's hairstyles during their time playing for Mayo. Around the time, there was also a lot of media speculation that Sven-Göran Eriksson would lose his job as English coach because of his sexual indiscretions in the "Fariagate" scandal. My attitude to all of this is very simple: if you are the Kerry manager I don't care if you are homosexual, heterosexual or metrosexual as long as you lead Kerry to the All-Ireland. If you are a Kerry forward, I don't care how you score in your private life as long as you score frequently on the pitch and I don't care if you wear hair-bands, lipstick or frilly knickers as long as you can steer the ball between the posts.'

DUNNE DEAL
During one of Eileen Dunne's first ever news bulletins in 1984, she was reading out the sports results for the six o'clock news, wearing this beautiful blouse her mother bought her. When she came off air, she was told that the blouse was see-through.

ALL THAT GLISTENS IS NOT GOLD
A wife comes home to find a prominent GAA star who has no shirt on and is glistening with body oil. She is very surprised and asks him why.

He replies, 'You said I never glisten.'
'No. I said you never listen.'

GET SHORTSY

Leitrim's first All-Star, Mickey Quinn, recalls one day that has gone into folklore: 'We were playing Mayo on a live game for RTÉ and a melee broke out and the Mayo manager, John Maughan, came running onto the pitch in his shorts. He passed a comment to Gerry Flanagan and Gerry floored him. In our view, Maughan definitely deserved it, but it is probably not the thing to do on live TV! Pat Spillane and the pundits were outraged but it did Flanagan's reputation no harm in Leitrim!'

HAIR-RAISING

Few players ever pushed themselves harder for Mayo's quest for an All-Ireland than Tom Parsons. After his *Laochra Gael* episode earlier this year, there was a consensus on social media that Tom really deserved an All-Ireland medal for his . . . magnificent hair!

CAT-TY

Dónal Óg Cusack is another former star known for his style. As a pundit, one of his most memorable moments came in 2022, after the All-Ireland club finals, when Harry Ruddle scored an incredible goal for Ballygunner with the last play to beat Ballyhale Shamrocks by one point. When asked to comment on that match, he referred back to the story which had emerged that week where footage had shown West Ham player Kurt Zouma failing to respect his cat around his home in London. 'Between Zouma and Ruddle,' said Cusack to Joanne Cantwell, 'it hasn't been a good week for cats.'

AND HERE IS YOUR HOST

One of the news stories of 2023 was the announcement of Patrick Kielty as the new presenter of *The Late Late Show*. While he was still under sixteen, Kielty was part of the Down squad that won the All-Ireland minor football crown in 1987. James McCartan and Conor Deegan helped Down defeat Cork by 1–12 to 1–5 in that game at Croke Park. Future Cork stars Stephen O'Brien and Don Davis were on the losing side that day.

Kielty has a nice line in self-deprecation: 'I played minor for three years. I was a sub on the team in 1987 – that's why we won. I was only sixteen when I made the minor team in 1987. My brother was on that team that won. I want to make that very clear. I played in 1988 and 1989 and we won nothing in both those years.'

11

FROM A JACK TO A KING

Jack Lynch Enters Politics

Jack Lynch has a unique claim to fame. He was the first man in history to have won six senior All-Ireland medals in consecutive years, 1941–6. He used his fame as a Cork star to launch his career in politics and went on to assume the highest office in the land. For a brief time I was his neighbour in Rathgar. When I questioned him about his time as Taoiseach, he laughed and told me a fable about politics:

'While walking down the street one day, a female head of state is tragically hit by a car and dies. Her soul arrives in heaven and is met by St Peter at the entrance.

'"Welcome to heaven," said St Peter. "Before you settle in, it seems there is a problem. We seldom see a high official around these parts, you see, so we're not sure what to do with you."

'"No problem, just let me in," says the lady.

'"Well, I'd like to, but I have orders from higher up. What we'll do is have you spend one day in hell and one in heaven. Then you can choose where to spend eternity."

'"Really, I've made up my mind. I want to be in heaven," says the head of state.

'"I'm sorry but we have our rules." And with that, St Peter escorts her to the elevator and she goes down, down, down to hell. The doors open and she finds herself in the middle of a golf course. In the distance is a club and standing in front of it are all her friends and the politicians who have worked with her. Everyone is very happy and in evening dress. They greet her, hug her, and reminisce about the good times they had while getting rich at the expense of the people. They play a friendly game of golf and then dine on lobster. Also present is the devil, who really is a very friendly guy and who has a good time dancing and telling jokes. They are having such a good time that, before she realises it, it is time to go. Everyone gives her a big hug and waves while the elevator rises. The elevator goes up, up, up and reopens on heaven, where St Peter is waiting for her.

'"Now it's time to visit heaven."

'So, twenty-four hours pass with the head of state joining a large number of contented souls moving from cloud to cloud, playing the harp and singing. Before she realises it, the twenty-four hours have gone by and St Peter returns.

'"Well then, you've spent a day in hell and another in heaven. Now choose your eternal destination."

'She reflects for a minute, then answers: "Well, I would never have expected it. I mean, heaven has been delightful, but I think I would be better off in hell."

'So, St Peter escorts her to the elevator and she goes down, down, down to hell. The doors of the elevator open and she is in the middle of a barren land covered with garbage. She sees all her friends, dressed in rags, picking up the trash and putting it in bags. The devil comes over to her and lays his arm on her neck.

'"I don't understand," stammers the head of state. "Yesterday I was here and everyone was on the golf course and we ate lobster and caviar and danced and had a great time. Now it is a wasteland full of garbage and my friends look miserable."

'The devil looks at her, smiles and says, "Yesterday we were campaigning. Today you voted for us!"'

THE LONG FINGER

Jack Lynch also had a way with words. He once made a bold policy statement that, 'I would not like to leave the repeal of the contraception laws on the long finger.'

ELECTIONEERING

As a boy, Lynch was known for his speed. Hence it was said of him that he was so fast he could do a minute in thirty seconds.

He once joked to me: 'A good speech isn't one that proves that the minister is telling the truth but that no one else can prove he's lying.' He also enjoyed Oscar Levant's comment that, 'A politician will double-cross that bridge when he comes to it.'

During the 1977 General Election campaign Jack went to visit an old folks home to canvas for votes. One woman had a bad-tempered face and her voice seemed remarkably like a dog growling and she insisted on telling the prospective Taoiseach her life story. She said she went to the dentist to have her false teeth adjusted for the fourth time because they still didn't fit.

'Well,' said the dentist, 'I'll do it again this time, but no more. There's no reason why these shouldn't fit your mouth easily.'

'Who said anything about my mouth?' she answered. 'They don't fit in the glass.'

In his later years, Lynch was occasionally asked to reflect on the ageing process. He loved George Burns's comment on turning eighty: 'I can do all the things today I did at eighteen, which tells you how pathetic I was at eighteen.'

A TIDY SUM

As a pupil at the famous North Mon, Lynch had a keen appreciation for the role of the Christian Brothers in Irish life generally, but in the promotion of hurling in particular. He especially admired their commitment and the dedication they inspired in others.

He once told me the story of a clever little boy at an expensive and liberal private school who was underachieving badly, particularly in maths, so the parents, devout atheists, sent him to a very strict Christian Brothers establishment. He returned after the first day, tiny school bag brimming with books, and locked himself in his room for three hours with his homework. This went on for a few weeks and at the end of his first month he returned with his interim report card, which showed that he was first in his class in maths. His delighted parents asked what had awakened his drive and he said, a bit grimly, 'I knew that it was a serious subject when they showed me the guy nailed to the plus sign!'

12

I NEARLY SH*T MYSELF

David Brady's Car Is Stolen

After Mayo sensationally beat Dublin in the 2021 All-Ireland semi-final, a Mayo fan asked: 'What do you say to a Dub in Croke Park on an All-Ireland final day?'

'A portion of chips please, with extra Mayo.'

Former Mayo midfielder David Brady is a man of strong opinions and often makes the news for his sometimes controversial comments.

In 2017 he was at an engagement in Harcourt Street in Dublin one evening. He parked his car beside an Aviva van. When he came out, he found his car was stolen. As he had a number of highly confidential patient records for his work in the car, in his own words: 'I nearly sh*t myself.'

Brady has a number of contacts in the gardai, so he rang the guards, the superintendent and the drugs squad. They duly arrived on the scene to investigate.

Then a group of ladies arrived whose car was parked in 'his' spot. He asked them what time they had parked their car. When they told him 6.30 p.m. he answered that it was not possible because he had parked his car there at 7.10 p.m. Then they showed him their ticket and he knew that they were not lying.

The seeds of uncertainty were sown in his mind.

He walked around the corner.

What did he see?

There were fifteen Aviva vans and his car was in the middle of them!

Brady showed commendable honesty: 'I made a complete fool of myself.'

SHUT THE F**K UP

In February 2019, after Corofin beat Gaoth Dobhair in the All-Ireland club semi-final, Brady was in the spotlight again. He took to social media to raise questions about the Donegal side's commitment. 'They will, when the dust settles and time passes, in a quiet moment, ask did they pass up on the opportunity of a lifetime ... posting multiple pi**-ups won't win you an All-Ireland and that's not what winning is about.'

After winning the Ulster title, former Donegal All-Star Kevin Cassidy had posted several videos showing the exuberant celebrations in Gaoth Dobhair. His response to Brady was: 'Shut the f**k up. I'm not even a midfielder and I would still take you to the cleaners, you muppet.'

RADIO GAAGAA

Brady is a regular on Newstalk radio's *Off The Ball*, where he is interrogated by the presenter Joe Molloy. The popular broadcaster at one stage bumped into Dave Moore from Today FM's 'Dermot and Dave'. Moore was with his children and said: 'Kids, Joe works for OTB on Newstalk.' His eldest child quipped: 'Oh yeah, Snoozetalk.' His mortified father turned to Molloy and said: 'No idea where he got that.'

THE BARE ESSENTIALS
Like all Mayo fans, David Brady has been very hungry for Mayo
to win the elusive Sam Maguire Cup. He has pledged to make
great personal sacrifice to assist them on the road: 'I'd wear a
pink G-String for Mayo to win the All-Ireland.'

He acknowledges, though, that the popular view in the
county is that the team will not be winning soon. 'Every man,
woman and monkey is nearly writing them off in Mayo.'

TURF WARS
John O'Mahony came close to bringing Sam Maguire to Mayo
in 1989. Later he would serve as a Fine Gael T.D. One of the
recurring issues he had to deal with was the protests about the
restrictions on turf cutting in Irish bogs. He was amused by a
headline in a national paper which read: 'Fine Gael under fire
over turf wars.'

Johnno made a cutting response: 'At least we got a blaze of
publicity.'

RIVALS
As a former manager of Mayo and Galway, few people are better
equipped to appreciate the rivalry between the counties than John
O'Mahony. The rivalry continues as was evident when Marty
Morrissey commented to the editor of the *Connacht Tribune* and
Galway super fan, Dave O'Connell, in advance of President Joe
Biden's visit to his ancestral home in the West of Ireland in 2023:
'Mayo deserve their day in the sun, don't they, Dave?'

O'Connell's response was: 'They got their day in 1951.'

13

GUARD OF HONOUR

The GAA and the Gardai

There's a story told about a famous footballer of yesteryear – a garda who got into a heated altercation with a member of the public and some hard words and, allegedly, a blow were exchanged. The affronted civilian in question went straight to complain about the garda to his superiors. As he made his complaint, copious notes were taken and when the garda's name was identified, the officer in charge mentioned casually, 'the footballer'. The complainant went a whiter shade of pale and asked in a whisper: 'Is that who he is? God, I don't want to get him in trouble. I'm dropping all charges.'

GARDA PATROL
Matt Connor, Páidí Ó Sé, Jerry O'Connor, John Morley, Aidan O'Mahony, Eddie Brennan, Josie Dwyer, Ciara Gaynor, Tony Davis, Larry Stanley, Seamus Bonner, John McCarthy, Pillar Caffrey, Frank Cummins and Ollie Baker – just a small selection of GAA greats who served or serve with distinction as gardai. Discretion prevents me from naming the prominent

72

GAA personality and garda who called on the Official Secrets Act in telling me the following story. To protect his identity further, I have changed the location of the story and relocated it to Roscommon. The names have been changed to protect the guilty.

In 1985 inter-county star Danny decided he was going on a search for love. He headed for Roscommon's premier nightclub, Rockfords, on the Saturday night of the Halloween bank holiday weekend. Fifty per cent of all marriages in Roscommon back then began in Rockfords. As if to show how serious he was, he bought a new shirt and some Old Spice aftershave. Whenever he was asked if he liked classical music, he would always say, 'I love the music in the Old Spice ad.'

It was time for the first slow set of the night. Out of the corner of his eye, he saw a vision in long black hair. He can still feel the acceleration in his heartbeat and the tremor in his voice as he asked her to dance. The song was 'The Power of Love' by Jennifer Rush. He wondered if it was an omen.

He knew everything hinged on whether she would stay with him for the second dance. He could feel the tightness in his chest as he asked her if she would stay on. She said yes. The second song was Fergal Sharkey booming out: 'A good heart is hard to find.' Danny felt the song was a sign from God. He had always believed that the idea of love at first sight was 'a load of old nonsense'. But when Danny looked deep into her sparkling ocean-blue eyes, he just knew that she was 'the one' for him. From that moment on, every corner of his heart would be hers.

Eight weeks passed. On Christmas Eve he brought her to the square in Roscommon town, which hosted the biggest tree in the county. Shakin' Stevens was singing 'Merry Christmas Everyone' over a car radio. Danny asked her what she would like for Christmas. She replied immediately: 'Nice jewellery, new clothes, lovely ankle boots and a fabulous handbag.' Then she asked him what he would like.

As he said 'all I want for Christmas is you', he got on his knees and pulled out a diamond engagement ring. There were tears of joy in both their eyes after she said yes. Danny knew deep in his soul that he would never be unhappy or lonely again.

The following Christmas, they were married and held the reception in Hayden's Hotel in Ballinasloe. The sun was shining and the weather was unseasonably warm and, in the conditions, his new bride glowed like a princess in her wedding photos. It was as if heaven was smiling on him. Danny could not believe that such a level of happiness existed as he felt that day and could feel in his bones that he was the luckiest man in Ireland, if not the world.

Christmasses came and went. Then on Christmas Eve 2021, on the anniversary of their magical engagement, his wife left him for a member of the gardai. For the next year everybody he met offered him words of consolation. Some seemed more upset that there was a guard involved than that she had walked out on him.

On Christmas Eve 2022, Danny was driving home from Roscommon when he noticed a garda car behind him. The squad car started to flash his lights. Danny went into panic. He hit the accelerator of his Volkswagen Golf and drove at ferocious speed all the way home. When he pulled into his driveway, the garda car followed him in all the way.

A guard walked up and Danny rolled down his window, even though he was hyper-ventilating and extremely agitated.

'Excuse me, sir, but do you know you have been doing 183km per hour in this vehicle? This is very serious with all the talk there is at the moment about road safety. I am afraid, even though it is Christmas Eve, I am going to have to prosecute you.'

Danny's breathing was still too intense for him to speak.

'I can see you are very, very distressed but, nonetheless, I have to ask: 'What is your name, sir?'

'DDDD . . . Da, Da . . . Dan . . . Danny,' gasped Danny.

'What is your surname, sir, please? Danny. Why is that name ringing a bell for me. Oh my God. Now I know why. You are the Danny that my colleague ran away with your wife. Now I understand why you had such a reaction when you saw the squad car. You were so upset about what happened that you drove like a bat out of hell. Sure, it's no wonder you were scared out of your wits after what that so and so of a guard put you through. We will forget that this ever happened. Let me just wish you a very happy Christmas. And on my own behalf, let me apologise that my colleague ran away with your wife. I hope one day you will forget the pain and the heartbreak.'

By now, Danny's breathing was back to normal. He looked up at the guard and shook his head sadly.

In a soft voice he gently whispered: 'Ah, guard. You don't understand. The reason I was driving so fast is that I was terrified that you were going to bring her back.'

SPEEDIE

Pat Spillane once had a run-in with a guard. He was once punched after a match as he left Croke Park stadium when he was set upon by a group of disgruntled Donegal fans after his commentary on *The Sunday Game*. The incident happened following Donegal's famous win over Cork to reach the All-Ireland Senior Football Championship final in 2012:

'I once got punched by Donegal supporters on Clonliffe Road after a game. That day I ran to my car and was driving a bit fast when a Ban Garda stopped me. "You are speeding, sir!" she said, and I told her that I had just been attacked by a group of supporters and that they could still be after me. It was like running with the bulls in Pamplona.'

TEARS ARE THE SILENT LANGUAGE

Much of the antipathy for Spillane turned to sympathy when he broke down in tears as he remembered his late father after Kerry's All-Ireland final win in 2022, in his final *Sunday Game*.

He recalled how clashes between Kerry and Galway mean a lot to him after his father passed away two days after the 1964 All-Ireland final:

'It's a lovely way to finish my time in *The Sunday Game*, I'm a passionate Kerry man and we knew there were a very talented bunch coming through, but talent doesn't necessarily mean All-Irelands.

'Just from a personal point of view, in 1964 my father was a selector for Kerry against Galway and the night before the game he had a pain in the chest. He wouldn't go to the doctor, went to the game the following day as a selector and was dead on Tuesday.

'Kerry v Galway matches to me always bring back this memory and my father never saw us play, the three sons. And today the three sons have nineteen All-Ireland medals and his two grandsons today, Killian and Adrian, have two more, and he would have been proud of twenty-one senior All-Ireland Football medals in his house. It's just a special day, a special day.'

Tears are a reminder that we are more than the moment.

14

COME ON THE ROSSIES

Roscommon Win the 2019 Connacht Final

The world of Gaelic games has produced its own classic hits. After Roscommon beat Galway in the 2019 Connacht final, the *Roscommon Herald*'s Kevin Egan tweeted his unique adaption of a famous piece of Norwegian commentary:

'Gráinne Seoige, Eamon Ó Cuiv, Nora Barnacle, Michael D. Higgins, Ronán Mullen, Gideon Ouseley, Joe Canning, Bishop Eamonn Casey, that ould wan that charges a fiver to read palms on Shop Street.

'"YOUR BOYS TOOK ONE HELL OF A BEATING!"'

TOPICALITY
Two days after Brexit happened in 2020, Roscommon travelled to play Fermanagh in the League. Shannonside commentator Willie Hegarty observed: 'Roscommon became the first team to play a league game outside the EU since 1972.'

TO THE POINT
Even during the bleakest days of the Coronavirus crisis there were moments of humour, like the club official in Roscommon who

remarked: 'We obviously were preparing for the virus long before everyone else. Our defenders were never closer than two metres to anyone. Our goalie never caught anything. Our forwards never passed anything on. And, of course, our committee members were always washing their hands for everything.'

LEGAL DILEMMA

Roscommon great, Karol Mannion, is a legal eagle. During one of his first cases he was asked to defend a thief. Karol asked him: 'Have you any money?'

'No, but I have a sports car.'

'Okay, then, you can sell that to pay me. Now, what are you accused of stealing?'

'A sports car.'

IN TOO DEEP

Roscommon lost to Galway in the Connacht Championship in 2021 playing ultra defensive football with most of the players behind the ball. This caused one fan to observe that if Roscommon were any deeper they would be in Munster.

SEASONAL

As a young boy, Roscommon's most legendary footballer, Dermot Earley, had a keen interest in music. When he was in infants class, he was asked if he could name the four seasons. Dermot replied: 'No, Miss, but I know Frankie Valli was one of them.'

MEMORY LOSS

When Dermot was eight, his mother asked him; 'What did I say I'd do to you if you ate the chocolate cake?'

Dermot replied: 'My memory is as bad as yours. I can't remember.'

SWEET

Dermot's one weakness was that he had a sweet tooth. He joked that when it came to cake, apple tart, biscuits and ice cream he could resist anything but temptation. Hence, he renamed my considerable stock of digestive biscuits as 'Suggestive biscuits'.

NO SUPER-VALUE

C. S. Lewis claimed: 'Friendship is unnecessary, like philosophy, like art . . . it has no survival value; rather it's one of those things which give value to survival.' My friendship with Dermot Earley continues over ten years since he left us.

In a dislocated age like ours, our often frail and brittle lives are glued together by an ever-decreasing circle of constants. Dermot was born into a life punctuated by work, family and religion, a world which lingered like a whisper in his subconscious.

Although the winds of change have swept through the country in the most dramatic of ways since his childhood, the one constant was his family – they still kept his feet firmly on the ground. A few years before he died, he rang his mother, Kitty, shortly before he was due to travel down to Castlerea to give a talk about temperance. During the conversation she casually remarked: 'I see you are coming down to Castlerea.'

'That's right.'

'They don't think much of you.'

'How do you mean?'

'They are only charging three euro for the entrance fee.'

They talked on for a while and, just as he was finishing, Dermot asked: 'Will I see you on Tuesday night?'

'At what?'

'At Castlerea for my talk.'

'Do you think I would pay three euro to go and hear you?'

15

STRICTLY COME RIVALRY

Kerry v Dublin

When Tipperary erupted in celebration after finally ending a sixteen-year wait for a Munster hurling title in 1987, their neighbours in Kilkenny bided their time before delivering a none-too-subtle reminder of how long the blue and gold had been absent from the main events.

As Tipperary supporters headed through Urlingford and Johnstown on their way to Dublin for the All-Ireland semi-final clash with Galway some weeks later, they were greeted by large roadside banners proclaiming, 'Croke Park this way.'

COME DANCING

In Gaelic football the most celebrated rivalry is between Dublin and Kerry. A humorous window into the rivalry between the counties came in the Spring of 2019 when former Dublin star, Denis Bastick, competed on the popular TV series *Dancing with the Stars*. One Kerry fan commented: 'At the end of every dance he looks like someone who has left the immersion on.'

TUFF STUFF

No other man had ever lost five All-Ireland finals to the same county, but that was the late great Brian Mullins's fate against Kerry in 1975, 1978, 1979, 1984 and 1985. The Dublin legend's philosophy was: 'You lose with grace and dignity, but you don't ever like it. Anyone not hurt by losing a big match is playing the wrong game, for the wrong county.'

He always had advice for younger players like Charlie Redmond: 'Charlie, if a match is passing you by, do something, get booked, start a skirmish, do anything to get yourself into the match, to make the other team take you seriously. If you need back-up in the row, don't worry, there will be plenty with you.'

Redmond jokes: 'Whenever I tell that story people say to me, "Jaysus, Charlie, you didn't need much encouragement to start a row yourself."'

STAR STRUCK

Size matters.

However, it may not be a barrier to sporting success. Ranelagh's favourite son, Ken Doherty, established himself as an icon of snooker – winning the World Championship in 1997, and almost winning it again the following year only to lose to John Higgins. When I spoke to Ken in Ranelagh he explained:

'My father loved the snooker. He used to watch *Pot Black*. It used to only come on the TV every Thursday for half an hour on BBC 2 and they would fit two single frames in the half an hour. Once I saw Alex Higgins play. He was running around popping balls – completely different to the other guys – I was completely fascinated.

'I asked Santa for a little snooker table that year. I was only eight, it was 1977, and I woke up Christmas morning and there was a little snooker table at the end of my bunk bed. From then on, I was completely hooked.'

Then Jason's Snooker Club in Ranelagh became his second home:

'When I used to go into Jason's, and this is a true story, they used to give me a biscuit tin for me to stand on. You know the old Jacob's biscuit tins? I would stand on it and take a shot and then I would kick it around and play the other shot. I used to start to beat the older boys my brother's age – four and eight years older than me – and they used to hide the biscuit tin.

'It became a stature thing, bragging rights. I just wanted to get better and better and every day. I would get off the bus past my mother's house, straight into Jason's, schoolbag under the table. I would be cleaning out the ash tray, sweeping the floor, just for the free game on the table. Until my mother would send my sister round to say that your dinner was on the table, get home!'

Kerry great Kieran Donaghy never needed to be perched on a biscuit tin. As the Covid-19 crisis struck, a zealous guard arrested Donaghy. He alleged that the 'Star' had strayed beyond the permitted two-kilometre zone during the government's lockdown. The judge dismissed the case saying, 'Sure, he's so tall that one of his strides takes two kilometres.'

LEAVING ON A JETPLANE

Another Kerry giant was Eoin Liston. He rejoices in the nick-name 'Bomber'. Everybody knew him by that name, it seemed. However, one day he was on plane from Cork to Cardiff and a passenger affectionately shouted 'Bomber' at him. Sadly, the airplane crew were not GAA fans and when they heard 'Bomber' they initiated a security alert.

NOEL, NOEL

With four league titles, three Munster crowns and an All-Ireland triumph under his belt, Noel O'Leary is a huge figure in Cork football circles. The Cill na Martra man won two Mid-Cork JFC titles. He first joined the senior team in 2000 for the National League and made his championship debut in 2003 in a loss to Limerick. He will always be remembered for his clashes with Kerry wing-forward Paul Galvin, especially the right hook that sent him to the line against Kerry in 2009, where Galvin was also red-carded for his involvement. Off the field, though, he faced more serious challenges. In the space of a year and a half at the turn of the century, he lost his best friend, his cousin and his brother.

One of the most impressive people I have ever met is Oisín McConville. He told me about his toughest opponent:

'Noel O'Leary marked me a couple of times. He was a hardy bit of stuff. He was working in Dublin. He was picking two boys up for training. They were on the Naas dual carriageway and a stone came up from a lorry in front, hit the windscreen and the windscreen shattered. He stopped the car on the side of the road, pushed the windscreen out while pulled over on the side of the road. The two boys were in the car, and he drove home to Cork with no windscreen. The two boys were lying down in the back of the car because they were frozen with the cold. That's the sort of boy he was.'

16

THE LYONS DEN

Tommy Lyons Manages Dublin

A manager's job is a tough one. At thirty-eight, Roddy Collins got his dream job in football as Bohemians manager, the team he supported as a boy. It was a tough task, though. The club was in a relegation battle. He needed a midfielder and a forward. He found two players who had just come back from playing with Hong Kong Rangers through an agent. Roddy asked his man in the UK to fax through their names and signatures so he could get them registered before the transfer deadline. He wanted to play them against Cork City that weekend. The striker's name was Dean Martin. 'Dean Martin? Are you winding me up?' said Collins. The agent told him to trust him. Collins did, naming the player in his side. 'Number eleven,' announced the stadium announcer at Turner's Cross through the loudspeakers: 'He's not a singer, he's a winger – it's Dean Martin.'

GAA managers and coaches seldom attract the same mass devotion that Pep Guardiola or Jurgen Klopp attract. However, they do bring a unique style. The late John Morrison was one of the great personalities in the GAA. When he coached Mayo, he famously sent the Mayo players a Valentine's card that year 'from Sam with love'.

Armagh's Paul McGrane was among those he got to practise catching balloons above their heads to improve their fielding technique. When he coached Donegal, Morrison gave all his players a nut. It was to remind them of Brazil and the skill and quality of their football team. If you don't find that puzzling, there is something very wrong with me.

THE LYONS CLUB

One of the most colourful and flamboyant managers was Tommy Lyons, who led Dublin to the Leinster title in 2002. That Christmas, Tommy gave his best friend the gift of a barometer.

When his friend looked unsure Tommy said, 'No pressure.'

ACCURACY

A fee-paying rugby school on the southside of Dublin challenged a northside Christian Brothers school to play a game of hurling. The date was arranged and the Christian Brothers boys decided to adopt a gentlemanly stance and send the college a telegram which read: 'May the best team win.'

The southsiders sent a telegram in reply which read, 'May the better team win.'

A NOSE JOB

The Dubs were pioneers. Long before cosmetic surgery had become fashionable, Jimmy Keaveney had a nose job. Playing for Dublin against the All-Stars in Chicago, Jimmy was being marked by a Kerry legend. They 'clashed' and Jimmy's nose ended up just under his eye. At half-time Dr Pat O'Neill noticed his star forward's problem. He got six of the Dublin players to hold the big full-forward down and with considerable force and after much screaming on Keaveney's part, and his blood flowing more freely than the Niagara Falls, O'Neill forcefully pushed the nose back to where it should be.

FEAR CRUA

Keaveney loved one of Seán Boylan's protégées, Colm Coyle. Colm took Seán's place on the Meath sideline – or at least he would have had he not been suspended. As a teak-tough defender, Coyle embodied the stereotype of tough, hard Meath players and as a result had the odd problem with referees!

I enjoyed Colm's reaction after the Monaghan team he managed some years ago beat Armagh: 'We planned for every eventuality, including if we had a man sent off. I told them what Meath did every time I was sent off!'

One Meath fan joked: 'There was once a street called after Colm Coyle, but they had to change the name because no one crossed Colm.'

EMERGENCY ACTION

Meath attracted much criticism when they were accused of 'roughing up' Peter Canavan in 1995. Two years later the Tyrone superstar was playing for Ireland in the Compromise Rules series. One of his teammates was Colm Parkinson, still only a year out of the minor ranks. Peter the Great called the Laois teenager over to him. Parkinson was expecting some great tactical insight as Canavan whispered into his ear. What he actually heard was: 'Cover me while I take a pee.'

17

THE PIANO MAN

Limerick Win the 2018 All-Ireland

The marketing of the All Blacks rugby team has been incredible. Sales of the famous black jersey have soared by the use of imaginative slogans such as: 'All jerseys keep you warm but only one makes you shiver.'

In recent years the GAA has upped its game massively in terms of marketing, particularly around the times of All-Ireland finals. They now have their own rituals. They begin the night before with *Up for the Match*.

A second ritual is that winning All-Ireland finals inevitably leads to a winter team holiday. There is no scandal like a sex scandal and Ger Loughnane provided plenty of ammunition for the chattering class after Clare's historic All-Ireland triumph in 1995. His eyes shine mischievously as he recalls it:

'We did something in Clare that was totally innovative. We had just won the All-Ireland for the first time in eighty-one years and something special had to be done to reward the players. I decided we would set up a Holiday Fund Committee that would be totally independent of the county board. I contacted

Johnny Callinan, who had played with me for Clare, who is a brilliant guy and a solicitor in Ennis; Gerry Kelly, a great Clare supporter and one of the most popular publicans in Clare, and Seamus Hayes, who wrote for *The Clare Champion* and they raised the funds for the holiday. I went into the travel agent and was looking for something different, and I began to look at the East and stumbled on Thailand.

'Back in 1995 everyone associated going to Thailand with Bangkok and with sex. Here you have a team full of bachelors going to Bangkok. When the news broke, all hell broke loose!

'We didn't mind. This was an exceptional achievement and we were going to do something exceptional to mark it. It was a holiday of a lifetime in a totally different culture. We had an absolutely fantastic time and the incidents that happened will be remembered forever but can never be recorded in any book!'

He adds a further layer to the story:

'The one criterion for our holiday destination was that it had to be a place where nobody knew anything about hurling. So, it came down to a straight choice between Thailand or Tipperary!'

NO THANK YOU FOR THE MUSIC

A third ritual is that All-Ireland finals are also associated with drink. The times are a-changing. In 2018, after Limerick won their first All-Ireland hurling title in forty-five years, the decision was made to break with tradition. During the lengthy months of celebration afterwards they did not bring the Liam MacCarthy Cup to a single pub.

A fourth ritual of All-Ireland victories is the singing of songs. Limerick won great plaudits for their players' skill in winning the All-Ireland. None more so than hurler of the year, Cian Lynch. His teammates, though, are less flattering. Shane Dowling went public on his one great vice: 'His taste in music is absolutely shocking.' Indeed, the finger of suspicion was pointed at Lynch when Limerick were found guilty of crimes against music by playing Westlife in the sacred sanctuary of the Croke Park dressing room after they captured the title.

In marked contrast, their manager, John Kiely, won acclaim for his more classic sensibilities. His party piece is 'The Piano Man'.

In June 2023, Limerick won their fifth Munster final in a row. One Limerick fan told him his new party piece should be ABBA's 'The Winner Takes It All'. Given that Limerick only beat Clare by a point and that the Banner were very controversially denied a late free to draw the match, a Clare fan suggested Kiely's song should be Frank Sinatra's 'Luck Be a Lady'. Other Banner fans suggested Amnesty International should investigate the travesty. One claimed it was the 'greatest miscarriage of injustice since Nelson Mandela was detained all those years in Robben Island'.

MISSED OPPORTUNITIES
John Kiely was less than impressed by a fringe player with the team. He said to him, 'It's a pity you didn't take up the game sooner.'

'You mean I'd be better now?'

'No, you would have given up the game long ago.'

FRIENDS IN LOW PLACES
The GAA's most infamous link with music came in 2014 during the shambles over the cancellation of the Garth Brooks series of concerts in Croke Park because of a dispute over licensing laws.

Some cynics were very unsympathetic to the huge loss of revenue for the GAA with the news of the cancellation of the concerts – on the basis that they had agreed to three concerts a year but then went for eight. Hence, the new name, the NGAA: The Not Great Arithmetic Association.

FUMING

The steam was coming out of the ears of veteran journalist Vincent Browne when Limerick won twelve All-Stars in 2021. He was furious because Limerick did not win all fifteen All-Stars.

18

SPYGATE

Donegal v Kerry

Before the 2014 All-Ireland football final, the mother of Donegal full-backs Eamon and Neil McGee was asked if she worried about her two sons playing in the match. As both are towering over six foot, she smiled philosophically and said: 'Have you seen the size of my two boys?'

AN ACT OF FAITH
Going into that final, Kerry's James O'Donoghue was the favourite to win footballer of the year. Hence the caption in Croke Park: 'In JOD we trust.'

BEATING THE BLANKET
Kerry beat Donegal with both sides playing very negative styles and making multiple mistakes. Hence one fan's tweet after the match: 'In a game that both sides seemed to want to lose, Donegal seemed to want to lose it more.'

EXORCISM

Joe Brolly was characteristically understated: 'Kerry were like the little girl in *The Exorcist* whose head revolves as she machine-guns the walls of vomit.'

GENESIS PART 2

In the Kingdom they do not take things lying down. So, one fan responded by rewriting the Book of Genesis: 'In the beginning God said, "Let there be light." Joe Brolly replied: "Say please."'

FOOTLOOSE

After the final, as there was so little use of the foot pass in the game, one letter writer to *The Irish Times* expressed his frustration:

'Congratulations to Kerry on winning the All-Ireland Volleyball Championship.'

19

GIVING IT SOCKS

Cyril Farrell's Management Style

Hurling managers have different styles. The phlegmatic Brian Cody brought unprecedented success to Kilkenny. That is why Eoin Larkin wrapped up his All-Ireland acceptance speech in 2012 by adapting the Donegal anthem: 'Cody's winning matches.'

THE TINKER MAN

Ger Loughnane was from 'the tough love' school of management. He was the drill sergeant who prepared his army for battle. He illustrates with an example:

'Fergal Hegarty, "Hego", came out of nowhere in 1995 from the under-21 side. If ever there was a "made hurler" it was him. He was very athletic and his job was to win possession and move the ball on. He did massive work in 1995 and 1996 and was great in our first All-Ireland win. In 1996 against Limerick he was easily Clare's best player and almost held the game for us. He was chasing Ciarán Carey for that final point and only for he fell he might have stopped him.

'After that his form dipped. I still can't figure out why. I tried everything but maybe I was too cutting with him. That's always the problem with a made hurler. You knock the best out of him while you can, but you know that it won't last. He's a fantastic character in a pub and is a wonderful mimic – mostly of me!

'We had desperate set-tos in training as his form declined and he was always complaining to Dalo (the team captain Anthony Daly) that I was too hard on him. There was one night we nearly fell out. I was making the point that a good player needs to be a good thinker. He got his wires crossed and went to Dalo afterwards and said, "Did you hear what he said to me? He called me a tinker." Dalo had heard what I actually said and thought it was hilarious!'

A ROOM WITH A VIEW
In July 2020 the GAA tentatively began playing club fixtures again after the shutdown of games because of the COVID-19 crisis. So restricted were the attendances that Anthony Daly joked that he was going to bring a stepladder with him to watch over the fence to see Clarecastle play.

GALWAY BOYS
If you go to the library every day you will eventually read a book. Cyril Farrell believes that there is an analogy there for GAA management. He had a different style which was much more player-friendly. He was just thirty years of age when he led Galway to only their second All-Ireland hurling title in 1980. Two more titles followed in his second incarnation as Galway manager in 1987 and 1988.

He had an idyllic childhood. Then all changed utterly when his beloved father was killed in a farming accident. The tragedy has given Cyril a keen sensitivity to the suffering and needs of others – and an ability to relate to strength and vulnerability in equal measure.

Cyril returned home from a trip one morning with such a tiny amount of change in his pocket that he gave his last penny to the porter. Forgetting this, when he was approached by a homeless man at the bus station, he invited the man, with characteristic generosity, to dine with him for breakfast in the local restaurant.

After a slap-up-meal, Cyril got on his feet to pay the bill only to discover there was nothing in his pocket. The man, seeing his predicament, paid for both of them.

Mortified with embarrassment, Cyril said, 'Come with me in a taxi to my home and I will pay you back.'

'No way,' replied the man. 'You've caught me for a meal, but there's no way you're getting a taxi fare out of me as well.'

SWEETS FOR MY SWEETS

As Galway manager, Cyril's caring nature was evident in a plethora of ways. He was a manager who was ahead of his time but not in the area of diet. He wanted his players to have the best of everything and after training they had steak and chips. However, this was not enough for Cyril. He sent the players home every evening with a pocket full of Club Milk bars.

On match Sundays the team had Mass in the morning, but Farrell always instructed the priest beforehand to say a 'nifty' Mass.

INTERVIEW TECHNIQUE

Critical to the success of the team was their legendary half-backline – one of the greatest in the history of hurling – of Pete Finnerty, Tony Keady and Gerry McInerney. The 1980s were a time of deep recession in Ireland. For many, the most important piece of paper was their ticket to America. Given the lack of employment opportunities, to the consternation of Galway fans, Gerry McInerney had to go to America for work. Cyril Farrell went into overdrive to find him employment back in Galway. He arranged an opportunity for Gerry and brought him home from the States for a job interview.

The interview was going brilliantly and was nearly over when the prospective employer noticed that the Galway star was not wearing any socks and asked him why.

McInerney shrugged and said: 'Ah it's still too hot in New York to wear socks.'

UNTO US A CHILD IS BORN

In 2004 Kevin Walsh was coming to the end of his illustrious career with Galway when he pulled a hamstring in training. In agony he went to call his wife, who was heavily pregnant at the time, only to discover that he had forgotten his mobile phone. As he drove to the hospital for treatment, he spotted a phone kiosk and stopped off to call his wife and let her know he would be home late and why but didn't let her say anything. After he got treatment he was surprised to find that there was nobody there when he returned home. Once he'd retrieved his phone, he rang his wife and asked her where she was. He nearly fell over when she replied: 'I'm in labour.'

'Why didn't you tell me?' he asked her indignantly.

'You wouldn't let me,' she replied.

20

MAGIC MOMENTS

The Fans Rule, Okay

The GAA experience is at once particular and universal – especially if you are a fan.

I LOVE ME COUNTY
Some people are very competitive. Eighty-two-year-old Cliff Richard went toe-to-toe with the much younger Stormzy for the Christmas number one album at Christmas 2022. When Chris Evans suggested to Sir Cliff: 'May the best man win,' Cliff responded quick as a flash: 'Don't say that. It might be him.'

Passion is the engine that drives all sports. Gaelic games are no exception. Witness Davy Fitzgerald's antics on the sidelines at any match. Then there is his motto: 'Hell for f**king leather.'

Who will ever forget John Mullane's *Braveheart*-like *cri de coeur*, 'I love me county'?

There is the passion of the ex-player. A case in point is Offaly player Daithí Regan's reaction to what he considered an uninformed comment: 'Hindsight is the foresight of a gobshite.'

Regan has also spoken of how Offaly took their defeat to Clare in the 1995 All-Ireland final with good grace: 'Although we lost there was an amusing end to the games. Not surprisingly the Offaly party was a muted affair and this was not to Johnny Pilkington's liking and he dragged a few of us to what he said would be the best party in town. Where did he bring us? Only to the Clare hotel! The chairman of the Clare County Board, Robert Frost, invited Johnny to say a few words. Typical of Johnny he said, "We'll keep those Kilkenny f**kers down and ye keep those f**kers down in Cork and Tipperary and we'll have a few great years together."'

DESPERATELY SEEKING SAM
There is a teashop in Westport and it has as its Wi-Fi passport: MayoforSam

HOLD ON TIGHT
Sometimes fans use interesting exhortations to motivate their team, such as the Armagh supporter, an aerobic talker who can work himself into a sweat just by a conversation, or more accurately a monologue, who roared out as the Orchard County shocked Monaghan in the 2019 Qualifiers: 'Stick to your man like sh*te to a blanket!'

During the controversial 1988 All-Ireland football final, a Meath fan shouted out to defender Liam Harnan: 'If you can't mark him, injure him.'

Sometimes fans can be cruel. After Cork put 5–31 past Waterford in the 1982 Munster final, the joke around Youghal was that Waterford had confused the scoreline with a train timetable.

CHANT OF THE DAY
Before Meath played Dublin in the Leinster final in 2019, an anxious Meath fan boldly parked his car in Archbishop's House

in Drumcondra. Just when he thought his troubles were over, some of the Dublin fans started chanting at him: 'We know where your car is parked, do-dah, do-dah.'

WEXFORD'S WONDROUS FAN

Wexford's most famous fan is the immortal broadcaster Liam Spratt. Some of Liam's famous quotes include:

Liam: 'What was the traffic like today, Billy, when you were travelling up?'

Co-commentator Billy Byrne: 'You should know, Liam, I was in the same car as you.'

Then there was the time when Liam mistook Waterford goalie Clinton Hennessy for former soccer international Clinton Morrison.

'And a great save from the Waterford goalkeeper Clinton Morrison ... wait, no ... sorry ... Clinton Hennessy in the Waterford goal. Got the wrong colour there, Billy.'

Another mix-up involved Wexford's most famous referee Dickie Murphy: 'Dickie Watch looks at his Murphy' and: 'The game is in and the ball is on.'

21

HAIR-RAISING

Clare v Tipperary

There were moments during his managerial career which provided the cue for Ger Loughnane to show the softer and more mischievous side of his nature:

'In 1995 we went to Thurles to train on the pitch ten days before the Munster final. The man who normally supplied food to us after training gave us his van, to take food down to Thurles with us. I volunteered to take the van, which may not have been the cleverest idea as I had never driven a van before! I had my son, Barry, with me and we were to pick up Frank Lohan on the way. We came to a T-junction and I couldn't find the brake without looking down. There was a woman crossing the road. I went right across the road, barely avoiding the woman, and just before hitting the footpath I managed to turn the van around. Then I was able to look down and see where the brake was.

'We collected Frank and put Barry in the back of the van, which was nothing but a freezer, because all the food was frozen. When we got to Tipperary town, we stopped because it was so hot, and we decided to get a cool drink. We went back and opened the door for Barry. He was nearly frozen alive!

'On the way home we had a race back to Shannon, between us in the van and Jamesie (O'Connor) and Seánie (McMahon) in another car. It was that kind of atmosphere that lightened up the whole thing on the way up to the Munster final.'

FEELING BLUE

Loughnane was adept at turning any unusual situation into an opportunity for a good laugh:

'Before the All-Ireland in 1997 our team sponsor, Pat O'Donnell, made a presentation to the panel and management. He gave each of us a blue and yellow towel and tiny silver bell. The morning of the All-Ireland, Tony Considine (one of the selectors) was fuming. He told me, "The dye from that f**king towel ran. I'm f**king blue all over." I replied, "It wasn't the dye from the towel that ran. It was the dye from your hair!"'

GUESS WHO

Despite Loughnane's happy capacity for weathering hostility, the strains that had been mounting mercilessly over the years as manager, strains whose ravages the obsessive in him deflected, took their toll. The biggest casualty was his hairline. At the peak of the Clare team's success, there was a table quiz in Shannon. For one of the rounds, they showed pictures of well-known people when they were young. A photo of Loughnane was included from back in the days when he had really long hair. When one of the teams was asked to identify his photo they answered: 'Princess Diana!'

Ger has since lost all his hair. He held on to his comb, though. He just can't part with it.

MEDIA MANAGEMENT

Throughout his management career, Loughnane was called a lot of things but one person he was never compared with was Mother Teresa. Yet they had one thing in common. Mother Teresa famously said, 'Facing the press is more difficult than bathing a leper.' During his tenure as Clare manager, Loughnane had a stormy relationship with the media. Before the 1995 All-Ireland he said of his media interviews: 'I say nothing but I never stop talking.'

WINING AND DINING

In 2002, Loughnane was having a quiet meal with his wife Mary in a restaurant in Ennis. Out of the corner of his eye, he noticed the then *Sunday Tribune*'s hurling correspondent Enda McEvoy entering the restaurant. A natural-born mischief-maker, Loughnane dispatched his wife to make contact. Enda was hardly seated when Mary approached him and said, with Nicole Kidman-like acting skills, 'I'm very sorry, sir, I'm going to have to ask you to leave.'

Enda was gobsmacked. 'What do you mean?'

'Well, sir, the last time you were here, you were caught on video camera leaving after your meal without paying your bill.'

McEvoy was stunned, 'But ... but ... but I've never been here before.'

A pantomime developed with an exchange along the lines of: 'Oh, yes you did.' 'Oh, no I didn't.' The journalist could not believe he was being accused of such an offence and was getting increasingly bewildered and distressed. Eventually, he heard the loud laughter coming from another table and turned around to see Loughnane splitting his sides laughing.

22

THE PAT FROM PAT

Joe Brolly Gets Sacked

Broadcasting is hazardous on many levels. During the 2022 World Cup, the abbreviations used on the RTÉ website for the England v Iran game were: ENG v IRA.

Joe Brolly knows all about the hazards of broadcasting.

My first encounter with Joe was memorable. I smiled as I went to approach him and held out my hand to him. His exact greeting was: 'Jesus, that tie you are wearing is absolutely hideous. People should have to get a license to wear a thing like that.'

Brolly described being invited to a revival of Brian Friel's *Dancing at Lughnasa* in the noughties. During the interval, Mrs Friel came over to him and said, 'Brian would like to speak to you. He makes me go to the shop and get the *Gaelic Life* every week. He sits in the kitchen and laughs.' When Friel met him, he said: 'I have to tell you: every week I read you. Atrocious literature, but very funny.' Joe's response was: 'Honestly, that is what's going on my gravestone.'

Mayo fans generally have a less benign attitude to Joe claiming: 'Brolly is so full of himself that his email is gmail@ joebrolly.com.'

Straight talking is Joe's forte and it is not an overstatement to say that from time to time it gets him in trouble. On *The Sunday Game*, during the 2019 All-Ireland final, at half-time in the drawn game, Brolly questioned the judgement of referee David Gough for the sending-off of Dublin's Jonny Cooper for fouling David Clifford on a third occasion. Brolly claimed the Meath match official had been 'clearly influenced by the propaganda coming from Kerry'.

Joe was describing how Dublin were bringing their 'democracy of excellence' to their drive for five against old rivals Kerry. Then he said with great irritation to Pat Spillane, 'Can I just finish the point? Can I just finish the point please? STOP PATTING ME.'

Brolly's comments led to him being dropped for the replay. Joe humourously tweeted: 'If anyone has a spare ticket for the replay, I've just been let down.' One enterprising club was quick off the mark to promote its draw for tickets:

'Hi Joe, we're running draw [sic] for a pair of tickets for both ladies and mens' finals, only €10 a line ♣ will I stick you down for 1?'

A few months later, Brolly said he was shocked how his years with the national broadcaster ended, in the wake of the drawn All-Ireland final: 'I loved every minute of it – to be palling about with the greats of Gaelic football, and to have the red carpet into Croke Park of a Sunday, and to be part of the national conversation. I was there for twenty years and, genuinely, I loved it and the fun we had. For it to end so abruptly, and, I thought, cruelly, I have to say. I'm a big boy and I'm freelance, but I have to say, I was shocked.'

The former Derry star complained he felt *The Sunday Game* had become increasingly scripted: 'When I came into *The Sunday Game*, I loved it. We were free to express our opinions. I felt that I could actually talk about football the way the lads in the pub talk about it. No one in the pub says: "Kerry had a 25.7 productivity rating in the first five minutes, but, in fact, that increased to 31.2% in the second quarter of the first half." You would be taken away by the men in white coats.

'It started to become statistics-driven and then we began to get sent scripts, before the All-Ireland football final: "You'll say this and then he'll deal with that and you'll deal with that." You know the way you pick out a package of analysis, which I always loved doing, and we were told what to pick out. I rang him and said: "You don't need me, you need a newsreader, you need a narrator." Eventually, the ground just shrank under me.'

Brolly admitted that he had great fun on his last appearance on *The Sunday Game*, for the drawn All-Ireland final: 'We had a brilliant day and there was some controversy during the game. The referee, who is a good pal of mine, gave a decision, and I had a bit of a blast at it.

'It was good fun. I went on the Dublin side for it. You have got to throw in the odd hand grenade. I can imagine people on their sofas, some clapping and enjoying, some ready to tear their hair out.

'Then, I got a series of warnings after that. For example, I was told that "Your position in RTÉ is probably untenable now – because, at eleven minutes past three, you said to Pat Spillane, 'would you stop patting my arm?'" I said: "Have you lost your f**king mad marbles?" Me and Pat are like an old married couple.'

Brolly's contract with RTÉ was not renewed at the end of 2019 after contact between himself and Head of Sport Declan

McBennett. Subsequently, Brolly joined subscriber channel eir Sport.

The affair had an unexpected postscript in February 2020. A motion was tabled by the Clare County Council to have Brolly returned as an RTÉ GAA pundit. The motion was put forward by Councillor Gerry Flynn and was backed by Ann Norton and PJ Ryan. Flynn said, 'I have put forward the motion and I have got a couple of my colleagues to co-sign it. I am a sports fanatic and I am suffering from withdrawal symptoms since he was removed from the RTÉ panel. He was a fantastic guy – I loved watching him play the game and I loved watching him analyse it.

'Where I'm coming from, maybe it's PC gone mad, I don't know. But I think RTÉ are basically sterilising all analysts now into a position where it's scripted, and it's taken away from the enjoyment of the game. I'm only giving you this from the point of view of my constituents and my good self.

'It wasn't just the punditry. He was entertaining and he was knowledgeable as well. For a state broadcaster that is funded by public money to be carrying on like that, I wouldn't be happy with it. So, I decided to put the motion to Clare County Council and it will be directed towards the Minister for Communication and the Minister for Finance.'

Well known impressionist Conor Moore of Conor Sketches fame tweeted about the motion: 'Well @JoeBrolly1993 what you think of motion 31 to be debated at Clare County Council?'

The motion was debated on 24 February 2020 and defeated 24–3.

One councillor who opposed the motion said, 'The only brolly I want to see at a Clare match is one in the hand of a Clare fan if it's raining.'

GOOD COUNCIL

At the 2020 GAA Congress, the motion about the introduction of the black card in hurling generated great emotion. It was resoundingly defeated. One delegate got the biggest laugh of the day when he said, 'This motion would be as welcome in Antrim as Joe Brolly would be if he went back into RTÉ.'

UNORTHODOX TACTICS

Brolly is a free spirit. He still coaches underage footballers in Belfast, using some unorthodox methods. To get his team to score goals, he placed a blow-up doll in the goals. 'Now, you won't see it in any coaching manual,' he quipped.

DIRECTIONS

Joe was the guest speaker at a fundraiser for the Louth County Board. He stopped for a coffee in Dundalk and was asked by a tourist: 'Is there a B&Q in Dundalk?' The ever-helpful Brolly replied, 'No, but there's an "r" and "h" in Drogheda.'

EVERYBODY'S CRAZY ABOUT A SHARP DRESSED MAN?

In the summer of 2023, Joe had a pop at the dress sense of a former colleague on *The Sunday Game*: 'Fair play to Jackie Tyrell dropping into *The Sunday Game* studio on the way to his wedding.'

Tyrrell turned defence into attack in response and highlighted Brolly's departure from RTÉ by tweeting: 'Only keeping your seat warm for you Joe. Oh wait . . .'

One of Brolly's most consistent themes in recent times is that the passion is gone as GAA is becoming a 'national embarrassment' on RTÉ. One of the examples he cited was: 'As Éamonn Fitzmaurice was droning on, a friend of mine texted, "F**k me, Brolly, I wouldn't be surprised if Fitzmaurice started into a decade of the rosary."'

23

POACHERS TURNED GAMEKEEPERS

GAA Greats Become Pundits

What does Tommy Walsh have in common with Elvis Presley?

A shared love of banana sandwiches.

The Kilkenny legend has followed a long line of former stars who have made the switch to broadcasting fame. Such is his brilliance on the airwaves that during the Championship Tommy is always on our minds as it's now or never for the big powers of hurling.

Though Tommy Walsh hurled with Tullaroan, his home address is Ballycallan. This was a fact which teammate John Hoyne regularly highlighted. Walsh, however, had a classic response: 'Me father told me that when they were building the house at home, they built the main part of the house in Tullaroan, but they built the toilet in Ballycallan. So, we eat and sleep in Tullaroan. But we go to the jacks in Ballycallan.'

GOING GLOBAL

For those personalities who have retired, media involvement affords them the platform to continue their happy addiction to the small and large dramas created by players when they suspend accepted reality in favour of a private, if heightened, version of it on the pitch. As a television pundit their task is to inform, enthuse and to entertain, drawing on the depth and authenticity of their experiences.

Former Sligo great Eamonn O'Hara has become a regular on RTÉ. His appeal is international: 'I got a text from friends on holiday in Portugal. They were surprised to see a Portuguese boy approaching wearing a Sligo jersey. When they turned around they saw the number eight on his back with the word O'Hara!'

Although at the time it was not funny, O'Hara now laughs at a case of mistaken identity: 'We were playing Westmeath in 2006. I was given a second yellow card for a foul, even though I was forty yards away at the time. The linesman fingered me because he mistook me for Sean Davey because we have the same colour. I'm naturally like this. Sean gets his colouring from a sunbed. It was farcical more than anything else.'

THE WHEELS ON THE BUS GO ROUND AND ROUND

O'Hara is tongue-in-cheek about the rivalry between his native Sligo and Roscommon. O'Hara has a riddle that perfectly captures the great love Sligo fans have for their near neighbours.

Q: 'What is big and yellow and goes b-b-b-beep?'

A: 'The Roscommon bus backing into the garage in June having gone out of the Championship typically early.'

THE EARLEY YEARS

Few current players act as analysts now compared to previous times. In the late 1980s, for example, Paul Earley was a regular analyst on *The Sunday Game* even though he was still playing for Roscommon and had been an All-Star a few years before.

He worked well because he matched his deep knowledge of the game with a bit of humour.

One of his best moments came after the 1988 All-Ireland semi-final when Mayo, managed by John O'Mahony, put up a credible showing before losing to mighty Meath. At the end, Michael Lyster asked Earley: 'Will Mayo be back?'

Quick as a flash, Paul replied, 'I hope not!'

ADAM AND EVE

Colm O'Rourke became an analyst in 1991 when he was still the best player in the country. In his autobiography, Liam Hayes deals with the ripples of discord that created on the Meath panel back in 1991, but O'Rourke was an inspired choice and was one of the best pundits you will find anywhere. His mind is as agile as an Olympic gymnast. When he talks about football he nearly always seems, quite simply, to hit the right note. You can't ask any more of an analyst than that.

Colm also came up with some good one-liners. In 2003, as Armagh's focus and obsessive will to win a second All-Ireland looked all-consuming, O'Rourke's incisive observation was: 'If Adam was an Armagh footballer, Eve would have no chance. Instead of an apple, he would have looked for a banana, as this is on the diet sheet.'

IF I WERE A RICH MAN

Dublin's towering midfielder, Ciarán Whelan, has gone on to be a top pundit on *The Sunday Game*. He was reminded of the gap between aspirations for riches and the reality when he attended his daughter's parent-teacher meeting. When the teacher had asked her earlier that day what she wanted to be when she grew up, she replied that she wanted to be a football pundit. The teacher asked: 'Why have you chosen this career?'

'I dream of making a fortune from working on RTÉ, like my father,' she replied.

'Your father makes a fortune from working on RTÉ?' echoed the impressed teacher.

'No,' replied Ciarán's little girl. 'But he always dreams of it.'

24

WHERE IS THE F**KING DOOR?

Roscommon Win Four Consecutive Connacht Finals

The four happiest years of my life came between 1977 and 1980 when I was still in school and Roscommon ruled the GAA world, at least in Connacht.

It helped that we had some phenomenal players like Danny Murray, who won the first of his two consecutive All-Stars in 1979. He was, though, humbled on one occasion: 'After we won the National League final in 1979, I went to Lucan, where my sister Helen was living. I decided to go there first and then head to the Roscommon team celebrations in the spa hotel taking place that evening. The meal in the hotel was scheduled to start about eight o'clock but when I got there the whole place was jammed. After about an hour trying to get in, I said to your man on the door that my name was Danny Murray and he said, "There are about ten Danny Murrays gone in here already." Then he just closed the door on me.'

ON THE BENCH

Danny Murray was famous in the squad for his propensity to have a steak for lunch before a big game. His happiest memories are of the players on the team: 'Probably the great character in the squad was Gerry Emmett. It seemed Gerry was the perpetual sub but it never got him down. The Connacht Council had a special celebration for us to mark the anniversary of one of our Connacht titles in McHale Park in Castlebar at half-time. Before the first half finished there was an announcement over the loudspeaker: "Would the 1980 Roscommon team please go the dugout." One of the lads asked, "Where's the dugout?" Quick as a flash Gerry interjected, "I'll show ye. I know every dugout in every county in Ireland."'

IN LOVING MEMORY

Emmett tells the story of approaching his club, St Ronan's, to put up a statue to him in his honour because he'd been down to Gorthaganny and seen the lovely statue of Dermot Earley. In his own version of the story, Emmett claims that the club were amenable to the request provided it would be one of him sitting in the dugout.

IN ALL HONESTY

Gerry Fitzmaurice was the rock on the team that many an opposing attack floundered on: 'We were in the dressing room for the 1979 All-Ireland semi-final and we were being psyched up for the game. There was a great passion and our trainer Tom Heneghan was giving a great speech to get us going. At one stage, he looked around at the whole team and said, "Is there anyone here that thinks a Dublin man is better than a Roscommon man?"

'We were all wound up and tensed up at this stage and ready to say, "No, we will tear strips off them."

'And Tom looked around and he said it again and no-one answered.

'He pointed to one fella, the most honest and truthful man you would ever meet in your life, who was on the panel at the time, and said to him, "What do you say, do you think these Dublin players are better than us?"

'With typical honesty he replied, "Well Tom, the way I look at it, some of them are and some of them aren't."'

LOST

Fitzmaurice adds: 'Another time we were playing Mayo in a big championship game and before the game, the captain was bouncing off the walls. He was psyching us up and, lined up from 1 to 15 behind him, we were all set to go out. As the captain was roaring, "Let's kill these f**kers, c'mon, follow me," he made a burst towards what he thought was the dressing-room door and of course we went after him.

'And, lo and behold, the captain was so pumped up, he didn't realise he had mistakenly gone into the shower area with us behind following him. The captain was still so psyched up about the game, he was saying in the shower, "Where's the f**king door, where's the f**king door?"'

SUPERMAC

A star of the Roscommon team was Tony McManus, not just because of his skill but because of the intelligent way he played the game. A revealing insight into the sharpness of Tony's mind came in a county final between his club Clann na nGael and Kilmore. At one point a Clann player grabbed the ball. One of his opponents called him by the Christian name. Instinctively the Clann player passed the ball to him and the Kilmore player raced up the field. Shortly after, Tony McManus won possession and the same Kilmore man yelled, 'Tony, Tony, pass the ball.' Tony swung around and said, 'If I was playing with you, I wouldn't pass you the ball!'

THE VIEW FROM WASHINGTON

Gay Sheeran played with Tony McManus before going on to manage the Rossies in the 1990s. He had a number of memorable moments in his career: 'I know it seems heresy to many people but the bond I felt and still feel for the players on the county team is much stronger than I do for the lads in the club. The reason for it is very simple: I spent so much time with them. When I was managing, I quickly found out that I was a lot older than I thought. We were playing a match on a wet day and Dermot Washington was wearing only one glove. The conversation unfolded as follows:

Me: "You're like Jimmy Mannion (the great Saint Brigid's stalwart who was sadly lost to the GAA world in March 2020). He would always wear only one glove."

Dermot: "Who's Jimmy Mannion?"

Me: "How can you not know Jimmy Mannion? He was on the Roscommon team that won the Connacht final in 1972 and got to the league final in 1974."

Dermot: "I wasn't born in 1974."'

FAMOUS SEAMUS

Seamus Hayden was a Roscommon midfielder in the 1980 All-Ireland final. After his inter-county career was over, he was in charge of a club team and they had a very high age profile on the team. One night Seamus rang one of the officials in Saint Dominic's club who was in the middle of a crisis meeting. The club had been going through some difficulties and could not get anybody to manage them. The meeting was going badly, and they were getting nowhere, so eventually the great Jimmy Murray, who was eighty-two years of age at the time, said he would train the team until they could get someone else to take over. At that moment Seamus's call came through and when the official answered he said, 'Hayden, you ugly hoor, how's it going?'

Seamus politely let this insult pass but when he inquired what was going on in the club, he got hit with a hammer blow when the official said, 'Well it's like this. Jimmy Murray has a dilemma. He's not sure whether at this stage of his life he should train Dominic's or else play for your team!'

BLESSINGS

Dermot Earley became a high-ranking army officer but for twenty years he was the undisputed star of Roscommon football. Traditionally, the army had a mission every Lent. In 1979 the mission was given by Fr Michael Cleary. In one of his talks he spoke about determination and compared determination with Dermot Earley going through with the ball for the goal, much to the amusement of the rest of the congregation. On that Ash Wednesday, Earley was going up to receive the ashes when Fr Cleary revised his blessing somewhat. Instead of: 'Remember man thou art but dust and into dust thou shalt return,' his blessing was: 'Up the Dubs.'

A REF'S BEST FRIEND

Dermot Earley was one of the greatest players never to win an All-Ireland medal. The closest he came to it was the controversial 1980 All-Ireland final when Roscommon lost to Kerry. The Roscommon fans were irate about the refereeing of the game. Legend has it that one of them approached the referee immediately after the game and said, 'Hi ref, how's your dog?'

The ref is said to have replied: 'What do you mean? I don't have a dog.'

The fan responded: 'That's strange. You're the first blind man I've ever met that doesn't have a guide dog!'

EXCUSES

During his stewardship of the Roscommon team, a fringe member of the squad missed a number of training sessions. Earley tried to make contact with him but with no success. He had to resort to leaving him messages in all kinds of strange locations. A few days later he got a message on his answering machine: 'Dermot, this is X. I'm sorry I missed the last four training sessions. My reasons were compelling and indescribable.' So ended the message and his brief and undistinguished career as a Roscommon footballer.

25

JERSEY BOYS

Kilkenny v Wexford

One of the best sources of comedy among GAA fans is the intenstity of feeling between rival supporters. A case in point goes back to the 1980s and early 1990s when Kilkenny's dominance ensured a bleak time for Wexford hurling. This was most obvious on the Wexford side of the New Ross Bridge, which separates counties Kilkenny and Wexford. It read: 'You are now entering a Nuclear Free Zone.' A Kilkenny fan added a message of his own: 'You've now entered a Trophy Free Zone.'

DANCING AT THE CROSSROADS

Rivalries of every level have been an integral part of Irish sport.

It was Ireland's first sporting civil war.

It took place twenty years before Keane v McCarthy in Saipan.

The Irish sporting nation was split right down the middle.

After he was sensationally dropped by the Irish rugby selectors on the tour to Australia in 1979, Tony Ward became embroiled in one of the most keenly argued controversies in the history of Irish sport. For three years a fierce debate raged:

who should wear Ireland's number ten jersey? Ward or Ollie Campbell?

Campbell thought he had finally resolved the Ward issue with a series of stunning performances that ensured Ireland broke a thirty-three year famine and won the Triple Crown in 1982. A few weeks later, Ollie was leaving Westport one morning when he picked up a lady of mature years who was visiting a friend in Castlebar Hospital. After an initial flurry of small talk, the conversation unfolded as follows:

Her: 'And what sports do you play? Do you play Gaelic?'

Ollie (as modestly as possible): 'No, I play rugby?'

Long silence.

Her: 'Do you know there's one thing I'll never understand about rugby.'

Ollie: (with all due modesty): 'What? I might be able to help.'

Short silence.

Her: 'The only thing I don't understand about rugby is why Tony Ward is not on the Irish team!'

Even after his retirement from rugby, Campbell still found his name linked with Tony Ward's. He was invited on Mike Murphy's radio show at one stage. Before the broadcast he was asked if there were any subjects he did not wish to discuss. He said: 'Tony Ward and South Africa' because he thought they had been flogged to death. The first question Mike asked him was: 'I see here, Ollie, that the two areas that you have said you do not want to be questioned about are South Africa and Tony Ward. Why is that?'

In 1996 Liam Griffin led Wexford to the All-Ireland. Some Kilkenny fans could not handle the new hurling order. One story illustrates this. That Christmas, a Kilkenny family went into Callan to do some Christmas shopping. In the sports shop the son picked up a Wexford hurling shirt and said to his twin sister, 'I've decided to be a Wexford supporter. I would like this jersey for Christmas.' His sister, outraged by the suggestion, slapped him on the face and said, 'Go talk to your mother.' The boy walked with the Wexford shirt in hand and found his mother. 'Mummy dearest?'

'Yes pet?'

'I've decided I'm going to be a Wexford supporter and I'd like this shirt for Christmas.'

The mother could barely speak with anger but eventually said, 'Go talk to your father.'

Off he went with shirt in hand and found his father. 'Dad?'

'Yes, son.'

'I've decided to become a Wexford fan and I would like this shirt for Christmas.'

The father hit the son a thump on the head and said, 'No son of mine will be seen in a yoke like that.'

As they went home, the father asked the son if he had learned any lesson that day. The son thought for a moment before replying, 'Yes I have. I've only been a Wexford fan for over an hour and already I hate you Kilkenny f**kers!'

Pat Spillane has a jersey problem too. One Mayo fan claims his head has got so big he can't take off his Kerry jersey any more.

BRIDESMAIDS

After leading Wexford to the All-Ireland title in 1996 Martin Storey produced one of the most memorable lines in a winning captain's speech: 'We have been described as the bridesmaids of hurling. Well, today we got married.'

WHAT'S THE STOREY?

The Wexford fans were not above taking the players down to size. A few days after their All-Ireland final triumph, a young boy walked into the bank, where one of the stars of the team, Tom Dempsey, worked. He walked up to Tom, who soon had a big smile on his face when the boy handed him his autograph book. His smile quickly faded when the boy asked, 'Would you be able to get Martin Storey's autograph for me sometime?'

FAST CATS

In 1988 Kilkenny minors, conducted by DJ Carey, were giving Galway an almighty hammering in the All-Ireland semi-final. At one point late in the game, the Cats were bringing on a sub. They were taking their time about it to the frustration of the Galway fans. Eventually one shouted, 'If ye don't hurry up he will soon be overage!'

26

BEAUTY AND THE BEAST

Pat Spillane Has a Moment

With man, most of his misfortunes are occasioned by man.
(PLINY THE ELDER)

Pat Spillane is probably the most celebrated former star turned pundit. When Martin McHugh dismissed Colm Cooper as a two-trick pony, Spillane responded by saying: 'It was a bit like saying the Pope isn't Catholic, the earth isn't round and Neil Armstrong didn't walk on the moon. It ranks with those three.'

He is phlegmatic about the hostility he sometimes attracts: 'Several years ago because of the success of *The Premiership* the people in charge of *The Sunday Game*, the editors and the directors, wanted to gizz it up and make it more punchy. They suggested to Colm O'Rourke and myself that we should ape what Johnny Giles and Eamon Dunphy did. Why can't one be thoughtful and analytical à la Giles and why can't one be a bit of a loose canon and be controversial à la Dunphy? In rare moments of vanity, I'm very pleased to think that I lived up to their instructions. I think I did a great job in the Giles role!'

TRAUMA

I am suffering from a serious, perhaps fatal, condition.

I have P.P.S.T.S.

It is Post Pat Spillane Stress Trauma Syndrome.

It all began on Valentine's Day 2020. I was having a quiet night watching a group of highly-strung young people on *The Late Late Show* 'love special'.

Then, for the last item, they produced two female agony aunts to give them advice on affairs of the heart. I felt my eyes were deceiving me because surely the man in the middle was not Pat Spillane?

Oh my God. It was.

Surely this was April Fool's Day?

It was not.

Then things got really surreal. The man I have spent half my life watching extolling the merits of geniuses like Michael Donnellan, Maurice Fitzgerald, Peter Canavan and Stephen Cluxton was suddenly singing the praises of . . .

Viagra.

The next day I convinced myself it was all a bad nightmare. To be sure, I watched the programme on playback three times the next morning. This did actually happen.

To make matters worse, Pat chose to speak about the trust his lovely wife Rosarii has for him. As only he could, he chose to illustrate this by claiming: 'If I went to America and I went into a big room and there were thousands of super-models in that room, naked, all trying to seduce me, and if there was a pint of beer at the end of the room, I would go for a pint of beer. That's trust.'

Trust me, you pay €160 a year on your TV licence fee for such wisdom.

A CHILD IS BORN

Spillane tells the story of when his first-born daughter Cara arrived, and the local priest both congratulated and commiserated all in one. Spillane clarified that: 'In rural Ireland when you have a baby you'd often be asked, "Is it a boy or a child?" But, in Kerry, they ask you: 'Have you the footballer?"'

27

MURPHY'S LAW

Dr Con's Medal Haul

The law demands the truth, the whole truth and nothing but the truth. Within the GAA, truth is much more nuanced. There are truths rather than truth because each county has its own truth.

Often there are fifty shades of GAA truth.

For generations in the world of Gaelic games, one of the most popular people has been 'Dr Con'. Until his retirement in 2019, Con Murphy served for forty-two years as the team doctor with Cork. His Wikipedia page was interesting. It recorded him as holding four county medals. That is correct but it is not the whole story.

In 1973 UCC won the county title and Con Murphy was one of eighteen players on the panel that day. He was handed a box of medals afterwards.

Afterwards, he gave out all the medals, including one for himself.

But . . .

There were still three medals left in the box.

Dr Con held on to the others.

Hence, he is the holder of four county medals.

TINA TURNER THRILLS

They do things differently in Cork. In Billy Morgan's first incarnation as manager of Cork, he employed two psychologists to get the team in the right frame of mind before playing a Munster final against Kerry.

The first guy had the job of calming the team down. Everyone had to close their eyes and picture themselves walking along the riverbank on a summer's evening with butterflies fluttering around them. There was the smell of freshly mown grass and the sounds of birds singing nearby. They had to imagine walking on a little path up a hill where there was a cabin and then walking into the cabin with seats inside and sitting down and feeling at peace.

The second psychologist had the job of getting the team all fired up and he was ready to have them play out of their skins when they got out on the pitch. The Cork team left the dressing room to the sound of Tina Turner singing 'Simply the Best' ringing in their ears. What happened? Kerry hammered the living daylights out of them that year.

OLYMPIC HERO

Billy's innovative methods did not always get the response he was hoping for. Another year, after Linford Christie won the gold medal in the Olympics, the mantra in the Cork dressing room was that the Cork team should take inspiration from Linford Christie. For ten minutes the team had the virtues of Linford extolled to them. When the inspirational words were finished, a very prominent Cork player, a household name, turned to another and whispered, in all sincerity, in a bewildered tone: 'Who the f**k is Linford Christie?'

FALLING STOCK

In 2019 two issues would relegate the state of Cork football down the agenda – the poor state of the pitch in Páirc Uí Chaoimh and the big cost overrun of the new stadium. One Kerry fan helpfully suggested that Cork needed the services of Bob the Builder.

28

WILL GALWAY BATE MAYO?

Mayo's Men Mountains

In 2019 Mayo began the Championship with renewed confidence fresh from their National League win and because James Horan was back as manager. First up in their Castlebar home were old rivals Roscommon, but then came one of those moments that can derange the emotional life when the Rossies ambushed them, as they did in 1986. The misery enveloping the county afterwards was palpable. Joe Brolly called it 'the disaster of disasters'. He went on to describe them as 'the nation's favourite tragic comedy unfolding again' and that it was 'more enthralling watching them losing than watching any other county winning'.

TWO'S COMPANY

This intense desire to win fuelled Mayo's 1980s All-Star midfield partnership of Willie Joe Padden and T.J. Kilgallon.

The joy of a Connacht title in 1981 quickly turned into bitter disappointment for Mayo's most iconic footballer, Willie Joe Padden, when Mayo faced Kerry in the All-Ireland semi-final:

'When we played Kerry in the All-Ireland semi-final in 1981 we did well in the first half but they gave us such a hammering in the second half that our goalkeeper, Michael Webb, said to me: "Every time I kicked out the ball I wondered would I have time to get back into the goal before the ball landed back in!"'

Padden's quick wit was shown when he was approached by a stranger in an airport who said: 'You're a dead ringer for Ian Botham.'

Quick as a flash, Willie Joe replied: 'Funny, I never get any of his cheques.'

CRIME AND PUNISHMENT

Mayo midfielder T.J. Kilgallon left his inter-county career with many happy memories to treasure of his colleagues in the green and red:

'One incident probably sums up the tight bond we had. We went for a holiday trip to the Canaries and one night Jimmy Burke was in a nightclub when a guy stole his wallet and ran outside with Jimmy chasing after him. Three of us happened to be coming in the opposite direction and we chased the thief into an alley. I'm six foot two but I was the smallest of our foursome. The guy had no escape and turned very contrite and handed the wallet back, saying: "Your wallet, sir." Let's just say it wasn't left at that!'

IN THE CLASSROOM

T.J. chose an honourable profession: 'My mother always had some reservations about my decision to become a teacher. She rightly pointed out that, at the time, teachers were very respected but had very little money. She used to say that I would be better if I had a job with a little less respect and a little more money!'

Then there are the strange answers T.J. got from some of his pupils, like when he asked: 'Who invented the barometer?'

The answer came immediately: 'Freddie Mercury.'

GOING TO THE CHAPEL OF LOVE

T.J. is proof of the old adage that the going to a wedding is the making of another. In his case the love of his life is an RTÉ personality:

'I met Eileen Magnier in 1990 and we got married two years later. She had no background in football. She's from Kilkenny and she's a cousin of Joe Hennessey. Whenever we are out, young people know Eileen because she's often on the news but they generally have no idea who I am. The odd time you hear someone say: "He used to play football." The galling thing is when the person they are talking to doesn't believe them because I don't look the part any more!'

MISSING IN ACTION

During his career T.J. witnessed some bizarre events:

'We were playing Galway in the Connacht Championship when Tomás Tierney "did a job" on Kevin McStay. Kevin was badly injured and had to go off. I was friends with Tomás and had shared a house with him at one stage but I couldn't believe that the referee, Seán Mullaney from Roscommon, wasn't booking him. I confronted Seán about it and he told me that the reason was that he had lost his notebook and couldn't book Tomás without it!'

THE TV DEAL

Cora Staunton is a legend of Mayo football. She helped make Mayo a superpower of ladies' football. Pat Spillane was a big fan of hers but used her success to poke fun at the Mayo men's team. 'There's a new series been made about Mayo footballers. It's called *Footballer's Husbands*.'

BORDERLINE

Roscommon fans have not always appreciated when Ballaghaderreen players go on to play for Mayo, despite the fact that they were born in Roscommon. The 2011 Connacht Final saw both counties contest a tight affair, played in almost Arctic conditions in the Hyde. In John Mullane parlance it was 'a day you wouldn't even throw out a milk-bottle'.

Whenever Mayo's All-Star forward, the Ballaghaderreen-born Andy Moran touched the ball, a lone fan, so thin that his shoulders looked like a coat hanger, approaching the shores of middle age, who had a way of presenting all his opinions as well-established facts, full of certainties that did have a sinuous power, was heard to boom out: 'Traitor, Traitor, Traitor.'

ON YOUR BIKE

In 1936 Seamus O'Malley captained the Mayo team to win the All-Ireland. He travelled to Dublin by train the evening before the match. On the day of the match, he announced that he could not stay for the celebrations and got a lift back to Mayo after the match. The Sam Maguire Cup was put in the boot of the car. He had to go to his work as a teacher the next morning. He left for work by bicycle with the Sam Maguire Cup strapped on his back. The times have changed.

29

UP FOR THE MATCH

An RTÉ Institution

Every year one of RTÉ's institutions is *Up for the Match*, where Jacqui Hurley and Des Cahill reach out to a very different audience than with programmes like *Love Hate*. The fact that the audience collapses into mirth when it emerges that two people who come from different counties have done the apparently unthinkable and married one another seems to be a mystery for young viewers. One tweeted: 'What the fock is this focking thing?'

BEAUTY SLEEP

The rivalry between Kilkenny and Tipperary down the decades has produced many great quips. On RTÉ's *Up for the Match* All-Ireland preview in 2014, former Tipperary captain Declan Carr said he could never sleep the night before an All-Ireland final and suggested that if you could sleep you were not properly up for the game.

Former Kilkenny great Michael Kavanagh was immediately asked if he slept the night before a final. He replied: 'It depended on who we were playing. If we were playing Tipperary, I slept like a baby.'

A TWIST IN THE TALE

The late Tim Kennelly had a fond memory of an earlier incarnation of the programme: 'It is important not to get carried away with yourself on television. I'll never forget the night before the All-Ireland final in 1980, the year we played Roscommon in the final. Jimmy Deenihan was interviewed, by telephone, from the team hotel by Liam Ó Murchú on RTÉ's special *Up for the Match* programme. Liam asked Jimmy: "An raibh tú ag feachaint ar an clár?"

'He replied: "Ní raibh. Bhíomar ag feachaint ar *Match of the Day*."

'Apparently the Roscommon players were watching it at the time and got a great laugh from Jimmy's answer. Mind you, it was probably the only laugh they got that weekend!'

PERENNIAL PROBLEMS

Mayo's old failings, like Kildare's, in the forwards department were once again exposed in the 2013 National semi-finals. This led Malachy Clerkin to observe in *The Irish Times*: 'Mayo and Kildare will be the dog against most teams but will likely find one to make them the lamp post the nearer we get to September.'

30

NOT ON BENDED KNEE

Con Houlihan Is Injured

Much of my love for Gaelic football was nurtured reading Con Houlihan's columns in the *Evening Press*. Con, though, was also a sporting ecumenist. He had a deep interest in rugby too.

I especially remember when Con wrote about a famous Scotland–Ireland game in which marauding Moss Keane scored a try despite the best efforts of the Scottish defence. Con's verdict was that 'a rolling Scot gathers no Moss'.

The Castleisland writer once described a new Irish international who was out of his depth: 'He was as confused-looking as a Kerry man in Paris.'

Con's favourite Dublin pub was Mulligans. Spotting a fellow journalist sitting sadly at the end of the bar in Mulligans, Houlihan said: 'There he is, poor fella, forgotten but not gone.'

Although he witnessed many brutal and violent incidents on the GAA fields, there was only one unforgivable crime for him: 'It is my belief that anybody who misuses the apostrophe is capable of anything.'

I once shared a meal of sorts with Con. He was less than impressed with the fare on offer and quoted John B. Keane to me on a Kerry man describing fat rashers: 'There wasn't as much lean in them as you'd draw with a solitary stroke of a red biro.'

When I asked him why he was drinking brandy and milk, he matter-of-factly explained: 'The brandy takes the shting out of the milk.'

He surprised me again when he told me that he had something in common with the Queen Mother. He read his favourite paper, *Sporting Life*, drinking his brandy and milk just like the Queen Mother at eight every morning would get her copy of the same publication brought to her bed accompanied by a large measure of gin and a bottle of tonic water.

PARISIAN WALKAWAYS

Con loved his biannual trips to Paris to see Ireland play France. At one stage he went with sportswriting colleague David Faiers. On the eve of the big game, the two men were enjoying a long, liquid session in the French capital. They were in a venue where Parisians and tourists gathered to hear beautiful women in alluring attire sing of affairs of the heart, and more carnal pleasures, and strange clowns cavorted in ways the priests of Kerry would not have approved of. Then, after a disagreement, the two writers abruptly decided to finish up and go their separate ways. To his horror and great surprise, the towering figure of Con was the victim of a mugging on his way back to the hotel, losing his money, his passport and, most terrifying of all under the circumstances, his match ticket.

The following afternoon and, with only minutes to go before the kick-off, there remained a vacant seat in the press box where Con was supposed to be. At that juncture, Faiers was approached by a stadium official who said that there was a

'Monsieur Oolahan' outside who claimed to be a member of the Irish press corps. Would Mr Faiers provide a description of his colleague so they might permit him access to the game?

'Of course,' Faiers replied, with a big smile. 'Monsieur Houlihan is a small, dapper (Con was perhaps the most sartorially challenged man in Christendom and beyond) gentleman . . .'

After a minute, though, he remembered there was honour amongst sportswriters as well as among thieves and Con was finally let in.

Another time, Con went to Mulligans for a liquid lunch to see that a poet of his acquaintance was waiting for him. The poet asked Con if he was familiar with the Russian poet Alexander Vvedensky who died on a prison train in 1941 (he has since acquired a new English-language audience when Pussy Riot's Nadezhda Tolokonnikova quoted Vvedensky at her trial in August 2012).

Con's reply was that Alexander Vvedensky was born in St Petersburg in 1904 and as a young adult became part of Leningrad's Futurist movement. Much of his work has been lost and destroyed and what remains, mostly published posthumously, is not very accessible. Con quoted from one of the poems:

'The only thing that is positive to the end is meaninglessness.'

He then quoted from *God May Be Around* (1931):

A star of meaninglessness shines,
it alone is fathomless.
A dead gentleman runs in
and silently removes time.

It was immediately obvious that his friend was less than happy with Con's familiarity: 'Well, Con, what would you say to a bit of horse-trading – the collected works in pristine condition in exchange for two tickets for Ireland's rugby international with England. What do you say, Con?'

After a short pause, Con replied: 'That is not horse-trading, that is ass-trading.'

BENDING THE KNEE
Con looked back on his own rugby-playing career with typical self-deprecation: 'I was never capped for Ireland but I was once knee-capped playing for Castleisland.'

DILEMMA
Con joked: 'I hate people who say literally when they mean metaphorically. It makes my blood boil.'

He also told me about the young Kerry woman who confessed to him: 'My boyfriend is twenty years older than me. He has tattoos all over his face, he has a ring in his nose, he has just got out of prison, he carries a gun. My problem is: how do I tell my parents that he is a Cork fan?'

31

THE LIMERICK LEADER

Éamonn Cregan Leads Offaly to Glory

In his twenty-year career with Limerick (1964–83), Éamonn Cregan's finest hour was at centre half-back in the 1973 All-Ireland final. In a tactical masterstroke, the Limerick mentors switched him to curb the menace of Kilkenny's ace centre-forward Pat Delaney.

Cregan would miss out on another All-Ireland medal in 1980 when Galway made the breakthrough. He scored 2–7 against Galway but his team lost by 2–15 to 3–9.

Cregan won three All-Star awards in 1971, 1972 and 1980.

A MODERN DAY MIRACLE

Cregan orchestrated one of the biggest miracles in hurling. In 1994 he tasted All-Ireland glory again when he coached Offaly to beat his native Limerick in the final, with two late goals in one of the most dramatic comebacks in living memory.

An old joke was revisited: 'Why aren't the Limerick team allowed to own a dog?'

'Because they can't hold on to a lead.'

SPEED MERCHANT

That Offaly team were a unique mix of characters and greatness. Liam Griffin described them as 'the Harlem Globetrotters of hurling' because of their skill. Éamonn Cregan remarked: 'If John Troy had speed, he would be the greatest player in the history of the game.'

A ONE-OFF

They also had the great Johnny Pilkington. The day before that All-Ireland, he was asked: 'What will it mean if ye win the All-Ireland?'

He replied: 'It will mean we will be drinking 'til Christmas.'

SO LONG

In 2021, former Offaly footballer Niall Geraghty announced his retirement – even though he had not played for the county in years!

While Mayo and Kerry fans were still reeling from a raft from their inter-county panels that same week, Geraghty offered a unique take on the retirement process with his tweet.

He wrote: 'I'd like to announce my retirement from @Offaly_GAA.

'After two championship sub appearances in 2014 and 2015, and a handful in the league, the time is right to call it a day.

'Thank you to the fans for always standing by me, literally, because I was on the bench on the terrace side.'

In response, Kieran Cunningham of the *Irish Star* congratulated him on 'great warm-ups over the years'.

GLORIOUS GLEN

In Kildare's great triumphs in the late 1990s, Glen Ryan was a central player. Two Kildare fans were settling down to a match in Newbridge when one realised he had left his wallet in his friend's Mercedes. He returned from the car park ten minutes later, pale and shaken.

'I've got bad news, Jim. A lorry has crashed into your Merc and the impact set it on fire. It's totally destroyed.'

'And I have some bad news for you,' said Jim. 'Glen Ryan is out injured.'

NEW RULES

Glen had a share in a pub in Newbridge. In the late 1990s, when Kildare had a very keen rivalry with Meath, it was rumoured that there was a sign in the pub which read: 'No Meath supporters served in this pub.' One day a man draped in the Meath colours came into the bar. 'I know you don't serve Meath fans, but I'm desperate for a drink and I'll pay £5 for a pint.'

The barman thought this over, then decided to serve the pint. It was gulped down in one go. 'Same again,' said the Meath fan. 'In fact I'll have two.' And he slapped a tenner on the bar. After a few minutes, he asked for another. The barman said tentatively, 'That's another fiver?'

'That's okay,' he said, pushing a fifty-pound note across the bar. 'I'll have a couple for the road. Keep the change.'

When the drinker had gone the barman put up a new sign: 'Only Meath fans served here.'

32

THE LONGFORD LEADER

Eugene McGee Steers Offaly to All-Ireland

It was the year England went to war with Argentina over the Falklands. The Taoiseach, Charlie Haughey, was due to meet the Prime Minister, Maggie Thatcher. Charlie spoke out in support of Argentina. The meeting never happened.

On the morning of the 1982 All-Ireland, the Offaly manager, Eugene McGee, was asked how seriously his players were taking their efforts to stop Kerry from winning their fifth All-Ireland in a row. Eugene furrowed his brow and said thoughtfully, 'Oh, very, very seriously. There are fellas here who are taking it so seriously that the last time a drop of drink touched their lips was – (dramatic long pause) – last Wednesday night.'

Pat Spillane offers the Kerry perspective on the defeat: 'We didn't underestimate them. They were just much better than we thought.'

An Offaly fan summed it up: 'Kerry for jokes. Offaly for Sam.'

MUSICAL MAESTRO
I once spent a Saturday evening in Eugene McGee's company as a spattering of stars flung over the dark heavens. We were

having a meal in a hotel when an intoxicated man came up to give McGee the benefit of his wisdom on Gaelic football. Eugene listened patiently for a few minutes before putting up his hand and saying: 'My good man, you obviously spend most of your life being ignored and that is exactly what I am going to do to you now.'

He also joked about the depth of his passion for the GAA: 'When my long-suffering wife hears me singing, very badly, in the shower "God only knows what I'd be without you" she knows I'm singing about the GAA and not about her.'

MARX-ISM

That does not mean he did not poke fun at them from time to time: 'To paraphrase Groucho Marx, I wouldn't like to belong to any organisation that would have me as a dictator. Trying to give well-meaning advice to the GAA is like chocolate. You know it's not good for you, but you go on eating it. For Cardinal Newman: "To be perfect was to have changed often." The logic of institutions is that to live well is not to change at all. Yet the GAA is, like buttermilk, not quite what it used to be.'

Eugene was frustrated sometimes by the pace of change within the GAA: 'Some officials think only: "Sure that's the way we have always done it." Yeah, and the captain of the Titanic used similar logic when he said the iceberg had only caused a small hole in the side of his ship!'

One thing that did not bother him was criticism on social media: 'I never worry about twitticisms. Most of that stuff is written by twits and half-twits.'

TWICE BANISHED

Although not the most distinguished player of all time, McGee retains a unique distinction as a player. He was sent off twice in the one game. He was playing in a club match for UCD and, in the first half, a player on his side was sent off but gave Eugene's name. In the second half Eugene was sent off himself but was too honest to give anyone else's name – so when the referee checked his report after the match, he couldn't understand how he'd sent Eugene off twice.

THE LONGFORD LEGEND
Jimmy Flynn was literally at the centre of the most successful period of Longford's history. His towering performances at midfield helped the county to beat the mighty Galway in the National League final in 1966. In 1968 Flynn helped Longford to take their only Leinster senior title. The most formative influence on his career was one of the most famous characters in the history of Longford football, Bertie Allen. As a boy, Jimmy played a nine-a-side juvenile match in Longford. Jimmy's side were winning a lot of ball and sending it in to the forwards, but they couldn't score. At half-time Bertie said that the four forwards were like Khrushchev, Eisenhower, Macmillan and de Gaulle they were so far apart.

THE OLD BOG ROAD
At the height of their fame in the 1960s, the Dublin-based Longford players were training in Longford once a week. Sometimes they would have two carloads of them travelling down to training. There were stories told about players coming out of various towns at night with too many drinks on board. One night, a few of the lads headed off to the Fleadh Cheoil in Clones but made a detour into a bog.

33

DOWN BY THE RIVER

Páidí's Motivational Style

Páidí Ó Sé's style was to fight fire with fire. When he became Kerry manager, one of the inner circle was wont to make mountains out of molehills about many small logistical issues. At first Páidí took no action. Then he discovered that the person concerned loved to go to bed early. Páidí took his revenge by regularly ringing him late at night, pretending to be deeply worried about some minor issue.

SPEED MERCHANT

After Páidí attended an Ulster final in Clones, he was less than pleased to find himself in a five-mile tailback. Lateral thinking was called for and Páidí's solution was to instruct the driver to activate the hazard lights and drive as fast as possible in the opposite lane. As motorists would imagine there was an emergency, no one would stop him. Oncoming traffic politely diverted into ditches and driveways, and in no time Páidí was safely at his destination.

EAGER TO PLEASE

Páidí psyched up Kerry before facing the Dubs: 'They think we're just a crowd of ignorant culchies from the bog. Let's not disappoint them.'

IN THE HOT SEAT

Páidí's finest hour as a manager came when he led Kerry to the 1997 All-Ireland. That was the game when Maurice Fitzgerald regularly broke through, the Mayo defenders falling around him like dying wasps, and kicked incredible points from all angles. There was a time Pat Spillane would have joked that if his mother had been marking Pat Holmes that day, she would have been man of the match. Not any more! After a replay against Galway, Páidí led them to another All-Ireland in 2000.

The wheels came off the wagon, though, in the 2001 All-Ireland semi-final when Meath beat Kerry by no less than fifteen points. Kerry went through a twenty-nine-minute spell in the first half without scoring and then could only muster a single point from substitute, Declan Quill, in the second half. After the match, Marty Morrissey asked a Kerry fan, 'Where did it all go wrong in Croke Park today?'

The fan replied, 'The green bit in the middle.'

RED IN THE BED

Páidí took his Kerry team's All-Ireland semi-final heavy defeat to Meath very badly.

A fan put the scale of the disappointment in Kerry well: 'It was like thinking you have gone to bed with Liz Hurley only to wake up to the terrible realisation that you slept with Red Hurley.'

MAGIC MOMENTS

A letter to *The Kerryman* newspaper praised Páidí's special powers: 'In Kerry we have not had much to be proud of lately but we like to think Páidí is the greatest magician of all time. He made Kerry disappear for the entire second half of the 2002 All-Ireland final against Armagh.'

ON THE BANKS OF MY OWN LOVELY LEE

In January 2003, Páidí O Sé got embroiled in a major controversy when he described the Kerry fans as 'f***ing animals'. One Cork fan suggested immediately that Kerry's nickname should no longer be 'the Kingdom' but 'the Animal Kingdom'. Another suggested that, in future, Cork should play all their home games against Kerry in Fota Wildlife Park to make the Kerry fans feel at home.

NOT FORGIVEN BUT FORGOTTEN

Despite his iconic status as a player, there are some Kerry people who will never forgive Páidí for his treatment of Maurice Fitzgerald.

A young autograph hunter was chuffed to bits when he got Páidí's autograph after a match. The following week he accosted Páidí again and got his autograph, and after the very next game he tried to get it again.

'Look,' said Páidí, 'this is the third time you've asked me for my autograph. What's going on?'

'Well,' said the youngster, 'if I can get eight more of yours, I can swap them for one of Maurice Fitzgerald's.'

Páidí was a bit nervous one day when he had to make the journey into Maurice's parish. His nerves were calmed immediately when an old man came to greet him and gave him a big smile and a most enthusiastic handshake and said, 'It's a great,

great pleasure to finally meet you in the flesh. You are a true icon of the game . . . What's your name again?'

LOVE IS ALL AROUND

Former Cavan manager Val Andrews was meant to be christened Joseph but because he was born on 13 February, a midwife fuelled on love suggested Valentine when he was a day old.

Val's coaching career began at a young age. His earlier forays with underage teams were not always an unqualified success. During one of his half-time talks, he looked out onto the pitch and, instead of having fifteen players, there were only eleven. In his own words, 'Four of them had f**ked off home.'

Val became a regular on radio programmes because he is not a man for soft talk. 'I don't agree with this Yankee school of "let's hug, kiss and breastfeed". Grow a set of a balls and mark your man, that's all a player needs to do.'

BORN TO RUN BACKWARDS

Managers have brought a number of new trends with them. Fitness gurus are all the rage. When 'the iron man from Rhode' Paddy McCormack was training Offaly for a year, his style of training was laps, laps and more laps. Frustration gnawed away at the players, and they eventually said to him, 'We're sick to death of all those laps. Tonight we're going to have something different.' Paddy thought for a moment and said, 'Okay, lads, that's fine. Turn around and run the other way for a change.'

34

EGGS-ACTLY

Peter Canavan Gets Attention

The famous Tyrone's three All-Irelands in the noughties would not have been possible without a number of great players, none more so than Peter Canavan. He is widely considered to be godlike in Tyrone. When one of his children was getting married, the presiding priest said at the start of the wedding ceremony, 'This is the first time I have said Mass in front of my employer.'

FRIENDS IN LOW PLACES
When Canavan played a charity match with Joe Brolly, the Derry pundit bowed down before Peter, to the amusement of the squad. 'Lower, lower,' Canavan said, to much laughter.

Canavan had the benefit of a great manager in Mickey Harte with the intense energy and drive that fuels him. Peter Canavan speaks of the transformation of his character: 'Back in his playing days, if there was a Vesuvius erupting on the pitch, the lava would be spilling from Mickey.'

EGGS-ACTLY

A great player's career is like a rose on a bush: it blooms brilliantly only to fade away. Peter Canavan's fame is destined to endure for many years. He captained the county to All-Ireland under-21 glory in both 1991 and 1992, and in 2003, despite struggling with injury, he captained them to their first senior All-Ireland,winning a second All-Ireland in 2005.

Some players, though, rely on more old-fashioned methods. Having almost won the 1995 All-Ireland final against Dublin for the county on his own, scoring eleven of his team's twelve points when they lost by a single point, it was a backhanded compliment to Canavan that he was singled out for 'special attention' by the Meath men in 1996 during the All-Ireland semi-final.

Two irate Tyrone fans were loud in their condemnation of the Meath team, particularly of their alleged ill-treatment of their star player, Peter Canavan. A Meath fan made an interesting and revealing slip of the tongue in response: 'You can't make an omelette without breaking legs.'

A GOOD NEWS STORY

The following year, Meath found themselves embroiled in controversy again with the infamous 'brawl' in the All-Ireland final replay. Seán Boylan sees the rivalry that developed between Meath and Mayo that year as a positive for the GAA:

'We had always enjoyed our rivalry with Dublin and I use the word "enjoyed" deliberately. Things did get very hot and heavy between us and Mayo that year but from the teams' point of view it was over and done with quickly. The Mayo fans were sore afterwards and, in their eyes, it was "the one that got away". Undoubtedly, when those situations arise there will be some who hold on to a grudge but a new rivalry, like the one that developed with Mayo and ourselves, breathes new energy into the GAA and provides lots of talking points for people. It helps bring the GAA more into the mainstream of Irish life. It is more than sport. It is a central part of people's lives. Do some people take it too far from time to time? Yes. But when people are more fired up by our games, that can only be a good thing for Irish life as a whole.'

With the replay won, Boylan thought he could relax. There was to be, though, yet a further twist in the tale:

'Back then the GAA hosted a lunch for the day after the final for both teams. It was a nice idea in theory but not very enjoyable if you were the losing team. So that day I walked to the door with Tommy Dowd and waited to be let in. There were two security men at the door and they refused to let us in. We didn't have official passes and they claimed not to recognise us. We calmly tried to persuade them at first, but they kept point-blank refusing us. So, things got heated. Eventually someone from on high in the GAA heard about the fracas outside and, much, much later than we ever expected, we were let in. It certainly killed the mood of celebration, I can tell you.

'The story was carried on the RTÉ news that night. I believe the GAA phonelines were jammed for the next week with people complaining about the way we were treated. I think it might not have been the GAA's finest hour from a PR perspective.'

THE SEQUEL

Boylan and his wife sought some serenity after the dramatic events:

'After all the hassle, Tina and I decided we needed a break for a few days. With all the media frenzy after the game, the problem was that there was no place where we would be able to go where people would not be hassling us and talking about the match. Eventually, we decided to go to Howth for the weekend. At first, we didn't have much intrusion but that all changed when we went to Mass on the Sunday and all these elderly women came up to talk to us. Every single one of them was an expert on Gaelic football!'

LEESIDERS

In 1987 Meath began a new and intense rivalry with Cork. In 1990 the sides met for the third All-Ireland final in four years, but this time it was the Leesiders that emerged on top. Meath full-back Mick Lyons went to his manager Seán Boylan after losing that game to Cork with a badly bruised face.

He said, 'I'm awful sorry, Seán.'

'Why?' Boylan inquired.

'When X gave me that blow into the face, I should have started an almighty row and that would have galvanised us.'

35

DOWN BUT NOT OUT

Ross Carr Hits the Big Time

Since Adam was a boy, great players have had a power to make the heart skip a beat.

Of course, they have also added to the gaiety of the nation for those of us not fit enough to barely move when going down an escalator.

Down's former All-Star forward Ross Carr was one of the greatest players of his generation and will never be forgotten because of some phenomenal points from distance. As Joe Brolly recalls: 'It was important to us that Down won the All-Ireland in 1991. We had nearly beaten them that year in a titanic game in the Athletic Grounds. We were a point up at the end when they got a free, 60 yards out. I was close to the ball at the time, and I heard Ross Carr saying to Enda Gormley, "I'm going to drive this over the bar." Enda told him, "Wise up you f**king eejit." But Ross sent it over the bar and they went through instead of us. But when they won the All-Ireland it inspired us because it made us realise how close we were.'

THE FIRST CUT IS THE DEEPEST

Ross Carr has a nice line in self-deprecation. One of the stories he tells against himself goes back to 1980, when he was just sixteen and was playing for the senior club in one of the biggest games in the club's history. He was incredibly nervous because he had not reached the highest standards of play at all levels. His poor mother prepared a great breakfast before the match that morning but he was just pushing the bacon after the egg on the plate because he couldn't conceive of keeping it down. He got up and went to the bathroom and on the way his mother drenched him in holy water to help him play well.

He came back and this time pushed the egg after the bacon but again he could not take anything. His mother got out her rosary beads and blessed him with them. His late father was quietly reading the paper and was seemingly oblivious to his plight but eventually he peered over the paper and asked, 'What's wrong, son?'

'I'm too nervous about the match to eat anything,' Ross answerd sadly.

His father then uttered the immortal words: 'Don't worry, son. You are sh*te. There's nothing you can do about that but there's no need to be hungry as well.'

(**Fógra:** Offaly legend, Michael Duignan, claims Carr robbed that story off him!)

ROOM TO IMPROVE

One of Ross Carr's teammates did not lack confidence. As Down manager, James McCartan Jnr steered his county to an All-Ireland final appearance against Cork. His talent was evident at an early age. He scored three goals in a MacRory Cup final and took Down to an All-Ireland minor title with his exciting and swashbuckling quality and because of his bravery, his courage and his electrifying confidence and self-assurance. As a player he won senior All-Irelands in 1991 and 1994. His father had played on three All-Ireland winning teams in the 1960s and James had inherited the winning mentality from his dad.

One famous story told about him sums it up. When he was nineteen he played for Ireland against Australia in the Compromise Rules. He was rooming with Jack O'Shea, one of the most iconic names in Gaelic football. An Australian journalist asked him, 'What's it like to room with a legend?'

James shrugged and said, 'You'd have to ask Jacko.'

36

A HOLE-Y SHOW

Antrim Reach the All-Ireland Final

The Donnelly clan, from beautiful Ballycastle, are the most famous dynasty in Antrim hurling. Over a hundred years ago, in 1907, Edward Donnelly co-founded the Ballycastle McQuillan Club and was its first chairman.

In 1989 his great-great grandson, Dessie Donnelly, won an All-Star as left full-back for his commanding performances that carried Antrim to the All-Ireland final that year. Dessie's team-mates included his brother Brian and cousin Terry, son of the legendary 'Bear' Donnelly, who hurled with distinction for club and county in the fifties and sixties.

Dessie Donnelly has a special place in his heart for his team-mates: 'In 1989, after we won the All-Ireland semi-final, we were training hard coming up to the All-Ireland final. To get a bit of a break, Paul McKillen and I went to see the All-Ireland football semi-final between Cork and Dublin. We were having a great chat before the game and as the players were coming on to the field I kind of noticed the big screen for the first time and I said to him, "This should be a great game today."

'Paul looked up at the big screen and then he turned around and asked me, "Is this game live?"

'I nearly died laughing!'

ALWAYS GUARANTEED

McKillen, though, is not the Antrim hurler who bought a JCB and set up his own business with the immortal slogan: 'With us you're guaranteed your hole.'

CLERICAL ERROR

People who are the most meek and mild in normal life can be transformed once they get on the hurling field. Former Antrim star Sambo McNaughton famously recalled marking Fr Iggy Clarke on his inter-county debut: 'My innocent childhood perception of the priesthood changed after that game!'

ARE YOU RIGHT THERE, MICHAEL?

Former All-Star Michael Duignan is a stalwart of Offaly hurling. He believes that playing on that team made him a better performer:

'In the 1990s Offaly were a big power in hurling, so if you were constantly marking Brian Whelahan or Kevin Kinahan in training, it really brought you on. Club hurling was also very strong in Offaly back then, so when I was marking Martin Hanamy or Hubert Rigney so often it also brought me on as a player.'

Who was the greatest character?

'There were so many of that Offaly team, but they were all characters in a different way, like Daithí Regan and John Troy. But it is hard to go beyond Johnny Pilkington. My favourite story about him came the morning after we won the 1998 All-Ireland final. Some of us went for a quiet drink in Doheny

Nesbitts. Somehow *The Pat Kenny Show* heard about it and rang the pub and asked for one of us to speak on the phone for the programme. To our surprise, Johnny volunteered to do so because, contrary to popular perception, he is a very serious lad and doesn't normally put himself forward. He had a great time with Pat and he was taking the p**s out of Pat for being a "great GAA man" which we all found hilarious.

'Pat's last question was about Michael Bond because Johnny was the man who had been fingered for getting rid of Babs Keating. "Well, now that he has won the All-Ireland, is Michael Bond's job safe for next year?"

'Johnny paused dramatically before he said, "I don't know. I haven't decided yet if I'll keep him on or not."'

37

THE CLASH OF THE ASH

Hurling Humour

Punditry has brought us many smiles – most of them unintentional! Soccer has given us gems like:

A team full of internationals.
Lee Dixon did his homework on Senegal.

McTominay needs to add goals to his reservoir.
Paul Ince goes to the well.

He doesn't score many, Declan Rice, but when he does they usually end up in the back of the net.
Steve McManaman

Nine times out of ten, if you give him three chances like that he'll score two.
Shaun Wright-Philips does the sums.

Richarlison has nineteen goals in forty games. You do the math, that's a goal a game.
Eni Aluko

They are going at it hammer and thong.
Gerry Armstrong got his knickers in a twist.

Champions League semi-final, it doesn't get any bigger than that.
Peter Crouch

He works his backside off and that's a massive thing.
A bum deal from Rob Butler.

He needs to take on Gareth Bale's mantelpiece.
Sam Ricketts is on fire.

They will struggle to score goals if they don't take their chances.
Dion Dublin

Didier Deschamps holds his plank for an hour every day.
Tony Cascarino leaves an arresting image.

The away team has won the last eight games, including five in a row.
Rob Phillips is not wrong.

He can count his lucky chickens.
Lee Hendrie cries fowl.

James Maddison got a good bird's eye view of it because he's lying down.
Ian Wright goes to ground.

CLASH OF THE ASH GOES VERBAL

As we all know, though, hurling is the real beautiful game. This chapter revisits some vintage hurling quotes:

If someone can market coloured gripe water, call it Coca-Cola and clean up worldwide, we should be able to sell hurling in Longford.
Liam Griffin

I'm always suspicious of games where you're the only ones that play it.
Jack Charlton when asked about hurling.

Just thinking of Tony Keady, I'd such time for the man. At half-time, looking at the piece on him there, it's so heartbreaking for him and his family. Just, look, whether it's Waterford or Galway, what it means to both those counties, looking over there at John Mullane, he's heartbroken. And I'm heartbroken for the people of Waterford. And I'm delighted for the people of Galway and that's the way it was always going to be today. What an occasion. What an emotional day.
Michael Duignan after the 2017 All-Ireland final.

If Wexford Hurling Ltd was a company and we had produced the results that we have over the last twenty-five years or so, we would have been declared bankrupt long ago.
Phil Murphy, *The Wexford People*

Dublin in rare new times.
The Irish Times' headline after surprise win of Dublin hurlers.

John Mullane: he shakes, he bakes, he scores!
Timmy McCarthy

Bogball and Stickfighting.
The late George Byrne's view of our national games.

If Offaly win the National League again this year it will be the greatest accident since the Titanic.
Paul O'Kelly of Offaly.

In the dust of defeat as well as in the laurel of victory, there is glory to be found.
J.J. Meagher

© INPHO / Donall Farmer

SPOT THE SLIOTAR
Glenmore and Eoghan Rua battle it out in the All-Ireland JHC final.

© Piaras Ó Mídheach / Sportsfile

A TOUCH OF CLASS
Meath's Emma Duggan has already established herself as one of the greats of the game.

EYE ON THE BALL
Brian Kelly rises
highest.

© INPHO/Colm O'Neill

**DID IT CROSS
THE LINE?**
Dublin's
Stephen Cluxton
desperately
stretches to
prevent a goal.

© INPHO/Donall Farmer

O HAPPY DAY
The Tipperary
minors celebrate.

© INPHO/James Crombie

© INPHO/James Crombie

THE CLASH OF THE ASH
Walter Walsh and Seamus Kennedy battle it out.

© INPHO/James Crombie

LITTLE AND LARGE
Aidan Bastick, son of former Dublin senior star Denis, stands in the Sam Maguire Cup.

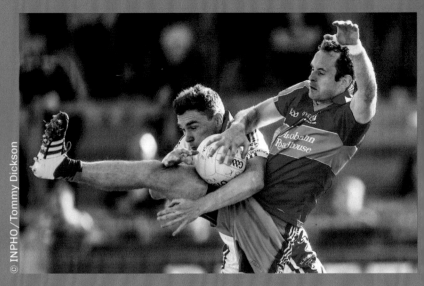

© INPHO / Tommy Dickson

FOR THE PRIDE OF THE PARISH
Ballymun's Carl Connolly with Paddy Andrews of St. Brigids battle for possession in the Dublin football final.

© INPHO / Tommy Dickson

GIRLS JUST WANT TO HAVE FUN
Johnstownbridge players celebrate winning the All-Ireland Camogie Junior Championship.

© Piaras Ó Midheach / Sportsfile

THE GHOST GOAL

Waterford's Austin Gleeson catches the sliotar, which was judged to have crossed the goal-line in the 2018 Munster Championship.

© Piaras Ó Midheach / Sportsfile

NO ORDINARY JOE

Joe Canning celebrates as he watches his late winner sail over the crossbar in the 2017 All-Ireland semi-final.

© Piaras Ó Mídheach / Sportsfile

© Piaras Ó Mídheach / Sportsfil

NIGHT RIDER
Semple Stadium groundsman and former Tipperary hurler Pa Bourke work on the field at 10 p.m. on a Saturday night after the 2015 All-Ireland Football Championship qualifier between Kildare and Cork.

THE HEAT OF BATTLE
Paddy Small of Dublin is fouled by Seán O'Shea of Kerry, late in the 2019 drawn All-Ireland Football Championship final.

© Piaras Ó Mídheach / Sportsfile

HAWK-EYE SAYS YES
A fan erected an unofficial hawk-eye sign for the 2019 Walsh Cup final between Wexford and Galway.

DADDY'S GIRL
Paddy McGrath and his daughter Isla
Rose after Donegal's championship
win over Derry.

COS YOU'RE A DREAM TO ME
Nickie Quaid and Cian Lynch
savour that winning feeling after
the final whistle against Galway.

HI-JACK
Jack McCaffrey of Dublin looks on as the ball goes out for a '45, when
Seán Kelly of Galway cleared his goal chance, after the ball came off the
post early in the second half, as umpire Tom O'Kane looks on.

CATCH OF THE DAY
Stefan Okunbor of Kerry catches the throw-in ahead of Darragh Tracey of Limerick.

TUNNEL VISION
Dublin captain Ciarán Kilkenny with the O'Byrne cup after the O'Byrne Cup Final.

JERSEY BOYS
Tony Kelly of Clare and Seán Finn of Limerick during the Munster GAA Hurling Senior Championship Final.

The miracle of the GAA is that it works so well despite itself. Paranoia, self-doubt, trenchant conservatism, fear of outside sports and veneration of the past are all key parts of the GAA psyche. In order to love the GAA, you have to swallow these faults whole.
Keith Duggan, *The Irish Times*

He is hurling's outsider artist, a Van Gogh whose ability to do things differently is not entirely unconnected with a certain eccentricity of approach . . . Davy Fitzgerald is Irish sport's punk rock genius. Occasionally obnoxious, frequently noisy and always ready to defy authority.
Eamon Sweeney

It's f***king bullsh*t, as you can see yourself.
Galway's Johnny Glynn responds to suggestions that Galway had only Joe Canning in attack.

Frank Murphy knows as much about high performance sport as I know about the sleeping habits of the Ayatollah.
Dónal Óg Cusack after Cork's hurling and football teams exit the championship on the same weekend in July 2015.

To be a great goalie, you need a big heart, big hands and a big bottom.
Comment about a former Antrim goalie.

Ger Loughnane was fair, he treated us all the same during training – like dogs.
Anonymous Clare player

If you put monkeys on to play, they'd still pack Croke Park on All-Ireland final day.
Anon

I said to the manager, this is supposed to be a five-star hotel and there's a bloody hole in the roof. He turned around and said, 'That's where you can see the five stars from.'
Player on All-Stars tour.

I love Cork so much that if I caught one of their hurlers in bed with my missus, I'd tiptoe downstairs and make him a cup of tea.
Joe Lynch

A fan is a person who, when you have made an idiot of yourself on the pitch, doesn't think you've done a permanent job.
Jack Lynch

Remember, postcards only, please. The winner will be the first one opened.
The late RTÉ commentator Liam Campbell

Pessimists see a cup that is half-empty. Optimists see a cup that is half-full. But we haven't even seen the cup.
Sligo hurling fan

Jesus saves – but Jimmy Barry-Murphy scores on the rebound.
Graffiti in Cork.

We've got grounds which are state of the art and administration which is state of the Ark.
Ger Loughnane

I'm not giving away any secrets like that to Tipperary. If I had my way, I wouldn't even tell them the time of the throw-in.
Ger Loughnane on his controversial selection policy.

Never watch a Gaelic football match before hurling as it slows the mental reflexes.
Mentor to Cork hurling team in the 1960s.

Cork hurling games are like sex films – they relieve frustration and tension.
Joe Lynch

Broken marriages, conflicts of loyalty, the problems of everyday life fall away as one faces up to Joe Canning.
Anonymous Wexford player

He (Nicky English) spoilt the game – he got too many scores.
Antrim fan at the 1989 All-Ireland.

The GAA is an amateur association run by professionals. The FAI is a professional body run by amateurs.
Fan during the Roy Keane 2002 World Cup saga.

Cork are like the mushrooms; they can come overnight.
Jim 'Tough' Barry

Is the ref going to blow his whistle? No, he's going to blow his nose.
Commentator on Kilkenny FM.

A forward's usefulness to his side varies as to the square of his distance from the ball.
Galway fan during the 2001 All-Ireland.

When Sylvie Linnane is good, he's great. When he's bad, he's better.
Galway fan

I think of myself as a socialist hurler. I'm not too bothered who scores – as long as we win.
'The Viking', Cormac Bonnar

Ger Loughnane is paranoid. He's the Woody Allen of hurling.
Tipp fan

You should play every game as if it's your last, but make sure you perform well enough to ensure it's not.
Jack Lynch

There's only one head bigger than Ger Loughnane's and that's Birkenhead.
Limerick fan

If Babs Keating wrote a book on humility he'd be raging if it wasn't displayed in the shop window.
Offaly fan in 1998.

Babs Keating 'resigned' as coach because of illness and fatigue. The players were sick and tired of him.
Offaly fan in 1998.

Babs Keating has about as much personality as a tennis racket.
Offaly fan in 1998.

I didn't get Christy Ring's autograph, but he trod on my toe, though.
Anon

Hurling – it's all a matter of inches; those between your ears.
Kevin Armstrong

Everyone knows which comes first when it's a question of hurling or sex. All discerning people recognise that.
Tipp fan

Sylvie Linnane would start a riot in a graveyard.
Tipp fan

Sylvie may not be sugar, but he adds plenty of spice.
Galway fan

A Munster final is not a funeral, though both can be very sad affairs.
Ger Loughnane

Funny game hurling, especially the way Kerry play it.
Cocky Cork fan

Frank Murphy. The comb-over who rules the world.
Clare fan

And as for you. You're not even good enough to play for this shower of useless no-hopers.
Former Clare mentor to one of his subs after a heavy defeat.

There is nothing even vaguely intellectual about a Munster Hurling Final, yet a proper enjoyment of the game presupposes a sophisticated appreciation of the finer things.
David Hanly

The Kilkenny players took their sleeping pills too late because they hadn't fully woken up until after the match.
Dejected fan in 1966 after red hot favourites, Kilkenny, surprisingly lost the All-Ireland to Cork.

Rugby is a sport for ruffians played by gentlemen, Gaelic football is a sport for gentlemen played by ruffians but hurling is a sport for gentlemen played by gentlemen.
Anon

They wouldn't bate dust off a carpet.
Kilkenny fan prematurely dismisses Galway's chances before the 2001 All-Ireland semi-final.

Babs Keating has been arrested in Nenagh for shaking a cigarette machine, but the gardai let him off when he said he only wanted to borrow twenty players.
Waterford fan after Babs had predicted a heavy defeat for Waterford in the 2002 Munster final.

They haven't come to see you umpiring, they have come to see me hurl.
Christy Ring after a clash with an umpire.

Winning the All-Ireland without beating Cork or Kilkenny is an empty experience, but as empty experiences go it's one of the best.
Tipperary fan in 2001.

In Kilkenny an unscrupulous shopkeeper will try to slip you an All-Ireland medal for a euro, they have so many to spare.
Ger Loughnane

Brian Lohan was always an absolute gentleman off the field during his playing days but it was almost like he morphed into the Incredible Hulk once that famous red helmet was thrown on top of his head. He was such a quiet man who kept himself to himself but when he crossed the white lines, he turned into an animal of a player who would leave a trail of destruction behind him.
John Mullane

I was born at a very young age. I've never been a millionaire but I know I'd be unreal at it.
Shane McGrath

38

SLEEPING BEAUTY

Heffo's Help

Apart from their contribution on the field, the Dubs added to the lore of the game through players like Mick Holden, who furnished the game with some wonderful stories. Coming up to an All-Ireland final, Kevin Heffernan spoke to the Dublin team about diet and proper preparation. He told them if they had any problems sleeping before the final, they should get tablets from Dr Pat O'Neill. The first person in the queue was Mick Holden. Heffo said to Mick: 'I never thought you'd have any problems sleeping.' Holden answered: 'Oh these are not for me. I sleep like a baby. These are for my mother. She can never sleep the night before a big match!'

CREATIVE EXCUSES

One Saturday morning he was seriously late for training, much to Heffo's chagrin. The manager curtly demanded an explanation. Holden responded by saying, 'I was coming across town and I was stopped by the guards. They said I was a match for one of the guys that pulled that big bank robbery yesterday.'

A bemused Heffo asked, 'Really?'

Mick answered, 'No, but it sounds so much better than saying I slept it out.'

CARD GAME

In 1983 twelve-man Dublin beat fourteen-man Galway in the All-Ireland final. After the match one wag remarked: 'The referee went ape. He pulled out more cards than Steve McQueen did in *The Cincinnati Kid*.'

MIGHTY MEATH

In the 1970s Dublin's great rivals were Kerry but in the late 1980s and 1990s their most intense rivalry was with Meath. In 1983, after Dublin won the All-Ireland, they travelled to Navan for the opening round of the National League. The All-Ireland champions were welcomed on to the field by the Meath team lined either side of the dugout. While the team applauded the Dubs, a Meath player was caught by one photographer giving the champs the two fingers!

YES MINISTER

The former Minister for Defence, Michael Smith, told a story which reflects that hurling is no place for the faint-hearted. 'The toughest match I ever heard of was the 1935 All-Ireland semi-final. After six minutes the ball ricocheted off the post and went into the stand. The pulling continued relentlessly and it was twenty-two minutes before any of the players noticed the ball was missing!'

39

F**K OFF JOE

Joe Brolly Gets Told Off

Joe Brolly favours the direct approach. Nobody watching will ever forget his comment after that tackle on Monaghan's Conor McManus in 2013, when Tyrone's star midfielder cynically took down his opponent as he chased in on goal: 'He's a brilliant footballer but you can forget about Seán Cavanagh as a man.'

In November 2015 this writer organised a conference where Joe was the keynote speaker. At one stage he was about to relate a tale that could not be committed to paper. He asked if there were any journalists present. Mags Gargan put up her hand. Joe joked a more colourful version of: 'You write what I say and I will come after you with all I have. I know a lot more sinister people than you do, young lady.' Mags nodded assent, but obviously not sufficiently for Joe, so he added: 'Do not f**k with me.' Then, wondering if she was a tabloid journalist, Joe asked her what paper she wrote for. Mags got the laugh of the day when she replied, '*The Irish Catholic.*' Nobody laughed harder than Brolly at her answer.

One of Joe's topics was the banality of managerspeak and playerspeak – which quickly descends into the clutter of common cliché and which creates 'a conformist freak show'. He illustrated it with a fictional conversation between a random top player or manager and his good friend Marty Morrissey.

Marty: 'You've got Leitrim in the qualifiers today. It will be little more than a run out for you?'

Random Player/Manager: 'Well, Marty, Leitrim are a great team and we've got the greatest respect for them.'

Marty: 'But they lost to Mayo by thirty-four points in Connacht.'

Randomer: 'Well, Marty, we watched the video of that, and they certainly didn't do themselves justice. Seven of those goals came from uncharacteristic mistakes and fourteen of the frees they conceded were unfortunate. They are a great team and I've no doubt that they will have learned from those errors. We are under no illusions that this is a huge challenge for us today.'

Marty: 'But seven of their first team, including their left-footed free taker, right-footed free taker, goalie, midfielders, full-back and centre-forward have gone to America since the Mayo game. We're hearing that the bus driver has had to tog out today.'

Randomer: 'Well, that is right, Marty. But the under-21s and the three minors they've brought in are all quality players and the bus driver is extremely experienced. We know that if we're not at the top of our game, we'll not come through this challenge – so we are under no illusions that this is a huge challenge today.'

Marty: 'And, of course, the game is in Croke Park, where this Leitrim team have never played.'

Randomer: 'Well, Marty, the fact is Croke Park puts all the pressure on us. Leitrim are a great team and they haven't come here to make up the numbers, so it is a huge challenge for our players and we're under no illusions that this is a huge challenge.'

Brolly went on to bemoan the fact that the only time a top inter-county player makes themselves available for interviews today is when a commercial company hires them for promotional work – a practice he stated was 'as tacky as the child in the beauty pageant'. That was just his polite warm-up for his criticism of the GPA, which he described as 'a nasty, money-grabbing little cartel that has come to dominate the county game'.

In fairness, bland commentary is not the exclusive preserve of the GAA fraternity. The BBC pays Jermaine Jenas handsomely for such gems as: 'They have got to improve collectively as well as a group.' And: 'He's found out a lot about his players that he already knew.'

THE DIET

Joe Brolly reported that he had been shown earlier that year a weekly diary of an Ulster squad. Each week, the players were given a timetable containing minute detail. One vignette serves to illustrate: 'Tuesday morning: Out of bed by 8. a.m. Eat breakfast at home' – before prescribing exactly what that breakfast should be. Brolly found the mere suggestion ludicrous that any player should have to be told to eat breakfast at home.

He contrasted the strict emphasis on diet with a memory of staying in the Slieve Russell Hotel with the Derry squad when his team were in their prime, after winning what he calls their 'one-in-a-row' All-Ireland in 1993. A waitress asked Tony Scullion if he wanted the continental breakfast and himself and

Brian McGilligan almost fell on the floor, they were laughing so hard. Within minutes the squad were scoffing huge Ulster fries.

THE WINNER TAKES IT ALL

In his keynote speech, Brolly also pointed to the number of serious injuries that players are suffering today as a by-product of this trend of over-professionalism. He used the case study of 'our Nobel Laureate of skill', Colm Cooper, who has endured a spate of injuries and consequently, in his latter years, had 'negligible impact on the big stage, either toiling against blanket defences or limping through Killarney on crutches'.

He used the example of the 2015 All-Ireland final when Cooper: 'Spent most of his time in his own half, tracking Dublin's counter-attacking corner-back. The fact that the corner-back scored, and Gooch didn't, tells you all you need to know about modern county football.'

Then Brolly examined the transformation in Gooch's physique: 'At first, a lithe, supremely supple footballer, running riot in his first final against Mayo. In the end, a muscled, tight gymnastic physique.'

He also quoted Darragh Ó Sé's observation about Cooper: 'You used to see Gooch swigging a bottle of Coca-Cola and eating a bag of crisps. Now, he walks down the main street in Killarney sipping spring water and eating a banana.'

Brolly's next target was the win-at-all-costs mentality which had been imported from soccer. He cited the example of this trend infecting the GAA in the under-10 St Brigid's footballers he coached who had reached the final of an important Mid-Ulster tournament. As the game looked destined for extra time, the opposing midfielder launched a long ball which bounced on the 14 and went over the bar. The referee blew the final whistle. His charges sank to the ground. Half of them were crying and meant it. The other half were crying because it seemed the appropriate thing to do. Their man of the match, Oisin McDonnell, was weeping inconsolably. Brolly went to him, tousled his hair, and said, 'Ozzie, you have nothing to cry about. You covered yourself in glory out there today.'

The boy replied: 'F**k off, Joe.'

40

BIG MAC

Mayo's Misfortunes

Few players have had as many reality checks as footballers in the green and red.

The giant of Mayo midfielders, Liam McHale, tells a tale which he thinks is symptomatic of Mayo's fortunes in Croke Park in recent years:

'Before the 2004 All-Ireland final I saw that there were great odds on Alan Dillon scoring the first goal in the match. I called my wife, Sinead, and asked her to place a big bet for me. After five minutes, Alan, on cue, scored the goal and I did a dance for joy. Afterwards I learned that Sinead had forgotten to place the bet.'

STRAIGHT TALKING

McHale's capacity to tell it as it was during those years did not always endear himself to the football constituency in Mayo:

'In 2006 I was on RTÉ's *Up for the Match* programme the night before the All-Ireland final. Mary Kennedy asked me if

I was confident. I replied: "I would be confident if we weren't playing Kerry."

'I got some abuse because of that.'

LOST IN TRANSLATION

When asked for a funny incident from his career, Liam provides a classic:

'We were staying in Maynooth College for the All-Ireland semi-final the day Princess Diana died. On the Sunday morning I was walking down into the breakfast room with P.J. Loftus, who is a bit of a character. We were met at the door by the head priest, who is a very holy man.

'He said: "Howya Liam, howya P.J. Did you hear the awful news?"

'I immediately went into a panic because I feared that James Nallen or someone might be injured. He told us that Diana had died.

'P.J. Loftus replied, "F**k off."

'I asked, "How did she die?"

'The priest: "She was killed in a car crash."

'P.J.: "F**k off."

'Me: "What kind of crash was it?"

'The priest: "The paparazzi were chasing her."

'P.J.: "What the f**k was Pavarotti chasing her for?"

'At that stage, the priest said nothing and walked away in disgust!'

41

THE SLOW LEARNER

Pat Spillane Is Humbled

For many years there was nobody in the GAA world who annoyed me more than Pat Spillane. It is fair to say that I was not on my own.

My antipathy towards him can be traced back to when Kerry beat my beloved Roscommon in the 1980 All-Ireland final. During the first half, Spillane lay writhing in apparent agony on the ground. Twelve years later, I saw the video for the first time and my suspicions were confirmed.

'Is Pat Spillane really hurt or is he in line for an Oscar?' So Micheál O'Hehir wondered aloud as Gerry Fitzmaurice and Spillane were involved in an incident off the ball.

Afterwards Pat was prostrate on the ground and took an age to get up. Time went by and many efforts were made to assist his recovery, to no avail. About four minutes later, Spillane staggered up. It did not escape my attention that Roscommon were playing with a strong wind at the time. Within a minute Pat was flying up the wing like a March hare.

A Roscommon fan standing behind me in the Canal End was so miffed by this bit of gameship that he remarked, 'There's no doubt – the two worst things about Pat Spillane is his face.'

I knew in my gut that Roscommon's All-Ireland was lost. In my eyes, Spillane became evil incarnate. Each time he tormented the Roscommon defence, I whispered the two lines I could remember from a poem by my friend, the late Michael Hartnett, which cursed a cat thief and expressed the wish that the culprit's drunken uncle would 'lose his dole'. He was more severe on the man's only daughter, hoping that she might 'get up the pole'.

As the years passed, my admiration for Spillane the player grew and grew because, in full flight, he caused more problems than a trapeze artist with loose bowels. Once he retired, though, all my ill-feeling returned. As a pundit he regularly ridiculed teams from Connacht and became our greatest enemy all over again. For most of the 1990s it would have been easier to get a Connacht football fan to knit with sawdust than to pay a compliment to Pat Spillane.

Fast forward to August 2002. By an accident of history, I found myself in Spillane's company for an afternoon. Within a few minutes all my deep prejudices were dissipated. By that evening I would have walked over hot coals for him.

WORDS-WORTH

Ulster fans had a Pat Spillane anagram competition. Apparently, the best anagram is Pet Anal Lips.

THANK YOU FOR THE MUSIC

Spillane also has a particular place in the affections of Cork fans: 'In Cork, at the very mention of my name, they all burst into song. Mind you the song they sing is "The Langer"!'

42

LOST IN TRANSLATION

With a Little Help from Paidí's Friends

Páidí Ó Sé's passion for football was evident at an early stage after Kerry beat Meath in the 1970 All-Ireland final. Páidí was a boarder, so it was not possible for him to legitimately attend the homecoming celebrations. He arranged to borrow a bike from one of the day students, robbed a brush and dressed it up as a decoy in his bed and set out for Rathmore. When he returned, the college dean, Dermot Clifford, later to become Archbishop of Cashel, was waiting for him at the entrance: 'Ó Sé, there are more brains in that brush above than in your head.'

A HELPFUL HINT
Páidí went to boarding school with Pat Spillane. Following rigidly the rules whereby one must not complain about one's food, a young Páidí found a mouse in his soup, so he attracted the attention of the server. 'Please, Father! Pat Spillane has no mouse in his soup.'

ON GUARD

Páidí was a first-class storyteller and was well able to tell stories against himself. Many go back to his time as a garda. In 1979, after a league match against Cork, he went for a few drinks. The next morning, when he went in to report for duty in Limerick, he was feeling a bit off colour. He decided that the best way of concealing his discomfort was to take out the squad car and pretend to go on patrol but instead he pulled into a quiet field for a nap. A few hours later he was awoken by a great commotion and suddenly there were squad cars all over the field. Páidí stumbled out of the car to find himself face to face with the assistant commissioner who said, 'Páid, did you nod off for a little while?'

'I'm sorry. I'd an auld game yesterday and I just pulled in for a few minutes. What are all of ye doing here?'

'We're checking out the venue for the Pope's visit to Limerick next September. The Holy Father'll be saying a Mass out here. We're sussin' out the place for the security plan. Sorry to have disturbed you.'

After a shift ended it was customary for a garda to go out for a drink. Sometimes, though, this posed problems when the session carried on after closing hours. Early in his career, Páidí was dispatched one night to inspect a pub that was reportedly selling after hours. When he arrived at the premises, he was told to check it out before entering. 'I'm here now, over,' he radioed back to the station.

'Is there any activity there?' questioned the officer.

'Yes,' he replied. 'I can hear people shouting, I can hear laughter and I can hear glasses clinking.'

'And can you hear a cash register going?' asked the officer.

'No,' Páidí replied.

'Ah, you better leave it off, Garda Ó Sé, it could be our own crowd.'

CALENDAR GIRL

Páidí told me he once arrested a woman for stealing a calendar.

I asked: 'What sentence did she get?'

'Twelve months.'

CAPTAIN FANTASTIC

In 1985 everyone on the Kerry team had their hearts set on winning the All-Ireland. None more so than Páidí as he was captain. As Páidí was trying to gee up the troops before the game, he said, 'We really need to win this one.'

Mick O'Dwyer asked, 'For who?'

'For me.'

'Not for Kerry?'

'Well, for Kerry as well.'

In an effort to add impact to his words, Páidí smashed the ball as hard as he could on the ground. It bounced so high that it shattered the lights overhead. Glass flew all over the dressing room. Yet so absorbed were the team in the team-talk that not a single player noticed the incident.

THE CRAIC

Páidí always enjoyed the social side of the game. In the 1970s and 1980s winning All-Irelands became such a routine that as he ran on to Croke Park after Mick O'Dwyer had been trying to psyche the team up to play the game of their lives before an All-Ireland final, John Egan ran up and pulled Páidí by the togs and asked him, 'Where are ye going after the game, Páid?'

Páidí went on to manage Kerry to All-Ireland success in both 1997 and 2000. His style of management was very direct. Once, his half-time talk to his team finished with the immortal words: 'Get the lead out of your arses now and shake your heads up and get out there now.'

HIGH SOCIETY

Páidí was never afraid to talk about his famous friends like Gregory Peck, Tom Cruise and Dolly Parton. He was close to the late Charlie Haughey. Pat Spillane has the inside track on their friendship. '*Aithníonn ciaróg ciaróg eile.* It takes a rogue to know a rogue. I can say that as a rogue myself!'

Páidí had a fund of stories about the former Taoiseach. One of his favourites went back to Italia '90. After the Italian game, Haughey went into the Irish dressing room and, for the players brought up in Ireland, gave a rousing speech about the sporting sons of Ireland.

Loudly, Tony Cascarino asked Niall Quinn, 'Who is that bloke?'

'He is the Taoiseach.'

Then Andy Townsend asked Cascarino who their visitor was.

Cas replied, 'I don't know but Quinny said he owns a teashop.'

43

THE VAN

The Dubs Celebrate

I like people who are humble. Having won an All-Ireland as a player and six as a manager, including an unprecedented five-in-a-row, Jim Gavin had every reason to be proud. Yet he remained the personification of humility.

JAYO

Gavin brought in top people to his background team to help win again and again. In 1995 Jason Sherlock became the GAA's first pin-up boy when, at just nineteen years of age, he helped Dublin to win their first All-Ireland football final in twelve years. His was fame of pop-star proportions after his bootless goal against Laois, his decisive goal against Cork in the All-Ireland semi-final and his pass to Charlie Redmond for the winning goal against Tyrone in the All-Ireland final. Nobody had ever seen anything like it. Hence Marty Morrissey's unique question in the post-match interview: 'Is there a lady in your life?'

To his credit, Jason turned defence into attack: 'I know you with the girls, Marty!'

RELAX

The Dublin players liked to enjoy themselves and this helped to create a strong sense of collegiality within the squad. A ritual after a big match was that they met up on the Monday for some liquid refreshment. This proved problematic for one who worked as a van driver as his company monitored where the vans went from their office every day on their computers. So intent was the player in question on attending the drinking session that he paid a student to drive his van all around the city for a day.

MR PRESIDENT

In his autobiography, Bernard Brogan speaks of how Dublin's party days and habit of socialising for two days after games ended following 2009. Gilroy and Mickey Whelan insisted on it, although Brogan had an embarrassing episode in New York in March 2011. He'd been in the White House for St Patrick's Day celebrations and met then US President Barack Obama.

Brogan had been out the night before for a few glasses of . . . lemonade when he received a text message from Gilroy asking him to confirm he would be back to play against Mayo on 20 March. Brogan texted back: 'Yeah, can't wait, Pat.' Then he replied to a message from his pal Vinny with, 'In bits after Pasha (nightclub) last night! What a spot! Getting breakfast in Mickey D's now. Where r u?'

The problem was that it was not Vinny that ended up getting it. A minute later the phone beeped. Pat Gilroy: 'WTF? You're not starting tomorrow anyway!'

Brogan and a friend went to the airport the next morning and discovered the flight wasn't for another twenty-four hours. The day of the game. It probably comes as no great surprise to discover that Brogan did not start the next match either.

THE GLORY OF HIS ASS

Despite the humility he nurtured in his squad, some of Jim Gavin's players have attained high profiles and great adulation. An unusual case was that of Kevin McManamon. On Today FM's *Gift Grub* his bum was celebrated as 'it is so close to the ground it could mow your lawn'.

44

RUCK AND ROLL

Moss Stays Calm

At times, claims about the GAA's connection with rugby have been exaggerated. Former Irish out-half Mick Quinn's father was not a sporting man but he was very proud that his son played for Ireland. He seldom drank but when he did he really knew how to enjoy himself. Once, he was having a few drinks with John Joe Whyte of *The Irish Times*. He told John Joe that Mick had acquired his ability from him and that he himself played for Monaghan in the 1928 All-Ireland Gaelic football final – not even knowing at that stage if Monaghan had played in the final that year. The next day this story appeared verbatim in *The Times*. John Joe hadn't realised he was being wound up and did not bother to check out the facts.

WORDY

The young players on the Ireland rugby team looked up to Moss Keane as if he was God. New players from the north found his thick Kerry accent particularly difficult to decipher. The senior players devised a little ritual for those new players.

When Trevor Ringland was brought onto the team for the first time, Ciaran Fitzgerald put him beside Moss for dinner, and Trevor was in awe of him. They primed Moss to speak for two minutes in fast-forward mode. He was talking pure gibberish. Then he turned to Trevor and asked him what he thought of that. Trevor answered lamely, 'I think you're right,' not having a clue what Moss had said. Then Moss launched off again, only faster. The panic on Trevor's face was a sight to behold. He was going green. All the senior players were killing themselves trying to keep a straight face until Trevor found out he was being wound up.

BUTTERFINGERS

Moss enjoyed a good relationship with Dermot Earley. The two had become friends after attending a charity auction for GOAL in 1979. Dermot donated the jersey he had worn in the league final, which raised £100. He was not sure if he should feel complimented with the price or insulted when the buyer Terry Rodgers told him, 'My father was from Roscommon but thanks be to God he got out early.'

Moss brought the house down when he told how Ireland had lost narrowly to Wales in Cardiff Arms Park earlier in the year despite a breathtaking performance by Tony Ward. The game is best remembered, though, for Ireland's full-back and future Tánaiste dropping a ball which let Wales in for a soft try and earning Dick Spring the nickname 'Butterfingers' on *Scrap Saturday*.

In his own distinctive style, Moss held up a plastic bag and recalled how he had gone into the Welsh dressing room after the game to swap jerseys with Allan Martin, the Welsh forward. On his way out, big Moss remembered that Martin had not been a good man to buy a round of drinks on the Lions tour, so he went back inside and 'borrowed' Martin's tracksuit while he was in the shower, to compensate for all the drinks Keane had bought him on the Lions tour.

Moss also said you have to pick your fights. To illustrate, he recalled how he was once selected to play for the Welsh Barbarians against a touring South Africa team. The game turned violent, with numerous bouts of fisticuffs. At one stage, twenty-nine of the players on the field were fighting ferociously. Moss was the sole non-combatant. Asked later why he was so uncharacteristically Gandhian, Moss replied, 'I might die for Ireland but I'm f**ked if I'm going to die for Wales.'

45

FOOTBALL MADE SIMPLE

The Essential Guide to GAA Punditry

Gaelic football is a technical game with its own specialised vocabulary. Many people do not fully appreciate the nuances of football speak. The following glossary of terms may help readers to understand this culture more easily.

When a pundit says: This wonderfully historic ground.
What the pundit really means is: It's a proper dump.

When a pundit says: You have to admire his loyalty to the club.
What the pundit really means is: No other club would take him.

When a pundit says: Few players show such flair.
What the pundit really means is: He is a complete show-off.

When a pundit says: He's a player who relies on instinct.
What the pundit really means is: He hasn't a brain in his head.

When a pundit says: This match was not without its moments.
What the pundit really means is: It would be more exciting to watch the TV with the screen switched off.

When a pundit says: He has an interesting temperament.
What the pundit really means is: He's a complete nutcase.

When a pundit says: He shows great economy around the ball.
What the pundit really means is: He never gets near the thing.

When a pundit says: And the longstanding servant.
What the pundit really means is: He must be soon entitled to free bus travel.

When a pundit says: This goalkeeper is like Dracula.
What the pundit really means is: He can't cope with crosses.

When a pundit says: He's like a big jigsaw.
What the pundit really means is: He falls to pieces.

When a pundit says: You have to admire his competitive spirit.
What the pundit really means is: He is a psychopath.

When a pundit says: He's a seasoned veteran.
What the pundit really means is: He's past it.

When a pundit says: He showed great promise as a teenager.
What the pundit really means is: He is totally useless now.

When a pundit says: The referee had a poor view of the incident.
What the pundit really means is: The ref is as blind as a bat.

When a pundit says: He has a distinctive look.
What the pundit really means is: He has a face only his mother could love.

46

ULSTER SAYS YES

Observe the Sons of Ulster Marching On

Pat Spillane is the best-known critic of Ulster football with comments like:

'Right now, playing positive attacking football is about as useful as trying to empty Kenmare Bay with a fork. There have been games this summer when, if you wanted interesting viewing, you would have been better off watching *The Angelus*.

'The sad reality is that these cancers have spread throughout the country. Most tragically of all, even my beloved Kerry have succumbed to this disease, as was graphically illustrated in the Munster final. Regardless of how much natural ability a forward has, there is not much they can do without the ball. As Con Houlihan once said of a struggling Kerry forward: "He was like a gun-fighter roaming the streets without his gun."'

Spillane is not on his own when it comes to Ulster football. Kevin McStay had his tongue firmly in his cheek as he anticipated the throw-in of old rivals Tyrone versus Armagh: 'Welcome to the pleasuredome.'

LATE TACKLE

They take football very seriously in Ulster as revealed in former Ulster chairman Michael Grennan's dismissive response to the suggestion that the IRFU would have the chance to use GAA grounds for their World Cup bid:

'We have prostituted ourselves and the bottom line is, when you have prostituted yourself, the people who make the money are not the prostitutes but the pimps. We'll know how much the GAA got for making Croke Park available, but does anyone know how much the soccer or the rugby boys got out of it?'

TOUGHER THAN THE REST

The toughness of Monaghan football was emphasised in the observation that a late tackle in Monaghan was one that came the day after a match!

DOUBLE STANDARDS

Pat Spillane was the main speaker at a major gala of a prominent club in Ulster. At the end of the night, a spectator went up to the MC for the evening, Adrian Logan from UTV, and said, "Twas shocking to hear all that filthy language here this evening. That kind of talk has no place in the GAA.'

Adrian nodded and, just to make conversation, asked the man what he thought of Pat Spillane. Logan was surprised with his response: 'I can't stand that f**king c**t. He only talks sh*te.'

THE LAST SUPPER

There were happier visits, though, to Ulster. In 1994 Spillane did a function in Tyrone and in 2004 he returned to the same venue. His opening words of ten years previously were quoted back to him in full. Peter Canavan was in the audience in 1994 and Spillane began by saying: 'I look down the hall and I see before me Peter Canavan, one of the greatest Tyrone players of all time. They call Peter Canavan "God" up here. They call me a boll*x. I have eight All-Ireland medals and Peter Canavan has none.'

47

WHERE WE SPORTED AND PLAYED

Jack Lynch Wins Six All-Ireland Medals

Hurling heroes have to be truly exceptional to be recognised in Cork. One hurler who gained iconic status on Leeside was the late Jack Lynch. He took mischievous pleasure in recalling Frank O'Connor's claim that Cork had a mental age of seventeen. You had to leave at seventeen if you were to be happy and stimulated, whereas Dublin had a mental age of twenty-one.

In the early days of the revival of Cork's inter-county hurling fortunes, the late thirties and early forties, Lynch had many an argument with his teammates as to why Cork did not do better in a particular game. Whenever things got particularly heated, Bobby Ryng, of Carrigtwohill, a forward who had a speech impediment, used to intervene with 'no p-p-p-politics here'. Of course, politics then was the least of their problems, but Bobby used the tactic to completely defuse the situation.

Lynch had a famous altercation with Tony Reddin, the legendary Tipperary goalkeeper. During the white heat of a Cork–Tipp clash, Lynch charged into Reddin and in the process bundled both of them into the net. An irate Reddin roared, 'F-f-f-f**k you, Lynch. Try that again an' there'll be a f-f-f-f**kin by-election.'

LATE ARRIVAL

Lynch won five All-Ireland hurling medals with Cork. He also won an All-Ireland football medal. His football career left him with one enduring memory from the 1945 All-Ireland football final. Having completed his law examinations, he was in 'digs' on the southside of Dublin in Rathgar. He met the Cork team at 'Kingsbridge' Station on the Saturday evening. He told the selection committee he would not be at the hotel the next morning but would go straight to the stadium as there was a bus route near his digs which passed by Croke Park. He was waiting in a queue about twenty yards long. Bus after bus passed, each taking only a couple of people at a time.

At one stage, Lynch barged to the head of the queue. The conductor told him to go back and await his turn. He pointed to his bag of 'togs' and said he was playing in the All-Ireland Football final in Croke Park within the hour. The conductor said sarcastically that this was the best reason for breaking a queue that he ever heard but let him stay on.

He alighted from the bus at the junction of Drumcondra and Conyngham Roads and ran to the back of the Cusack Stand, where the dressing rooms were then located. He knocked at the Cork dressing room door to be greeted by an ominous silence except for the sound of footsteps slowly and deliberately pacing the floor, and this within only about fifteen minutes from the throw-in. The door opened. It was Jim Hurley, formerly Cork hurling midfielder, then Secretary of UCC and Chairman of the Cork Selection Committee. Lynch expected to be 'bawled' out.

Instead, he got: 'Hello, Jack Lynch, you were great to come'.

48

RING OF FIRE

Christy Ring Becomes the Best

On Cork hurling's roll of honour, pride of place goes to Christy Ring. In 1944 Limerick drew with Cork in the Munster Championship. In the replay the Shannonsiders led by five points, with fifteen minutes to go, as Mick Mackey scored a goal only to see it disallowed because the referee had blown for an infringement on him. To add insult to injury, Limerick spurned a scoring opportunity from the free in. Cork pegged back the lead to draw level and, in the dying seconds, the wizard of Cloyne struck. Never were truer words spoken:

> *Now Cork is bate,*
> *the hay is saved,*
> *the thousands wildly sing.*
> *They speak too soon,*
> *my sweet garsun,*
> *cos here comes Christy Ring.*

Cork had won the three previous All-Irelands and were bidding to become the first side to win the four-in-a-row. Ring's brother, Willie John, ran in from the sideline to tell Christy, 'If you get the ball into your hand, run with it because your man's legs are gone.' Seconds later, Ring got the ball and made a forty-yard solo run, which has become part of hurling legend, before unleashing a powerful shot for the decisive goal. After the match, Willie John asked Christy why he had not gone for safety and taken a point. Ring replied, 'That would be too easy. Anyone could have scored a point.'

BABE

Christy was famous for his commitment to training. One story that has gone into legend dates back to the time his wife gave birth to their first son. A few hours later Christy was said to have been on his way to training when he was greeted and warmly congratulated by a neighbour. When she saw his gear and hurley she said, 'I'm surprised to see you training just after your wife gave birth to your son.'

Christy coolly replied, 'I don't care if 'twas a young piglet she had. I'm not going to miss training.'

EAGLE EYED

Ring was very single-minded and once instructed a debutante on the Cork team to: 'always keep your eye on the ball – even when it's in the referee's pocket.'

TROUBLEMAKERS

Christy and a friend attended a seminar on coaching, in a church hall in Cork, one evening. The priest approached the great man apologetically and said, 'There are very bad acoustics here.'

Christy's friend replied reassuringly, 'Don't worry, Father. I'm not sure who these acoustics are but if they start any trouble we'll throw them out.'

For years and years Ring wreaked havoc on Tipperary hurlers. The great Tipp star Mickey 'Rattler' Byrne said to him at one stage, 'By God, Christy, we'll have to shoot you.'

Ring calmly replied, 'Ye might as well. Ye've tried everything else.'

PASSENGERS

One man does not make a hurling team, though Ring had his doubts. One Sunday he was jumping over the stile instead of displaying his pass as he went into a match. An irate county-board official, a former teammate of Ring's, caustically inquired where was the wizard of Cloyne's pass?

'I don't have it.'

'But Christy, you ought to have. You won no less than eight All-Ireland medals.'

The reply was fast and devastating: 'And if I hadn't been carrying passengers like you, I'd have won at least eight more!'

49

A MEDICAL MIRACLE

Tyrone v Armagh

Armagh fans in the noughties were not happy with the way the Tyrone forwards, especially Brian Dooher, would go to ground after any light physical contact – and perish the thought he might exagerate the nature of his injuries. They started a rumour that after a particularly theatrical fall, Dooher thought he was dead. When the Tyrone team doctor went onto the pitch he found it tough to convice Dooher he was still alive. Nothing seemed to work. Finally the doctor tried one last approach. He took out his medical books and proceeded to show the then Tyrone captain that dead men don't bleed. After a long time, Dooher seemed finally convinced that dead men don't bleed.

'Do you now agree that dead men don't bleed?' the doctor asked.

'Yes, I do,' Dooher replied.

'Very well, then,' the doctor said.

He took out a pin and pricked Dooher's finger. Out came a trickle of blood.

The doctor asked, 'What does that tell you?'

'Oh my goodness!' Dooher exclaimed as he stared incredulously at his finger. 'Dead men do bleed.'

CATCH UP

Clashes between Armagh and Roscommon provided many memorable moments down the years. In 1982 they met for a series of three matches in America. Before the first match some of the players had partied too hard and went onto the pitch in something less than the full of their health. At one point the ball was coming in towards the Armagh goal. Their accomplished full-back, Jim Kerr, went for the ball but was experiencing a form of double vision, and as he went up, he caught an imaginary ball, toe-tapped it and cleared it. Meanwhile, a Roscommon player had caught the real ball and stuck it in the net. When interrogated about the mishap, Kerr's response contained no admission of guilt: 'I got the ball I went for!'

FRANKLY SPEAKING

Tyrone legend, Frank McGuigan, was only the second player in history to play inter-county football at minor, under-21, junior, and senior levels in the one year. The first was Roscommon's Dermot Earley.

Roscommon's All-Star full-back, Pat Lindsay, played with McGuigan on an All-Stars trip:

'Frank was probably the most gifted player I ever saw, though he would probably be the first to admit he was never a hundred per cent fit. He loved life! I roomed with Frank for a while. It was an education! One time we stayed out all night and in the morning we went to a diner for breakfast. We had a massive fry-up. A very nice waitress came over and asked if we had enjoyed our meal. Frank was a big man and he replied: "It was so good I'll have the same again!"'

AN OFFICER AND A GENTLEMAN

By profession, Pat Lindsay was a prison officer. The 1958 memoir *Borstal Boy* is based on life in an English prison and borstal in the late 1930s and early 1940s as seen and experienced by Brendan Behan. One of the most striking features of *Borstal Boy* is the amount of humour and wit which occurs throughout it. Nothing has changed in this area since Behan's time.

Pat Lindsay believes that God gave us the imagination to compensate us for what we are not and a sense of humour to console us for what we are. A major part of living in this crazy, incomprehensible life is about seeing the light and humour in difficult times. Life is simply too short to be wasted on negativity.

Humour is particularly helpful in prison as a release from tension in an overcrowded environment. In 2003 the Corrections Department in Thailand held a laughter contest for its 250,000 convicts in an effort to relieve the stress caused by overcrowding in their prisons – a prize was awarded to the best laugh and the best joke by a prisoner. This may be an extreme example, but in a prison environment humour is a great way to avoid, limit or reduce conflict between prison officers and prisoners.

In his time in the prison service Lindsay came across many comic moments:

'New prisoners and officers are nicknamed almost immediately and some of the crispness and appropriateness of the names selected are just hilarious. A case in point was Johnny, who was committed to St Patrick's and despite his own best efforts he continually presented in an untidy state – he simply attracted dirt. Instantly he was nicknamed "Johnny Hoover".

'We had a humorous example of the need for great clarity in communication in Mountjoy in May 1988. There was a month-long prison strike and we had to bring gardai into keep the prison running. As the gardai are not familiar with the nuances of managing large numbers of prisoners in a confined space, we were worried that it would increase tension. One of our staff got the bright idea of giving a newspaper to each prisoner in the hope that reading them would distract them and keep things calm. He sent off somebody in a van to buy every newspaper he could in the local shops and he came back with his van full. He put the papers in bundles for each wing in the prison to make the distribution of them easier. He called over one of the gardai and said: "Give one of these to each of the lads." A short time later he decided to check if his masterplan was working. He was horrified to see that all round the prison the gardai were reading their newspapers. When he used the word "lads" the garda thought he meant gardai not prisoners.

'During a hostage-takers crisis in Mountjoy they were saying things like "We want transfers" and "We are being treated like dirt". Then they were following it up with "Will you be able to make sandwiches?" and "I'm looking for nasal spray". As the threads of their stories begin to unravel, what was revealed was a patchwork of confusion.

'At the time I did not appreciate it but years on I can enjoy the black humour of the situation, particularly when one of the hostage-takers looking for people to come in and speak to them said: "Contact f**king Houdini as well."'

50

HANGING ON THE TELEPHONE

Cork Win the Munster Final

Cork dramatically won the 1983 Munster final courtesy of a sensational last-minute goal from Tadhg Murphy. Cork full-back Kevin Kehilly rang Murphy a few days later only to be told: 'I'm sorry, Kevin, I can't talk to you now cos I've some-body with me. Ring me back in ten minutes.' He did and when he rang he got Murphy's answering machine. The message was: 'This is Tadhgie Murphy here. The man with the golden boot. Kevin, without me you wouldn't have won a Munster medal.'

OLD AGE AND FAILING POWERS

Throughout Kehilly's career, his Cork colleagues always kept him in laughs. The autumn of his inter-county football career was the era of the roving full-forward. He was the last of the traditional full-backs who marshalled the square and it was a big culture shock for him to have to start running halfway out the field and running back in again for the whole match. It was tough on his aging body. Billy Morgan was always winding him up before a match, saying, 'Kevin, keep close to the goal today. I didn't bring any oxygen!'

THE YOUNG ONES

Kehilly's inter-county career ended in 1989 when Cork regained the All-Ireland. Among the Cork stars of that team was John Cleary – a very accurate forward, though not the biggest man in the world. Before one of Cork's clashes with Kerry, Jack O'Shea came up to him and, in an effort to psych him out, said, 'You're too small and too young for a game like this.' Cleary said nothing until after the game when Cork emerged triumphant. As he walked off the pitch past Jacko, he softly said, 'You're too old for a game like this.'

PUTTING OFF THE INEVITABLE

In the glory days of the Kerry team, Páidí Ó Sé told the story of when Cork trailed Kerry by 2–19 to 0–5 at half-time. Kerry were to play with a gale-force wind in the second half. So desperate were the Cork mentors in the dressing room at half-time that they asked the tea lady if she had any advice for them. After pausing for thought, she said: 'If ye want to prolong yer stay in the Championship, the only thing ye can do is stay as long as ye possibly can here in the dressing room.'

STYLE COUNCIL

Not surprisingly, Pat Spillane has strong memories about Cork footballers:

'I gave a talk at the Jurys Sportstar of the Year awards: talk about meeting the enemies. Niall Cahalane was in the audience. He was probably the most difficult player I ever marked. I told the crowd that Niall had such a love of Kerry that he used to collect bits and pieces of my Kerry jersey by marking me so closely, all through the years.'

CRITICAL VOICES

Kerry are rightly seen as football royalty. However, in recent years, Kerry people are often indignant about the comments of Joe Brolly in particular, as he has discovered:

'On television you make a casual remark and people become suffused with rage. The odd time people will berate you for that. I recall travelling on a train to Dublin when a fella in a Meath jersey got up and said to me: "You f**king bollix." During an ad break in the Wexford–Armagh quarter-final, a man in his seventies burst into the studios and said to me: "You're a f**king joke, yourself and O'Rourke. You're Dumb and Dumber."

'I could say something relatively trivial and RTÉ got a thousand emails. I said something about Paul Galvin after he kicked someone off the ball or something against Armagh in 2006. I said: "That's unbelievable and he's a teacher. That's real corner-boy stuff." Jesus Christ. All hell broke loose.'

Brolly was unfazed by the controversy:

'The Kerry manager Jack O'Connor then was supposed to be furious. I am told that in his book with Tom Humphries he has a go at me for "crossing the line" but I never read it. I reviewed it but I never read it! I'm like Alan Partridge. He was interviewing a woman and asks her: "Is it true that you . . .?" She answers: "Of course I did. Did you not read my book?" Alan replies: "No, I never read the books." In my review I said O'Connor's book was unlikely to trouble the Pulitzer Committee!'

LAST WILL AND TESTAMENT

A Clare farmer was making out his will the day after Clare, then managed by Páidí, lost to Waterford in the 2007 Championship.

His solicitor was surprised at one of his clauses: 'To Páidí Ó Sé I leave my clown suit. He will need it if he continues to manage as he has in the past.'

FANCY DRESS

Another Clare fan joked after the match that Páidí was going to a fancy-dress party dressed as a pumpkin. He was hoping at midnight he would turn into a coach.

51

BROKEN ENGLISH

Tipperary Have Hard Times

Injuries can wreak havoc on a player. Given his injuries, Babs Keating once said to Nicky English, 'Nicky, if I had legs like yours, I'd be wearing nylons.'

The one and only Babs is a man who knows all there is to know about the vagaries of hurling fortunes. He once said about management: 'It's a very short distance between a slap on the back and a kick in the arse!'

For his part, Nicky English has known setbacks too: 'If I had ducks, they'd drown.'

SYLVIE HELPS OUT

With time running out and Galway's victory apparently secure in the 1988 All-Ireland hurling final, Nicky asked the referee how much time was left. The ever-helpful Sylvie Linnane butted in immediately to say, 'In your case, a year and five minutes!'

SPAT-GATE

During Babs Keating's 'second coming' as Tipperary manager, after a poor performance against Limerick, a critic said that Babs was past his best. Keating was not going to take this comment on the chin. Instead, he went on Tipp FM and said: 'To me he is an arsehole and always has been an arsehole.'

SLIOTAR-GATE

Tipperary and Cork games during those years were noted for their skirmishes over sliotars. At the time, the GAA had not imposed a standard sliotar for big matches – so most teams used the O'Neills models whereas the Cork lads used the Cummins version. Cork were wont to try and sneak an advantage against Tipp by using that well-known Irish political tactic of playing 'cute hoors'.

When Tipperary got a close-in free, one of the Cork backs would start a bit of a row and one of his colleagues with smash the ball into the net as a gesture of solidarity. In the confusion, the Cork goalie would puck out 'the' sliotar but having replaced it with a much older, heavier model which would make it much harder to strike with the kind of power that would yield a goal. Babs, though, quickly wised up to the tactic and famously went behind Dónal Óg Cusack's goal and drew the umpire's attention to the fuss, much to the annoyance of the Cork camp. The Cork rebels, though, had the last laugh. They countered Babs's monitoring of the situation in 2005 by cleverly selecting the oldest, deadest sliotar they could find and writing Tipp on it with a marker and holding it for when Tipperary got a penalty and slipping it to Eoin Kelly and fooling him into thinking it was a Tipperary sliotar. When Kelly stood up though to take the shot, he quickly realised the error of his ways because he was unable to get his customary velocity behind the shot and the penalty was saved.

ACHIEVEMENT IS IN THE EYE OF THE BEHOLDER

Michael Doyle had the virtually impossible task of succeeding Nicky English as Tipperary manager. One of his most courageous decisions was to take off star forward, Eoin Kelly, in a match against Galway. Kelly was being marked by the great Ollie Canning and was struggling. The Tipp fans, though, felt he should have been switched rather than replaced. Kelly was phlegmatic: 'I did pretty well. I held Ollie to just a point.'

STAG

In the 2021 Munster final, Tipperary led Limerick by ten points only for Limerick to crush them in the second half. Afterwards, a Tipp fan posed the question: 'What's the difference between Tipperary and a stag party?'

'A stag party would never lose ten p(0)ints.'

52

MUSCULAR MEATH

Meath v Dublin

It was the time when Meath and Dublin were drawing more often than Michelangelo and when Colm O'Rourke was voted footballer of the year. O'Rourke won two All-Ireland medals, three league titles and three All-Stars. However, what he will probably be best remembered for is his part in a four-game saga which enthralled the nation in the first round of the Leinster Championship in 1991. At a time when Ireland was going through soccer mania after Italia '90, and when the nation was under the spell of Jack Charlton, the series of games showed that reports of the GAA's demise were premature.

Despite their intensity the four-game saga did produce one moment of light relief. Paul Curran was dropped for the third game but came on in the second half and scored the equalising point. A few nights later, Dublin manager Paddy Cullen had a team meeting with the players and did some video analysis with them. Cullen was severely critical of the forward's first-half performance and turned to Curran and asked him: 'Where were you in the first half?' To the hilarity of his teammates Curran replied: 'Sitting beside you, as a sub on the bench Paddy!'

BARR-ED

The rivalry between fans can be nasty or it can be witty. When Dublin played Meath in the 1996 Leinster final, Meath's Tommy Dowd was in a clash of heads with Dublin's Keith Barr. Some time later Keith's brother, Johnny, was also in the wars with Tommy. After the match, Tommy was going up for an interview when he banged his head against a bar in one of the barriers – an injury which subsequently necessitated four stitches. As he held his head in agony, a passing Dublin fan said to him: 'I see you made the hat-trick.'

'What do you mean?' Tommy asked.

'Johnny Barr, Keith Barr and iron bar!'

SQUARE BALL

During a Dublin v Meath game in the 1990s, the Dubs fans were giving Meath goalie Mickey McQuillan a bit of stick. A few started throwing coins at him. Mickey collected the coins, discovered he had fifty pence and he went over to the umpire and presented him with the money and said, 'There you are now. Any square ball that comes in, you know what to do! Put the money towards a pint.'

KELLY'S HEROES

Meath football has always been a place where the weak don't survive. Hence a club secretary's report which stated: 'Mick Kelly (the name has been changed to protect the guilty) made his championship debut in such a way that he will never be asked to make it again!'

53

FOREVER YOUNG

The Paula Pan of Camogie

The former president of the Camogie Association, Miriam O'Callaghan, described Máirín McAleenan as: 'one of the finest ambassadors that the game has ever had.'

In March 1986 Máirín made her senior debut for Down in Portglenone against Antrim as a wing-forward, in a game which Down won.

She has won a proliferation of honours including: Down Senior Championships; Down Senior League; Ulster Club Championships; Player of the Tournament Kilmacud 7s; Ulster Minor Championships; Ulster Minor League; Ulster Junior Championship; All-Ireland Junior Championship; All-Ireland Junior National League; All-Ireland Intermediate Championship; Ulster GAA Writers Player of the Year and Player of the Tournament Ashbourne Cup and All-Star awards.

Máirín's career has been enriched by her interaction with a number of characters:

'My clubmate, the age-defying Bernie Kelly, played every game with the experience of a veteran, and the enthusiasm of an eight-year-old. At forty-three years Bernie continued to power Liatroim's efforts from midfield, twenty-two years after helping her club to their first Down Senior title. Bernie possessed an indomitable and unquenchable will to win, as well as a Rolls Royce engine! She scored a goal in each of the All-Ireland Junior finals of 1976 and 1991.

'On the way to the Ulster Club Final in 1998, I was reading a newspaper article on the match. The journalist in question had put Bernie in the "veteran" bracket and questioned the wisdom of playing a forty-two-year-old in midfield at such a high level of camogie.

'Fully aware of the effect this would have on Bernie should she hear it, I said to her, "Do you hear that, Bernie – they reckon here that you're past it!"

'"Huh! Past it!" said Bernie. "I'll be hurling for Liatroim when I'm f***ing ninety!"'

54

THE MIGHTY QUINN

The Rattler Rules

Hurling was once cynically described in a British Sunday newspaper as 'cavemen's lacrosse'. In the debate as to whether hurling or football is the greatest game on earth there is only one answer in Tipperary. Hence Tony Wall's adage that, 'Football is a game for those not good enough to play hurling!'

RATTLE AND ROLL

Tipperary have given the game great players and characters, though nobody could top Mickey 'Rattler' Byrne. He was a small man but, pound for pound, he was the toughest man you could ever meet. He could mark guys from Wexford three or four stones heavier than him but he would never be beaten. He was a great corner-back for Tipp but also a wonderful storyteller. He did not have much time for all the talk players have today about their injuries, especially about their 'hamstrings'. He always said that the only time in his playing days he heard anybody talking about hamstrings was when they were hanging outside a butcher's shop.

EMERGENCY EXIT

One day he went to New York with Tommy Doyle, who was making his first flight and was very nervous. He sought comfort from the Rattler, who told him, 'Don't be worrying, Tommy. There are two parachutes under the seat; you put one on, jump out, count to ten, press the button, and you jump to safety. What could be simpler?'

'But what happens if the parachute doesn't open?' asked Tommy.

'That's easy,' answered the Rattler. 'You just jump back up and get the spare one.'

LAST MAN STANDING

It is claimed that one of Tipperary's greatest-ever goalkeepers, Skinny Meara, from Toomevara, trained in the summertime by opening the doors of his barn, standing in the great gap and stopping swallows from flying in and out.

BILLY'S KID

In the 1950s one of Tipperary's star forwards was a young Billy Quinn, whose three goals in the 1954 league final helped Tipp beat Kilkenny that day. Billy was the father of Niall, who served Irish soccer with such distinction. Although soccer claimed Niall's career, his love of hurling remained unabated.

Niall's uncle, also called Niall, was a fine hurler. Back in the 1940s one summer he was selected to play for Tipperary against old rivals Cork in a championship match – which was a dream come true for any hurler. Niall arranged to be picked up by team-mates outside a famous pub called the Horse and Jockey. As he waited for his lift, he spotted a red squirrel. So taken was he by the squirrel that he decided he would pass up the opportunity to play against Cork so that he could catch the squirrel and make it his pet. Hours later he returned home in triumph with his prize to be greeted by baffled neighbours who wondered why he hadn't lined out for Tipp. Quinn had no regrets. He played again for Tipp and kept the squirrel for years.

A COLLECTOR'S ITEM

Niall Quinn paid a small fortune for a hurley signed by Jimmy Barry-Murphy at a charity function in London only to discover later that Jimmy hadn't signed it at all!

PRIDE

Despite his pride at Niall's great success in soccer, Billy still felt the game was no match for hurling. He put his foot in it in 1990 when a journalist came to interview him about Niall after he scored the famous goal against Holland in the World Cup. When he asked Billy if he was proud of Niall, Billy said without thinking, 'To tell you the truth, I'd rather if he had won a Munster medal!'

THE WINDOWS OF WONDER

The family, though, did pay a price for Niall's devotion to hurling. As a boy, Niall always had a hurley in his hand. One famous day in Killarney, Babs Keating scored a last-minute goal from a free. That was the day when a mentor came on with a towel and was supposed to have switched the ball and swapped a wet one for a dry one to make it easier for Babs to score. Niall was about five at the time. He was practising frees in the back garden after the match and his mother, Mary, was doing the ironing when the window was shattered to smith-ereens by Niall's sliotar. Mary nearly dropped dead with the shock of the shattering glass. All Niall said afterwards was, 'I was only doing Babs Keating!'

SHOCK AND AWE

Niall went out for a few drinks one night with a few friends and they were joined by Manchester United legend Norman Whiteside. The youngest in the group turned to Norman and asked: 'Did you play a bit yourself?'

Whiteside instantly responded: 'Who was the second youngest player to play in the World Cup finals?'

The young man replied: 'Oh my God, it was you.'

Whiteside shook his head: 'No. The second youngest was Pelé. The youngest was me.'

55

GARDA REPORT

Seán Boylan Revives Meath's Fortunes

The face of Meath football was changed forever with the appointment of the great Seán Boylan as county manager in 1982. Shortly after he became coach, Dublin were playing Meath in Croke Park. Seán wanted to make a positional change during the match and walked down along the sideline behind the goal in front of the Hill and all the Dublin fans were jeering him and slagging him. It was all in a good-natured way and there was no malice in it whatsoever. Because he was so new in the job, and Meath weren't having huge success at the time, a garda came racing up to him and thought he was just a fan! Boylan had a fierce problem convincing him that he was actually the Meath manager. After a lot of cajoling, Boylan eventually persuaded him of his identity and he said to him, 'You do your job and look after the spectators and let me do my job and look after these lads on the pitch.' After they had finished their 'chat' Boylan walked back in front of the Hill again. This time the Dublin fans gave him a great ovation. They thought he was a hero because he had stood up to and had a big row with a guard!

HELL AND BACK

Under Boylan's stewardship, Meath carved out a reputation for never being beaten until the final whistle sounded. Hence Martin Carney's evaluation of Boylan's boys: 'Meath are like Dracula. They're never dead 'til there's a stake through their heart.'

After their clashes with Cork in 1987 and 1988, in particular, Meath got the reputation of being hard men. Seán Boylan attended a funeral in 1989 and met a young recruit to the Meath panel who took the wind out of the manager's sails by claiming, 'When I die I want to go to hell.'

A bemused Boylan asked, 'Why do you want to go down there?'

'Well, now that I'm on the panel I want to be one of the lads in every way. If all the things that are said about them are true, the only possible place they could end up is roasting in the fires of the hell!'

DUB-LE TROUBLE

In the 1970s Dublin brought new glamour to Gaelic football. The Dublin players became like pop stars and, accordingly, some of them had great appeal for women. One Saturday night one of the players took a young lady in his car up the Dublin mountains and got immersed in a passionate embrace. What they had forgotten was that the Don Tidey kidnap was on at the time and the gardai were on the lookout for suspicious activities and suspicious 'vehicles'. The couple were at an advanced stage of undress and the car windows were very steamy when there was a knock on the window. The Dublin player hadn't time to react when a flashlamp was beaming on him. The garda was so embarrassed when he recognised the star of the Dubs that all he could say was, 'Can I see your driver's licence, please?'

DOCTOR, DOCTOR

Another star of that team was David Hickey, who went on to become a distinguished medical professional. Hickey joked that he had overheard one of his female patients complaining about him. She said, 'I've been under my doctor for six months but he hasn't done me any good.'

Before the 1977 classic All-Ireland semi-final between Kerry and Dublin, the Dubs were bemused when Hickey yelled in the middle of a training session: 'Typhoid! Tetanus! Measles!'

Kevin Heffernan asked, 'Why are you doing that?'

Hickey replied, 'Oh, I want to be the guy that calls the shots round here.'

56

A LOAD OF BULL

Sligo's Supremo

Like Tyrone's Iggy Jones and so many players from the West of Ireland, Sligo's Micheál Kearins missed out on an All-Ireland medal. Micheál Ó Muircheartaigh furnished the definitive epitaph to Kearins's career: 'Some players are consistent. Some players are brilliant but Micheál Kearins was consistently brilliant.'

His first Railway Cup game was against Leinster in Ballinasloe. At the start, as he was moving into position before the ball was thrown in, he noticed his immediate opponent, Paddy McCormack, digging a hole along the ground with his boot.

He said, 'You're young Kearins, from Sligo. I presume you expect to go back to Sligo this evening.'

'Hopefully,' Kearins replied.

'If you don't pass the mark, you have a fair chance of getting back.'

Barnes Murphy gives a different context to that story:

'A lot of people know the story of Micheál Kearins's first game with Connacht, marking Paddy McCormack. What they don't know is the postscript. Mickey was switched off Paddy and Cyril Dunne went on his place. Cyril went up to Paddy and said immediately: "Watch yourself or I'll give you a box." Paddy was very quiet for the rest of the game.'

BRILLIANT BARNES

In 1974 Roscommon needed a replay to beat Sligo in a National League semi-final. Sligo's Barnes Murphy was rewarded for a string of fine performances through the year with an All-Star award. There is one Sligo player, though, who is most associated with Murphy:

'Micheál Kearins had a serious side and a funny side. We were travelling to a match one day and Micheál, unusually, was coming on the team bus with us. It was often said that Sligo were a one-man team. Someone asked Micheál how the team were going. He replied: "I'm feeling great today!"'

BULLISH

Murphy reflects with amusement: 'In 2008 Micheál had a confrontation with a bull and the bull won. Micheál has put on a bit of weight since his playing days, and when a friend of mine heard the news, he rang me to inquire if the bull was okay!'

57

THE FLAIR FACTOR

Quick Wits in the GAA

Down the years, many Gaelic footballers have added to the gaiety of the nation with their comments and their antics on and off the pitch. This chapter celebrates some of them.

NOTHING BUT THE TRUTH

Former Laois star Colm Parkinson was being interviewed on Newstalk radio and remarked that whenever there was a controversy it was always branded a 'scandal' in the county. The interviewer, Ger Gilroy, asked: 'Why is that?' Parkinson calmly replied: 'Probably because we were always drinking.'

TALL TALES

Parkinson was also characteristically candid when asked about his own evaluation of his performance when playing for Ireland against Australia in the Compromise Rules series and marking a player who had a big physical advantage over him. 'The first time I tried to tackle this big fella I was holding on to his jersey and he started to run down the pitch. I don't think he even noticed I was holding on to him.'

NOT A LION KING

Joe Brolly is honest enough to admit that he baulked at the prospect of playing International Rules for Ireland: 'I was asked about it a few times and I couldn't run away from it fast enough. I'm too much of a coward!'

A TALL TAIL

After Armagh beat Down in the 2008 Ulster semi-final, the Armagh manager Peter McDonnell explained, using the term in its broadest sense, that: 'We were riding the donkey close to the tail.'

An analyst is essential to the national TV audience in moments like this to decipher its hidden treasures. Happily, Joe Brolly rose to the plate and explained: 'Riding the donkey close to the tail? I presume that's something you do in south Armagh. It's a very odd part of the world.'

CAPTAIN FANTASTIC

One of Gaelic football's great gentlemen was Dermot O'Brien. He captained Louth to their only senior All-Ireland title in 1957 and had more fame as a singer and smashed records with his biggest hit *The Merry Ploughboy*.

One of Dermot's favourite stories was about the Louth player of the 1950s who on a visit to America was chatted up by a woman in a bar. To put it very charitably, she was less than pretty and was as heavy as the combined weight of Louth's two midfielders. At first the Louth player was immune to the woman's charms. His attention, though, was captured when she told him that her mother had only two months to live and the dying widow had inherited a multi-million dollar fortune from her husband. Now the daughter stood to inherit everything. The Louth player was moved to action.

Two weeks later he was married . . . to the mother.

ANONYMOUS

In 1984 Dinny Allen was the only Cork player to be chosen on the Team of the Century of players who never won an All-Ireland. Five years later he put that omission to right when he captained the Cork team to win the All-Ireland. A lot of hurlers on the ditch alleged that Allen had not contributed much to winning Sam. As a result, Dinny christened himself the 'non-playing captain'!

HARE-RAISING

In 1985 Paddy Quirke played for his club, Naomh Eoin, against the Westmeath champions, Brownstown in, the first round of the Leinster club hurling championship. One of his teammates was asked a few days later how bad the pitch was. He replied, 'Well the grass was so long a hare rose at half-time!'

QUIRKE-Y

Carlow dual star Paddy Quirke played senior football and hurling with the county in the 1970s and 1980s. The highlight of Quirke's career came when he was chosen as the dual All-Star replacement. He also played hurling in San Francisco and found it really tough and physical. At one stage he put in his hurley, angled with the bas to the ground, to block an opponent; got a severe belt across the face; and was taken off and rushed to hospital. He had no social security cover, but his friends who were with him decided he was Patrick Foley (a genuine holder of social security). So, all of a sudden, he was somebody else. The only problem was when Paddy heard the name Patrick Foley being called out in the hospital, he forgot that was supposed to be him and had to be reminded who he then was.

At that stage he was not in very good shape and was expecting some sympathy from the doctor. Instead, all he said was, 'Were you playing that crazy Irish game?'

CARLOW CLUB COMMITMENT

A man concerned about warped priorities was a gentleman of the cloth at an emergency meeting of a club in Carlow. Sixty players had been on a weekend tour of Amsterdam for a sevens tournament, at which they were ignominiously dumped out of in the first round, one short week after they had failed to drum up fifteen players to play a side twenty miles down the road. A member of the touring party to Amsterdam responded to the priest's criticism: 'Well, Father, to the best of my knowledge, there are no ladies of the night there.'

58

AH REF

Tough Men

It has been said that junior club football in Wicklow has produced so many injuries that it has generated more breaks than KitKat.

COMMERCIAL INCENTIVE

John O'Mahony tells the story of a referee who was having a very strange game:

'He was scrupulously fair to everyone but allowed one of the midfielders on one team to run wild and to virtually decapitate half the opposition without getting any censure. In fact he clocked up enough offences to merit eight or nine red cards but hadn't even a free given against him.

'As was his normal practice, the referee had a quick review of his performance after the game with his umpires and linesmen. They said that generally he had done well but they asked him how on earth he could have allowed the midfielder to go unpunished.

'The referee calmly replied: "Well, lads, it's very simple. It's like this. I sold that guy a tractor two weeks ago and he still hasn't paid me. Sure, if I sent him off, he'd never pay me."'

THE LIFE OF O'REILLY

Wicklow have always produced great footballers, though never enough at the one time. Among their greatest was Gerry O'Reilly in the 1950s. His favourite character in the game was Kit Carroll from Dunlavin, who played with him on the Wicklow minor team. Like Gerry, he was fond of a pint after a game. What was unusual about Kit, though, was that after a match he would have an auction at the bar for his socks and jersey and would always get a pound or two to fund his drinking.

Gerry attributes the failure of the Wicklow team in the 1950s to the inadequacies of the county board. He claims that the men on the county board were so incompetent they couldn't even pick their own noses.

THE ROAD LESS TRAVELLED

A prospective young bank official was being interviewed for a job in Wicklow. The bank manager was chairman of the local club and said, 'We need a centre-half forward with courage and a strong set of hands like yours.'

'Sorry, sir,' said the lad. 'I don't know a thing about football.'

'No worries. We need referees too.'

OBVIOUS BIAS

Sometimes, though, referees are their own worst enemies. After two midfielders were embroiled in a serious entanglement in a club match in Wicklow, the captain of the home team asked, when the referee finally blew his whistle: 'Who's the free for, ref?'

The referee replied: 'It's for us.'

GOD V THE DEVIL

At one point God challenged the devil to a football match. The devil agreed provided the match was played in Wicklow.

'Remember,' said God, 'we have all the good footballers up here.'

'Yes,' said the devil, 'but we've got all the referees down here.'

GET YOUR MAN

A club team in Wicklow was facing defeat. At half-time the coach roared some fight into them. 'And you John, it's about time you got ferocious.'

'What's his number?' said John.

59

SUPERQUINN

Leitrim Heroes and Anti-heroes

Mickey Quinn was Leitrim's first All-Star. He admits to playing a leading role in the infamous 'battle of the fog':

'Aughawillan were playing Clann na nGael in the Connacht Club Championship but the match shouldn't have gone ahead. The fog was so bad you couldn't see the goalie kicking out the ball. Things heated up when two of our players were hit. I think it was me who really started it off! I "had a go" at Jimmy McManus and soon the whole set of players, subs and supporters were involved. The referee had a hard time getting law and order back but the game was a great battle in every sense.'

The match did have an amusing postscript though:

'Jerome Quinn played for Aughawillan against Clann na nGael that day and really dished it out to some of the Clann lads and developed a reputation as a hard nut. That was one of the reasons why Aughawillan versus Clann was renamed "the Provos versus the Guards". We were playing Roscommon in the Connacht Championship in 1990 and, before the match,

P.J. Carroll had an unusual mind game planned. He said: "Jerome Quinn, they all think you're f**king mad in Roscommon. What you need to do is pick up a clump of grass, stick it in your mouth and eat it in front of your marker's face. He'll sh*t himself." Jerome was wing half-back and was marking a lovely, skillful player. Sure enough, Jerome did as he was told and you could see the Roscommon player's legs turn to jelly!'

DOG-GONE

Mickey's interest in hunting has led him to become friends with Ger Loughnane. Dogs are at the top of Loughnane's hierarchy. He is a big fan of Tom T Hall's song which claims that there are three things in this world that are worth a solitary dime: old dogs, children, and watermelon wine. Ger claims: 'I never drank watermelon wine but I'd agree with him about the other two.'

SCAPEGOAT

Of course, Leitrim's most legendary footballer is Packy McGarty. He once told me about one of his first club games as a minor. At that stage it was hard to field a team. There was one guy roped into playing for them and he was provided with boots, socks, a jersey and the lot. They were thrashed and, of course, when that happens everybody blames everybody else. When unflattering comments were put to the new recruit, his riposte was, 'Well you can't blame me. I never got near the ball!'

THE BITTER WORD

A Leitrim football fan was shouting abuse at one of their corner-backs: 'Take that useless c**t off, he's good for nothing.'

Another fan interjected: 'That's terribly insulting. Imagine if he was your son.'

The first came back with an unexpected response: 'That useless f**ker is my son!'

60

WHO IS THE FAIREST OF THEM ALL?

Peter the Great

Although he played with a very serious manner, Peter Canavan also has a light side. In 2003 he was speaking at a reception to launch his book. All the Tyrone team were there apart from the delayed Owen Mulligan. Canavan explained to the crowd that Mulligan was late because his mother had bought him a new mirror and he was still admiring his reflection.

LEG OVER
Canavan showed a new side of himself after he became a pundit with Sky Sports. Commenting on the Munster semi-final replay, he remarked on the small dressing rooms in Páirc Uí Chaoimh: 'Senan (Connell) was telling me about a National League match that Dublin played here. It was that dark that one of the Dublin players, when he was changing, actually put his leg into someone else's shirt.'

FLYING WITHOUT WINGS
Great players have to be careful what they wish for. Peter Canavan and Owen Mulligan died and went to heaven.

St Peter greeted them, and said, 'I'm sorry, gentlemen, but your mansions aren't ready yet. Until they are, I can send you back to earth as whatever you want to be.'

'Great,' said Canavan, 'I want to be an eagle soaring above beautiful scenery.'

'No problem,' replied St Peter, and *poof!* Peter the Great was gone. 'And what do you want to be?' St Peter asked Mulligan.

'I'd like to be one cool stud!' was the reply.

'Easy,' replied St Peter, and Mulligan was gone.

After a few months, their mansions were finished, and St Peter sent an angel to fetch them back. You'll find them easily,' he said. 'One of them is soaring above the Grand Canyon, and the other one is on the bottom of a fridge in Omagh.'

MUGSY

That Tyrone team had some big personalities. None more so than Owen Mulligan. Joe Brolly tells a great story about him:

'It was the summer of 2005. I was walking through the tunnel beneath Croke Park, past the dressing rooms and out through the coach exit, exhilarated by what I had just seen, when there he was, standing big in the evening sun, bleached blond hair, looking left and right. It was Owen Mulligan and the big man was standing alone. Restless. He saw me and came over. "You were great today," I said to him. He said, "Never worry about that. Is there anywhere we can go for some quiet pints?" "Owen," I said, "you look like Sid Vicious, you've just scored the greatest goal ever seen at Croke Park. Your days of quiet pints are over." Quiet pint maybe. Not pints.

'Owen used to, as he put it, "go on the beer" every now and again, and one of his go-to excuses on those occasions was that his grandmother had died. From the bar one night, he rang Mickey Harte. "Mickey, I can't make training tonight, my granny has died." There was silence. Mickey said, "I thought she died last year." Owen said, "That was my other granny."'

THE LIFE OF RYAN

Tyrone's Ryan McMenamin was one of the most tenacious defenders in the modern game. In his own words: 'I know a lot of people think the way I act on the field is the way I act in life. If I did that, Jaysus, I'd be in Maghaberry. I'd be in jail.'

This aggression was most graphically illustrated at a league game in Omagh in 2009 when he grabbed Kerry's fashion guru Paul Galvin in the groin area. Amongst a section of the Kerry GAA fellowship he was immediately rechristened 'Holden McGroin'.

DANCING QUEENS

In the noughties Armagh and Tyrone pioneered a new style of defensive football and were seen as trailblazers for the other counties to follow. This was not seen as part of the natural order by the purists, in Kerry in particular. Anthony Daly recalls meeting Tomás Ó Sé and the Kerry defender said: 'I'm sick of that northern crowd. If they went set dancing twice a week, we'd all be set dancing twice a week.'

THE BOY FROM THE COUNTY ARMAGH

Kieran McGeeney captained Armagh to their only All-Ireland in 2002. As Kildare manager he has been involved in a few controversies. When questioned about them he could either talk up the situation: 'If anything goes wrong anywhere it seems to be my fault. Next thing I'll be blamed for the Famine and Fianna Fáil.'

Alternatively, he could talk down the situation: 'It was more tickling bellies than anything else' – on his sideline spat with the then Meath boss Séamus McEnaney.

THE FAB FOUR

Of course, what made Tyrone's 2003 All-Ireland victory all the sweeter for their supporters was that it came over their old rivals Armagh.

Four men went climbing a mountain, each claiming to be the most loyal fan in the country: one was from Armagh, one from Tyrone, one from Tipperary, one from Waterford. When they climbed the mountain, the Tipp fan said: 'This is how much I love Tipperary.' With that he jumped off the mountain and died instantly.

The Waterford fan said: 'This is how much I love Waterford.' With that he jumped off the mountain and died instantly.

The Tyrone man said: 'This is how much I love Tyrone.'

With that he pushed the Armagh man off the mountain.

KEEPING DOWN WITH THE JONES

In 1956 Tyrone narrowly lost the All-Ireland semi-final to the eventual champions Galway. The undisputed star of the Tyrone team at the time was Iggy Jones. The semi-final was a match that Jones was never allowed to forget. He had a goal chance to win the game when they were trailing by just two points. He made a run and cut in along the in-line. You don't score goals from there so he was looking for a teammate to pass to but there was no Tyrone forward there for him. The Galway goalie, Jack Mangan, was toward the near post. Jones thought to himself, 'I'll not get it past him but I'll get it over him.' He punched the ball over his head in the opposite direction to which he was travelling. Unfortunately, Mangan got his hand to it and Tyrone's chance for victory was gone. Thirty years later Iggy went to a school to speak to the children and this boy came up to him and said, 'My dad told me you were the man that lost the All-Ireland for Tyrone!'

PAYING THE PENALTY

In John McKnight's first year with Armagh seniors, in 1953, they got to the All-Ireland final only to lose to Kerry. Armagh got a penalty and Billy McCorry took it. He was a great man to take a penalty and had never missed one before but, like Liam Sammon in 1974 (having never missed a penalty for Galway, his penalty was saved by Paddy Cullen in the All-Ireland final), Billy missed.

McKnight was involved in an amusing postscript to the incident shortly after. He was playing for UCD in a club league game in Belfield. It had been alleged that just as Billy was going to take that penalty a Kerry player ran across him. It went through McKnight's mind, in that club match, that he would do something similar. After the ball was kicked, he struck his foot out and the ball made contact with it and looped up high in the air and landed gently into the goalie's arms. The penalty didn't have to be retaken but there was a serious 'rumpus'.

History repeated itself in 1977. Paddy Moriarty had a penalty saved in the All-Ireland final by Paddy Cullen. Moriarty was forcibly reminded of the link between the two penalties in the graveyard at Bill McCorry's funeral when he was asked, 'How does it feel to be the only Armagh man alive to have missed a penalty in an All-Ireland final?'

61

NUDIE

Monaghan's Maverick

One test of fame is when you are known simply by your first name: Bono, Gay, Miriam – no further introduction required. In Gaelic football circles the name 'Nudie' elicits instant recognition as that of Monaghan's most famous footballer, Eugene 'Nudie' Hughes. Nudie helped Monaghan to three Ulster Senior Football Championships in 1979, 1985 and 1988.

Nudie was well able to hold his own in any company. One player who gave him a lot of problems, though, was the Kerry forward John Egan. Ulster were playing a Railway Cup match against Munster, and Nudie was marking John. They were standing talking because Nudie always talked to opponents even though he would be told not to. At one stage John said, 'What's that man writing down on that piece of paper? He's a right looking eejit isn't he?' As Nudie turned to answer, John was sticking the ball into the net.

In 1988 Nudie used that same trick on Cavan's Damien O'Reilly. He was marking him in the Ulster final. At one stage in the game Nudie said, 'Jaysus, there's an awful lot of people up on the hill. How many people would you say are up there?' As Damien looked up to make his guess, the ball came in between them and Nudie caught it without any obstruction and stuck it over the bar. O'Reilly was taken off him immediately.

TOO MANY MURPHYS

Nudie also made his mark on foreign shores. He played in England but his club game with Round Towers in New Eltham was cancelled. A few enterprising men came up from Bristol and got Nudie to play against Gloucester in a league final, totally illegally. He was the last brought on and about to hand his name, 'Brian Murphy', to the ref. The official from Bristol called him back and said, 'I'd better change that, as the other two I sent in were Brian Murphys and the ref would surely spot it.' They changed it to Aidan Dempsey and went on to win the match.

CLARE AND PRESENT DANGER

Monaghan were playing against Clare in a league match in Ennis. Some young lads started throwing stones at Monaghan's goalie, Bubbles McNeill. True to form, Bubbles began throwing stones back at them. The only problem was that he got so caught up with the stones that he completely forgot about the match. A Clare forward pumped a hopeful ball in from midfield and it went into the empty net. Monaghan lost the match by a point.

VIDEO DID NOT KILL THE RADIO STAR

Nudie has found new fame as a co-commentator and analyst on Northern Sound Radio Station. In 2016 when Monaghan got two goals to haul back Donegal's five-point lead he shouted: 'Forget the Euros. Forget the Leinster Championship. Forget the Iraq War. This is a real war in Cavan tonight.'

NOISY NEIGHBOURS

Monaghan 'enjoy' a great rivalry on the football field with Cavan. Their fans are never slow to invoke the stereotypical image of Cavan people revealed in stories like the Cavan footballer who gave his wife lipstick for Christmas every year so that at least he could get half of it back.

One story they tell in this context is about the Pope. He had a very, very unusual blood type. The doctors could only find one person in the whole world who had the same blood type – Paddy O'Reilly, the Cavan footballer. So, Paddy donated a pint of blood and the Pope recovered. As a gesture of goodwill, the Pope sent Paddy on £20,000. The Pope got ill four times in successive years after that and each time he got a pint of Paddy's blood and each time he sent Paddy £20,000.

The sixth time he got Paddy's blood the Pope sent him only a holy medal. Paddy was devastated and rang the Vatican to ask why he got no money this time. The Pope's secretary took the call and answered, 'Well, Paddy, you have to understand he has a lot of Cavan blood in him at this stage!'

That may be why Monaghan fans say that when the Cavan football team went on a short holiday, the hotel they stayed at put their Gideon Bibles on chains.

TRADITIONAL TESTINESS

It is among the oldest rivalries in Ulster football, and perhaps the bitterest. To paraphrase Monaghan's greatest poet Patrick Kavanagh, Cavan have tended to weave a snare that Monaghan might rue. There is mutual reciprocity when it comes to that sentiment.

Those in the know suggest that the origins of the animosity can be traced back to Cavan's narrow win in the 1915 Ulster final. Eoin O'Duffy was the godfather of football in the Farney county, and he did not take the defeat well. He was an IRA commander during the War of Independence and became the first commissioner of An Garda Síochána. However, he is probably most remembered as the founder of the right-wing Blueshirt movement, and he fought on General Franco's side in the Spanish Civil War. At an Ulster Council meeting following that 1915 defeat, O'Duffy complained of crowd encroachments, a disallowed goal and requested, or demanded, depending on which version of events is to be believed, that the match be replayed. Decisions were taken by those in the room and, as there was nobody from Cavan present, a replay was ordered. Cavan appealed to Central Council, won the appeal and kept their title.

A defeat to Monaghan in 1917 led to Cavan appealing because their bitter rivals had been 'late fielding'. They got nowhere but star of the 1947 team, John Wilson, told the story that Cavan had grown so fed up of Monaghan that they proposed setting up a fifth province – to be known as Tara – where they would compete against Meath, Westmeath, Louth and Longford. They were denied the opportunity by, in their eyes, 'short-sighted GAA administrators'.

Patrick Kavanagh regaled Charlie Haughey once about how Cavan and Monaghan met in the 1930s. Cavan were winning so handily at half-time that the team sat down on the pitch at the break, smoking cigarettes. Their full-back took things to a whole new level, stretching out for a siesta. The Monaghan players were a tad annoyed and felt badly disrespected. Charlie Haughey suggested that they should have rubbed it in by smoking cigars and drinking champagne and eating strawberries.

'Why would they need strawberries?' asked a puzzled Kavanagh.

From his throne of authority, Charlie rolled his eyes in frustration before growling, 'Everybody knows strawberries add flavour to champagne.' (Richard Gere makes the same claim in *Pretty Woman*.) When he told me that story Charlie nodded his head vigorously; in full agreement with himself.

INCLUSIVE

Anybody who has seen Nudie Hughes transform himself into Marty McFly alongside fellow Monaghan legend Declan 'Doc Brown' Loughman for Castleblayney Faughs's fundraiser knows his appetite for a laugh.

Cancer treatment hasn't knocked the spirits of one of Gaelic football's most affable characters. Having been diagnosed with colon and liver cancer, the three-time All-Star faced a fresh challenge with a characteristic smile:

'I'm very lucky that I can still interact with people in these times. When you crack a joke, when it's not being smart or insulting, when you can break the ice with strangers, it helps because everyone has their own challenges at the moment and we all need a laugh.

'I was in the Mater (hospital) and I was the second last in the line for chemo. A woman walked by and realised we were in the queue. She apologised but I just said to her, "Not at all — there's one for everybody in the audience. It's like the lotto — if you're not in, you can't win."'

62

FATHER AND SON

The Brollys

In his role as an analyst on RTÉ, Joe Brolly deferred to nobody, especially to Colm O'Rourke or Pat Spillane. Away from the cameras, the only man who Brolly yielded to was his father, Francie, who sadly passed away in February 2020. For his part, Francie was always happy to put his son in his place. In 2008 he told me, 'I played half-forward for Derry in the 1960s. Anyone who saw both of us play would agree that I was always a much better player than Joe ever was!'

TRINITY MAN
An Irish schoolboy basketball international, Brolly did not follow the conventional path of Ulster footballers: 'I didn't go through the St Pats Maghera, Jordanstown or Queens production line. My parents were folk singers so I boarded in St Pats, Armagh, and then I went to Trinity. One of my teammates in Trinity was Tadhg Jennings. He has a unique claim to fame. He is Kevin Heffernan's godson and, in 1974, Dublin were struggling to

find a freetaker. Tadhg was only eight at the time and he said to Kevin: "I've seen a man up in Marino and he never misses a free." Heffo was intrigued and went to see for himself. The rest is history. So, many a time during my Trinity career I would hear Tadhg saying, whenever he had a pint or two: "I'm the man who discovered Jimmy Keaveney."'

THE FIRST NOEL

Brolly is less reluctant to go hard verbally on a player. A case in point was his description of Cork's tough-tacking defender, Noel O'Leary. 'He has the face of a man that is not always given to clean living.'

PAY FOR PLAY

Brolly is perhaps the most high-profile critic of the Gaelic Players Association. It can be exclusively revealed, though, that despite the amateur ethos, the Derry squad were the first to engage in pay for play when they got an unexpected reward for their achievements:

'Our manager, Eamon Coleman, brought us to Ballymaguigan one night and said: "Lads, there's someone who wants to speak to you." In comes Phil Coulter. He was wearing a lemon suit and a lime tie. He presented each of us with a signed photo of himself and a commemorative copy of "The Town I Loved So Well." The reason he gave us that was that when *The Sunday Game* came to film our celebration the night of the final, we sang that song for them. On the cover of the record Phil had his arm outstretched in a Liberace pose. It is gathering cobwebs somewhere in my house.'

UPWARDLY MOBILE

Brolly got a new insight into sociological factors when he switched clubs:

'I gave up Dungiven when I was thirty-six because it was a 130-miles round trip, and I transferred to St Brigid's in Belfast. I've got five kids so that eats into your time. It gave me a new lease of life. The club is based on the Malone Road. Bob McCartney, the controversial Unionist politician, made a great comment on the changing demographic about the Malone Road – which used to be home to the Protestant aristocracy but now belongs to the Catholic nouveau riche. He said: *Tiocfaidh ár lá* has given way to *Tiocfaidh our la-di-da*! I became heavily involved in under-age training in the club and you see all the Bentleys in the car park. We got promoted to the first division but I started playing in the fourth division. It was hairy enough there, particularly as you get punched in the back of the head as you are hearing: "I'll give you a f**king All-Star."'

AGONY UNCLE

Brolly is also lighting up the world of social media with tweets like: 'If I have to endure marriage, I see no reason why it ought not be inflicted on the gay community.'

63

WHO SHOT MICHAEL COLLINS?

Cavan Critics

After Cavan lost to Tyrone some years ago, in a match they should have won in the Ulster Championship, the Cavan fans were dejected. Cavan's Cathal Collins had not had a good game and, as he trooped wearily off the field, the Cavan fans started shouting at him: 'They shot the wrong Collins.'

THE HEAT IS ON
P.J. Carroll managed Cavan in the early 1990s. Things were going badly for the team. At one stage he roared at one of his star players, 'Warm up, Donal. You're coming off.'

MISTAKEN IDENTITY
In the early 1990s a certain club in Cavan were facing an Intermediate relegation game. They fielded a ringer, a Meath county footballer, who a few years earlier had won an All-Ireland senior medal. He played under an assumed name. He caught the ball on his own forty, went on a solo run and scored a sensational point. One of the opposition management said: 'Jaysus, that lad

is brilliant. He should be on the county team.' His opposing chairman muttered under his breath: 'He is.'

CHAMPAGNE CHARLIE

Cavan's sole representative on the centenary team of greatest players never to have won an All-Ireland medal was the late Charlie Gallagher, who played at right corner-forward. In 1964 Gallagher went to America for the Kennedy games. On the trip he became close friends with Gerry O'Malley even though they were chalk and cheese as personalities. O'Malley, was very serious, religious and quiet: Charlie was devil-may-care. Every match Gerry played he had to win. Gallagher was always winding Gerry up and saying that if they ever met in a match he would destroy him – which drove O'Malley mad. In private, Charlie admitted that he would have hated to have to play on O'Malley.

Down's Joe Lennon was on that trip too. He had written a book about Gaelic football at the time and he brought loads of them out with him and sold them wherever he went. One day, Charlie went up to O'Malley and said, 'You know what. I'm going to write my own book about football.'

'Really! And I suppose we're going to see Gallagher on the front cover in full flight with the ball?' asked O'Malley.

'You will in my barney. You'll see the world's most beautiful woman!'

THE STRIFE OF BRIAN

One of the many incidents Derry's Brian McGilligan is remembered for goes back to one of his appearances for Ireland in the Compromise Rules series against Australia. The teams were coming off the pitch and one of the Aussies was chastising the Cavan midfielder, Stephen King. Brian was coming up behind

Stephen and wasn't very impressed with what he saw. He went up and knocked the Aussie's gumshield out of his mouth and stamped on it with his foot. Nobody ever saw anybody shutting up so quickly.

DRINK, DRINK, DRINK

The Cavan county crest motto is *Feardhacht is Fírinne*, which translates into English as 'Manliness and Truth'. One of the great exemplars of this was three-times All-Ireland winner Mick Higgins. Mick captained Cavan to an All-Ireland final victory in 1952. The first match ended in a draw. It was the first time the GAA brought the two teams together for a meal after the game. When Mick and some of the Cavan boys got to the hotel they ordered drinks – just bottles of ale and minerals. Mick went to pay for it, but the barman said it was on the GAA. Mick double-checked if he had heard correctly. Quick as a flash, once this was confirmed, one of his colleagues said, 'Forget about the ales and get us brandies.' For the replay, though, there was no free drink!

GETTING HIS TEETH INTO IT

The New York born Higgins found that management was a more frustrating experience than playing. He often told the story of taking charge of Cavan for a Championship match against Armagh. As the match reached its climax, Cavan's dominance was threatened as Armagh took control over midfield. Corrective action was required urgently and Higgins decided to send on a sub, big Jim O'Donnell, whose high fielding prowess was just what Cavan needed.

Jim, though, didn't seem to realise the urgency of the situation. After going onto the pitch, he strolled back to the sideline seeking a slip of paper with his name on it for the referee.

Moments later, O'Donnell was back again seeking a pair of gloves. Higgins forcefully told him to get back to his position immediately and not to mind about the gloves. A minute or two later, he was back a third time to ask, 'Mick, would you ever mind my false teeth?' As he calmly handed the manager his molars, Higgins's blood pressure hit record levels.

PETER THE GREAT

Mick Higgins was the Ulster manager when, arguably, Fermanagh's best-known player, Peter McGinnity, played his first match for the province against the Combined Universities. There were two other Fermanagh players on the team with him, Kieran Campbell and Phil Sheridan, which was their highest representation ever, as well as having Finn Sherry play for the Combined Universities. Four Fermanagh lads playing inter-provincial football on the one day was big news.

When the three Fermanagh lads went into the Ulster dressing room, first Mick said to Peter, 'Here you are, Kieran, here's the number 3 jersey,' and then he turned to Kieran and said, 'Here's your number 10 jersey.' It pulled them down a peg or two not to be recognised by Mick Higgins.

O BROTHER WHERE ART THOU?

One of the funniest incidents in Peter McGinnity's career happened in a club game when he was marking Barney O'Reilly. Barney enjoys a rare distinction of having won senior county medals in four different decades: in the 1960s, 1970s and 1980s with Teemore, and a Meath medal in the early 1990s with Navan O'Mahonys. Barney and Peter played for Fermanagh under-21s and they came up the ranks together. In one club match, the ball went up between Peter and Barney's brother, also called Peter, and a kind of ruck developed. McGinnity snatched the ball as

Barney came charging in to give his brother some 'assistance'. Happily for McGinnity, in the melee and confusion Barney struck his own brother instead of his illustrious opponent. As McGinnity was heading up the field with the ball before Barney started chasing him after, he said 'sorry' to his brother as he lay stretched out on the ground.

HAY EMERGENCY

One of McGinnity's heroes was Derry's Jim McKeever. Seamus Heaney described his fellow Derry man and Nobel prize winner John Hume: 'There was one among us who stood taller than all the rest.' He might have been speaking about Jim McKeever.

I was hugely saddened in April 2023 when Jim left us. In 1958 the GAA world witnessed a shock of seismic proportions when Derry beat Kerry by 2–6 to 2–5 in the All-Ireland semi-final. The Foylesiders were led to the promised land by a prince of midfielders, Jim McKeever. His ability to jump and catch the ball was the hallmark of his play. He could jump so tidily that he would be almost like a gymnast in the air, toes extended and fingers outstretched as he grabbed the ball, way above the heads of anybody else and then he would hit the ground, turn and play. In basketball parlance 'he could hang'. McKeever's mastery of his position was recognised in 1984 when he was chosen at centre-field on the Centenary team of greatest players never to have won an All-Ireland, partnering the legendary Tommy 'The Boy Wonder' Murphy of Laois.

Born in Ballymaguigan in 1930, his love of football was nurtured as a boy when his father brought him to games on the bar of his bike. The bonus of talking to him was experiencing the quiet, self-effacing warmth with which he spoke about a glittering career. At the age of seventeen, McKeever made his senior debut for Derry:

'I remember listening to the famous All-Ireland final in the Polo Grounds in 1947. I didn't think then that a year later I'd be playing in a challenge game for the county against Antrim. It wasn't until the following year, though, that I made my championship debut. When I was in my teens, Derry used to play in the junior championship. We didn't have a senior team then. At that stage there was a tremendous gap between Cavan and Antrim and the other seven counties in Ulster. We played in the Lagan Cup at the time, which featured the eight counties in Ulster apart from Cavan.'

The high point of McKeever's career came against Kerry in 1958:

'I have no recollection of great excitement when we won the Ulster final,' he told me. 'However, when we beat Kerry in the All-Ireland semi-final the response was sensational. I remember the great John Joe Sheehy saying to me, "That's a rattling good team you have there."'

Dublin beat Derry by 2–12 to 1–9 in the All-Ireland final despite an imperious display from McKeever in midfield:

'I have no great recollection of great disappointment when we lost the final to Dublin. We were happy just to be there. If someone told us a few years before that we would play in an All-Ireland final, we would have been absolutely delighted.'

McKeever was chosen as Footballer of the Year, much to the chagrin of some Dublin supporters, who felt that the honour should have gone to one of their stars like Kevin Heffernan.

In the following years, McKeever led Derry to National League finals, which they lost to Kerry, in 1959 and 1961 before his retirement in 1963. It was fascinating listening to a player of his stature. However, it was not his own achievements that really ignited the passion in his voice but his vivid description of the juvenile club match in Derry he watched the evening before that really enthused him.

Derry's first All-Ireland win in 1993 was a source of great pride to McKeever:

'It was very emotional when the full-time whistle went. The fact that all the years of disappointment have been wiped out with the 1993 side gave me a certain amount of pleasure. It was a unique occasion. The first time that something great happens is special, because there can never be another first time.'

One of the stories Jim told me lives in my memory:

'In 1965 I was selected as one of the fourteen hurlers and footballers to be guest players in the Cardinal Cushing games in New York, Hartford and Boston. The games were important to our hosts and to Irish-American spectators and we played them seriously, but it was the off-field events which were memorable. The highlight of the New York part of our tour was being greeted individually in Gaelic Park by Bobby Kennedy, who was at that time electioneering in New York. His brother, the President, had been assassinated two years earlier, and it was impossible not to sense a vulnerability and an exceptionalism in the presence of this small man.

'As a postscript to the tour, I learned on my return that the Ministry of Education in Belfast had refused to allow me time off to travel and deducted fourteen days' salary, which included two Saturdays and two Sundays. When many years later I retired, they further informed me that I had lost fourteen days' pension contribution and for years I have been a little poorer each month. In "our day" we really were amateurs and I have no regrets. The genuine friendships, the integrity of not being a "bought" sportsman and the rich, irreplaceable memories are ample compensation.'

Who was the greatest player of them all?

'It's so difficult to judge. The greatest fielder and the most stylish footballer was definitely Mick O'Connell.'

Who was his most difficult opponent?

'One of the toughest guys to play against was Galway's Frank Eivers,' he explained. 'He was just massive. You couldn't get near the ball with him standing there beside you.'

After his playing days were over, he went on to become a trainer and a manager with both St Joseph's College and Derry:

'I didn't enjoy it near as much as playing. Most times it's two nights' training but you've got to be thinking about games and planning ahead for them. Of course, it's a great buzz when you win but it can be very, very demoralising when you lose and you know your team has passed its peak. I know there are a lot of people interested in administration, but it was never for me. I don't think people appreciate how much stress is on the manager, especially trying to do the job in bits of free time. Anybody who says it's easy is not talking about the job I recognise.'

Jim noted some major changes in the game since his own playing days:

'I think the players of today are better than the players of my time in terms of fitness but not in terms of the skills. It takes a team five years to develop. Nowadays a bit of a win-at-all-cost mentality has crept into the game and only experienced players can handle that.'

McKeever's happiest memories were of the club scene. His club, Ballymaguigan, were playing Coleraine in a club game in Coleraine. The pitch wasn't very well marked. The crossbar was only a rope and there weren't any nets. The ball was bobbing around and somebody pulled on it. One umpire gave it a goal, the other a point. Both umpires gave the decision against their own team. The referee split the difference and awarded two points.

The really comic part of the story was that one of Ballymaguigan's best players, the late Michael Young, did not want to play as he had hay ready for baling and the weather forecast was not good. However, he was persuaded to play. When the controversy emerged, Young went up to the referee and told him that he should hurry up and make a decision, as he had to go home to bale the hay!

FLEET OF FOOT

Jim played with Ballymaguigan in a seven-a-side match one evening. Before the match finished darkness was falling quickly. They had a famous character in the side at the time who they suddenly saw tearing up the sideline with the ball. They could not believe the speed he was going at. They found out afterwards the secret of this new-found speed. As he was running, he was not bothering to solo the ball, but it was so dark that nobody could spot him.

64

THE GREEN AND RED OF MAYO

Mayo on Tour

Some players' careers are defined by a season. Kevin O'Neill was such a player. A Connacht title victory and an All-Star in his debut year in 1993 and he was still only a teenager. He seemed set to be the next big thing in Gaelic football, but injuries intervened. So did John Maughan – who for most of his time as Mayo manager did not select Kevin!

Football was in O'Neill's genes. In 1993 he made history when he became part of the first father-and-son partnership to win All-Star awards. His father, Liam, had won with Galway. In 1999 Kevin was back in a familiar territory – languishing on the subs bench when Mayo lost to Cork in the All-Ireland semi-final, as he had in both the drawn game and replay in the 1996 All-Ireland final. The dictates of a demanding job with an international financial company took him to America for three years but he continued to commute home to play for his beloved Knockmore. When he returned to Ireland, he was unable to continue to travel up and down regularly to Mayo because of work pressure, so he transferred to play club football in Dublin with Na Fianna during John Maughan's second incarnation as Mayo manager:

'Playing club football in Dublin rejuvenated me and gave me a new perspective. We play very skillful club football in Mayo but in Dublin it is much more physical. In 2004 I was playing well with the club but I didn't think it was my place to be ringing people up and telling them that. So, when Kerry trashed Mayo in the 2004 All-Ireland final I wasn't even on the subs bench!'

ON THE BENCH

It is surprising that O'Neill never got the nickname 'the judge' because he spent so much of the John Maughan eras on the Mayo bench. The elephant in the room has to be confronted. Why did John Maughan ignore a free-scoring forward like O'Neill when the county had so few natural scorers? He pauses for thought. This is a man whose bedside reading is a thousand-page tome on the history of the Romans. Still waters run deep. It is clear that he is walking a tightrope between answering the question as honestly as possible and being diplomatic:

'I am a very positive person. I am not interested in looking to the past and being bitter. I find it hard to put my finger on why he didn't play me. I guess you'd have to ask him. It wasn't because of lack of application. Since I was young, I have always pushed myself to the very edge when it comes to training. I was routinely scoring ten or eleven points in club games and I believe I could have made a difference in both the games against Meath in 1996. Likewise, I think I could have offered something in the 2004 All-Ireland final. Of course, now and again I think back to what might have been. I honestly believe that if you were to ask most of the players in the squad at the time, they would have said that my form was good enough to warrant selection.'

Did he ever confront Maughan about his exclusion?

'There were times when I felt like it but I always believe that football is a team game. If I had a blowout with John a week before an All-Ireland final it was going to be very disruptive for the team, so I kept my head down and my mouth shut. I thought the best thing for me to do was to try and play my way onto the team, but it didn't work for me. I don't bear him grudges and if he walked into the room now, I would talk with him.'

When the second Maughan era came to an end in 2005, O'Neill was brought back into the Mayo fold by new manager Mickey Moran. He showcased his scoring pedigree on the national stage once again when he scored two goals in the 2006 All-Ireland final and set up another for Pat Harte. The match itself was a big disappointment:

'Psychologically speaking, we were all wrong for the game, as was indicated by Kerry's devastating start, which meant that we were always playing catch-up. Scoring two goals was no consolation for me because the result was all that mattered. I still believe that was an All-Ireland we could have and should have won.'

O'Neill is well placed to comment on the rivalry with Kerry:

'Kerry are the benchmark for all football teams, so when we play them we are always keen to beat them. We did it in 1996 but, sadly, too often since we have fallen short in All-Ireland finals.'

THE ROLLING STONES

O'Neill has many happy memories of his time with Mayo:

'We went on a team holiday to Florida and discovered that the Rolling Stones were in concert there. We asked one of the lads, who will remain nameless, if he would like to see them play and he asked in all seriousness: "who are they playing?"

'We had great characters on the team like Anthony Finnerty. A sight to behold was Anthony doing his unique impersonation of Michael Flatley! Padraig Brogan was something else: both for his talent and his unique capacity to forget his teammates' names in big matches.

'We played Sligo one year, in Gurteen in Sligo, to officially open the local pitch. The local parish priest came on the field to throw in the ball. It had been raining all morning and there was loads of surface water on the new pitch. Seán Maher, our midfielder, was not a man to stand back in any game whether it was a challenge game, training game or A v B game. He was a real tough character on the field. Anyway, the local PP threw in the ball, Seán went up and caught it and proceeded to smash into the priest, landing the man of the cloth into a pool of water. That was Seán. He took no prisoners!'

FAT LARRY

Anthony 'Fat Larry' Finnerty holds a unique place in the affections of Mayo football. He was fat in the winter but lost a lot of weight in the summer. Once, some of the Mayo team went to the Cheltenham festival and heard a racket from one of the tents. They went in to investigate only to see Anthony having a crawling race with somebody else, to great hilarity.

THE ONE THAT GOT AWAY

In common with a whole generation of Mayo footballers, Kevin McStay has special fondness for Anthony Finnerty:

'Three days after we lost the All-Ireland final to Cork in 1989, everyone was very down. We were in Anthony's local pub, Mitchells, at about two o'clock in the afternoon and the place was packed. Someone asked him to say a few words to cheer them up. Anthony got up on a three-legged-stool and said, "I know ye all feel sorry for me and are cringing that I have to stand up like this in public, but I've got to be positive and look on the bright side. If I had got that goal I missed ye'd have been talking about me all winter but now that I missed it ye'll never stop talking about me." Needless to say, he brought the house down.'

65

RE-JOYCE

Galway Boys Hurrah

Brian Talty has already chosen his epitaph. Given that he experienced the fate so many times as a player, as a coach and selector it is: 'We were beaten by a point.'

The disappointments in the Connacht Championship in those years were offset by victories in the Gael Linn competition:

'The prize for winning it was a trip to New York, so that's why we put more into winning it than the Connacht Championship! We had some great times on those trips. My abiding memory is of rooming once with Billy Joyce. We were staying in the Taft Hotel. It should've been called the Daft Hotel! One day Billy was lying on the bed when of our teammates came rushing into the room in a state of high excitement shouting: "I've just got the news that I've won an All-Star."

'Billy coolly looked up at him and said: "Didn't I tell you that you'd get one?"

'Our colleague beamed and said: "You did." Then modesty took over and he added: "I didn't deserve one."

'Billy's response was immediate: "Correct."'

GILMORE'S GROIN

In 1983 Talty's Galway team showed all the signs of a good team when qualifying for the All-Ireland final – they won without playing well:

'Living and working in Dublin, I was trying to keep away from the hype as much as possible, which wasn't easy. I was having a tough year. I had a stomach injury for most of the season and was spending a lot of time on the physio's table. Nowadays, there would probably be a name for the condition like "Gilmore's groin" (after the great Galway star T.J. Gilmore) but back then there wasn't much understanding. My mother said: "It's all in your head."

'Billy Joyce never believed in injuries and met me one day when I was going to see someone who had a good reputation for dealing with my condition. When I told him where I was going, he said: "For Jaysus's sake, if I told you there was an auld wan with a magic cure you'd go to her." Years later I met Billy in Tuam on crutches and asked him what had happened. He told me that he was getting out of his car and he tore his Achilles tendon. I told him it was all in his head!'

LET'S BE FRANK

Talty's trips to America with the All-Stars did create some lasting friendships:

'Frank McGuigan was a great tourist. He'd play games after having had a few pints and still go out and grab great balls out of the air. I always wondered what he'd be like if he had no pints!'

TACTICAL INNOVATION

Talty saw some unorthodox tactical manoeuvres on those trips:

'One of my clearest memories is of playing at centre-field in Gaelic Park against Kerry. They had come up with this revolutionary move at the time, everybody does it now, which involves the midfielders switching sides. Tom Spillane had just come on the scene and I remember looking at my midfield partner, Moses Coffey, and saying: "What the f**k is happening?"

'The second match was in San Francisco and, before it, Moses came to me and said: "Don't worry. I will sort things out today." The first ball that came our way I heard a screech of pain and saw Tom Spillane sprawled out on the ground. There was no more crossing over that day!'

HIGH FIELDING

Laughter regularly punctuates Talty's conversation. Perhaps that explains why he looks as if he is set to become the Peter Pan of Gaelic football. The laughter is accentuated whenever Billy Joyce is brought into the conversation:

'Once, before we played a big match in Croke Park, Billy took us by surprise by asking: "Did ye ring the airport?" I didn't know what he was talking about and asked him why would we ring the airport. He replied: "To tell them not to have airplanes flying over Croke Park. I'm going to be jumping so high I don't want to be in collision with them."'

THE HARDER THEY FALL

Billy Joyce was not a man to take prisoners:

'When we were getting beaten in midfield by a particular player, Billy would turn to me and say: "Time to take the chopper out." The next ball that came our way, you would hear a thud and a sigh of pain. We were playing Roscommon in Pearse Stadium and it was an atrocious wet day. Before the throw-in, one of their midfielders said to Billy: "Tis an awful day for football." Billy looked at him and said: "You don't have to worry about it. You won't be out in it very long."

'He was right!'

66

EYE OF THE TIGER

Jimmy Magee Shines

Jimmy Magee had a few mishaps in his broadcasting career. A caller on his radio show rang in with a question. The only problem was that he started speaking in Irish and Jimmy's Irish was not up to a conversation with a fluent Gaelic speaker on the national airwaves. He knew he had to say something so as not to appear rude or ignorant, so he said, '*Agus ainm*?'

The reply was, 'Seán . . .'

Jimmy didn't know what 'address' was in Irish, so he asked '*As Corcaigh*?'

The reply was: '*Ní hea, as Luimneach.*'

Then he asked a question, but Jimmy hadn't a clue what he was saying. He had to think on his feet, so he began saying, 'Hello! Seán? Seán? . . . We seem to have lost him there . . .' But Seán was saying, 'No, you haven't! I'm here.' But Jimmy shot him down: 'No, we've lost Seán. We'll try him again.' So, he took him off the air, because he could think of no other way of getting out of it.

THE FRENCH CONNECTION

Jimmy was also famous for his coverage of the Tour de France. At the 1987 tour he went to the cyclists' medical area when he heard they had a new laser treatment as he had a sore leg. When he emerged, he found four waiting cyclists, one of whom was Sean Kelly, who said: 'So, you're the man who is holding us up. That's gas, we're riding in the Tour de France and Magee is in the tent!'

TELL IT AS IT IS

Jimmy Magee was always happy to embellish a story but he really loved ones where no embellishment was needed. One of his favourites was that of a prominent GAA personality who was driving home one night having drunk a glass of lemonade too many and crashed into another vehicle. He was irate when a member of the gardai told him he was in trouble and said: 'Do you know how I am? I will have this sorted out within the hour.'

He promptly texted the then Taoiseach Enda Kenny and wrote: 'Enda, I'm in a bit of bother here and need your help. Ring me as soon as you can.'

The only problem was that he mixed up the numbers and texted the Roscommon footballer Enda Kenny!

ELEGANT ELOQUENCE

The GAA has pundits noted for their tongue-in-cheek (or was it wishful thinking?) tone. A good example was Tomás Mulcahy after Brian Cody's achievement in leading Kilkenny to victory in the 2012 All-Ireland final replay over Galway: 'You'd be hoping now that maybe he would take time out, maybe to be cutting the lawn, or take up a bit of golf, or train the Kilkenny footballers for a change, or something like that. This is never-ending stuff.'

67

HAVING YOUR CAKE

Shane Curran Gets Blood on His Hands

The GAA needs characters. Roscommon's former goalkeeper Shane 'Cake' Curran is certainly one of them.

Curran first exploded onto the national consciousness in the 1989 Connacht minor football final. Roscommon trailed Galway by two points when they were awarded a penalty in the last minute. Peadar Glennon, corner-forward with the Rossies, placed the ball on the spot and stepped up to take the kick. Out of the blue, Shane raced forward and blasted the ball past the Galway goalie. There was chaos. Roscommon were presented with the cup but subsequently had the game taken away in the smokey GAA corridors of power. Eventually the Rossies won the replay ordered by the Connacht Council.

A CROWD FAVOURITE
A lot of people still remember the way Curran whipped the Roscommon crowd into a frenzy with his antics in Croke Park against Kerry in the All-Ireland quarter-final in 2003, not to

mention the way he scored a goal and an incredible point from the goalkeeper's position against Sligo in the Connacht Championship in 2004.

Someone once asked him: 'So what's a forward doing playing in goal for Roscommon?'

Curran replied: 'I'm trying to keep the ball out.'

MISTAKEN IDENTITY

At the height of his career, Curran was in a well-known nightclub when he fell into conversation with a complete stranger. The combination of the loud music and the effects of a few glasses of something stronger than lemonade meant that the communication levels were not as they might have been. As they shook hands before parting, Curran received an unusual request: 'Any chance if I give you my address you'd sign one of your CDs and send it on to me?'

A puzzled Curran inquired, 'Who exactly do you think I am?'

'You're the lad from the Saw Doctors, aren't you?'

QUICK THINKING

In 2000 Shane won a Junior All-Ireland Final with Roscommon. His manager, Gay Sheeran, has a vivid memory of the win:

'You never knew what would happen next with Shane. In the replay Kerry got a score and the Kerry lads were catching a breather. The referee turned his back and started running up the field when suddenly the ball went over his head and landed seventy yards up the pitch before Kerry knew what had happened. Karol Mannion was the only one alive to the situation and set up a point. We won that All-Ireland by a point. What the referee never realised was that Shane had kicked the ball out from his hands and that's why he got the ball up the field so quickly! That's typical of Shane. He could give you acute blood pressure at times but when his moments of madness came off, he could be a match-winner.'

BLOODY HELL

In 2003 Roscommon played Galway in the Connacht Championship. Before the match, Curran was in full Russell Crowe in *Gladiator* mode and intent on whipping the Rossies into a frenzy. He urged the team to give every last drop of blood to the cause. He stunned his teammates, though, by throwing a bag of blood on the dressing-room floor to stress the point. He told them that he had got the team doctor, Martin Daly, to take a pint of his blood to highlight the lengths he was prepared to go to for the team. To this day the Roscommon players are unsure if it actually was his own blood – but, knowing him, they think he might be crazy enough to do it.

STICKY STUFF

That was not the end to his stunts. He brought two pairs of gloves with him and put on the old pair and absolutely layered it with Vaseline. Before the match he ran up to the Galway goalkeeper, Alan Keane, to shake hands with him, hoping to cover his hands in Vaseline so that he would let in a soft goal as a result. Keane did and Curran smiled with relish at this prospect on his way back to change into his new gloves but, sadly for him, the Galway netminder Keane had the sense and sensibility to cop on to his tricks before the Vaseline did any damage and changed his gloves also.

And how was Curran rewarded for his cunning and unique motivational style?

Galway hammered Roscommon.

68

A MARTY PARTY

Marty Morrissey v Brian Cody

It was TV gold.

The ultimate awkward moment.

Marty Morrissey became a YouTube sensation after his interview with Brian Cody immediately after Kilkenny completed a historic four-in-a-row in 2009.

Tipperary were ahead with less than ten minutes to go, when referee Diarmuid Kirwan awarded Kilkenny a controversial penalty. With typical aplomb, Henry Shefflin smashed it to the back of the net to turn the game in Kilkenny's favour.

In the post-match interview Marty began by politely congratulating Cody on the win before having the temerity to ask the Kilkenny manager if he thought it was really a penalty.

The spectacle of Cody bristling with indignation was funnier than any pantomine.

In 2022 Marty starred in panto as 'the Magic Mirror' in *Snow White*.

HANDS UP

One of Cody's ace defenders, Noel Hickey, was recovering from a broken finger and was struggling a bit in training, which was most uncharacteristic. At one stage a ball came in which he would normally have caught, but Martin Comerford put up the hand and caught the ball and stuck it in the net. Conscious of the disapproving eye of Brian Cody on the sideline, and knowing there was no forgiveness for mistakes, Hickey said quietly to Comerford, 'If you put your hand up like that again it will be broken.'

R.I.P.

Two stalwarts of a club in Kilkenny were distraught. One said, 'Have you heard the bad news? Old Frankin is dead. And to think he was going to play left corner-forward for the Junior B team tomorrow.'

'My God. That's awful.'

'It's tragic! But wait a minute . . . Maybe we can get Micky Joe to fill in for him.'

TALES OF THE UNEXPECTED

Irish sports stars have a chequered history with speeches. Dungannon's most famous son is Darren Clarke. Darren played rugby at school for Dungannon Royal. Had he not chosen golf, he would have been a star rugby player. Like a lot of Irish men, from time to time, Darren takes a drink. He agreed to be best man at a wedding in West Palm Beach but didn't understand that weddings are different in America. There is a long wait for the best man to make his speech. Although the ceremony took place early in the day, Darren didn't get to speak until 11.45 p.m. by which time the wedding party had been drinking since early afternoon and Clarke was feeling like the father of the bride in Brendan Grace's famous sketch.

Darren grabbed the mic with gusto, determined to make a good first impression. He had prepared extensively for his speech and, despite the drink he had consumed, he remembered all his jokes. The only problem was that he spoke at such a speed and in such a broad Irish accent that none of the Americans in the audience could understand a single word he said.

When he was Tipperary hurling manager, Babs Keating faced the problem of rallying his team even though they were trailing at half-time by eight points. After a number of inspirational words, in an effort to instil confidence, he went around the team individually and asked each of them: 'Can we do it?'

To a man, they replied, 'We can. We can.'

He could feel the surge of belief invading the dressing room. Everything was going swimmingly until he turned to Joe Hayes and asked, 'Joe, can we do it?'

Joe replied, 'It's not looking great, is it, Babs?'

BELIEVE

Although Joe Hayes never got the acclaim of some of the star names on the Tipperary side, he was a fine player. He did not lack self-confidence. He once asked Michael Lyster: 'Who do you think is the best hurler in Ireland? And why is it me?'

BABS SPEAK

After Galway dished out a thrashing to his Tipp team in a league match in March 2006, Babs stirred up a hornet's nest when he said, 'I saw the Galway fellas shouting at each other from goalkeeper to corner-forward – our fellas are dead only to wash them.'

DIETARY POLICY

When Babs let a big-name player go from the Tipperary panel, the rationale for the decision was: 'He was putting too much butter on his spuds.'

ODDS ON

There is a great book to be written on GAA rumours. After being held scoreless in the 2012 Munster final, Tipperary's grapevine went into overdrive that Lar Corbett had bet on himself not to score in the game. As with many great rumours, there was not a shred of truth in it. However, one of his teammates, John O'Neill, knocked some fun out of it when he shocked his teammates at a team meeting by saying Lar suffered from poor communication skills. With every eye on him, O'Neill coolly informed Corbett that the next time he had a great tip for the Munster final he should share it with his teammates.

ALL IN THE DRAW

In 1981 Roscommon and Mayo qualified for the semi-final of the National League. The decision as to who would have home advantage was one of the many issues to be resolved on a crowded agenda at a meeting. To speed things up, the Roscommon county secretary at the time, Phil Gannon, was told to put the names of both teams on two pieces of paper and one was pulled from the hat. Roscommon got home advantage. The rumour afterwards was that Phil had written Roscommon twice.

69

HAND ACTION

Mick O'Dwyer Gets an Edge

Long before Ger Loughnane came on the management scene, Mick O'Dwyer was a great man to pull a stroke. In the late 1970s the Kerry team used the hand pass a lot. At one point people started to complain that they weren't using it properly. Micko was concerned that it would cost the team dearly in an All-Ireland final if the players were penalised for not using it properly. So, before the match he invited Paddy Collins, who was to be the referee for the big game, to a training session. Micko had each of his players doing all kinds of hand movements with the ball and every time he would ask: 'Is this okay, Paddy?' Each time, Collins would nod. When it came to the match, the Kerry team did what they liked with the hand pass because they knew Paddy Collins could not penalise them because he was the one who showed them how to use it.

SMALL TIME
Liam Griffin tells the story of how, in 2002, he attended a social function with the then Dublin manager Tommy Lyons and

Micko, who was still Kildare manager at the time. Tommy said to O'Dwyer at one stage, 'Micko, you and I will fill Croke Park this year.' O'Dwyer replied, 'Tommy, you and I wouldn't fill a toilet!'

PILGRIMAGE

Mick O'Dwyer's wife was known to organise trips to Lourdes. One fan asked Micko: 'Did you ever go to Lourdes?' The great man furrowed his brow and paused before inquiring: 'Did Kerry ever play there?'

THE BOSS

One of the biggest changes in the world of the GAA over the last fifty years has been the prominence of the manager. It began in the 1970s with Kevin Heffernan and Mick O'Dwyer. Some people, though, wonder if there is a mercenary reason behind all this and recount the story of the rich GAA manager, the poor GAA manager and the tooth fairy. They are in a room with a £100 pound note on the table when the lights go out. When the light comes back on, the money is gone. So, who took it? It's got to be the rich GAA manager because the other two are figments of the imagination.

Typically, Pat Spillane has a view on this topic: 'In cases where they are paying managers, the exact figures should be revealed. I know there is a fat chance of that happening. Lip service rules, okay. You have a better chance of seeing me beat Kylie Minogue in the competition for "Rear of the Year" than seeing any action on that front.'

THE POOR MOUTH

In response to rumours that GAA managers were earning a small fortune, Mick O'Dwyer replied: 'Ah sure, we're all going around with our arse out of our trousers.' O'Dwyer went further to explain his life of hardship: 'When I played we got a piece of orange at half-time, and if you were very quick you might get two.'

BLESS ME FATHER

Kerry football has produced many great characters, like Jackie Lyne. Jackie was a great player himself and produced three fine sons, who all played for the local club team; Dinny, Jackie and Frank, who was just ordained to the priesthood. Jackie referred to him as 'His Reverence'. Jackie always, always wore his hat. The only time the hat came off his head was during the consecration at Mass. After a club match Jackie was holding court in the pub, reliving the crucial moment in the match. 'Dinny kicked the ball out. Jackie caught it and kicked it in to His Reverence.' He paused his dramatic narrative to lift his hat at the mention of 'His Reverence'. The religious aura, though, was quickly dissipated as he came to the climax: '. . . and he kicked it into the f**king goal.'

THE GREAT DIVIDE

This little story is a small indicator of just how seriously they take football in Kerry. Maybe that is why it is said that there are two kinds of people: those who are from Kerry and those who want to be from Kerry.

SHADOW OF A GUNMAN

History casts a long shadow in the area in Kerry. Memories of the civil war lasted a very long time. This was most tellingly revealed in a conversation between a de Valera and a Michael Collins fan in the 1960s.

The Dev fan said: 'De Valera was as straight as Christ and as spiritually strong'.

The Collins fan replied: 'Wasn't it a great pity the hoor wasn't crucified as young.'

70

OFFALY SERIOUS

Offaly Win All-Ireland by the Back Door

Offaly's Pat Carroll was known for his dedication to hurling, as revealed in the following conversation:

    Pat: 'My hurley was stolen this morning.'

    Friend: 'That's terrible – where did you lose it?'

    Pat: 'In the car park.'

    Friend: 'Did the thieves damage your car much?'

    Pat: 'I don't know – they stole that too!'

WHISKEY IN THE JAR

Another Offaly hurler's dedication was not quite as intense. On the night of the presentation of the All-Ireland medals, he had a few glasses of orange juice too many and, as he drove home, he was unable to take a corner and drove his car through a farmer's wall, absolutely wrecking his car in the process. A passer-by was soon on hand and recognised the famous driver, even though the blood was pumping out of his forehead like the Niagara Falls. The Offaly hurler instructed the passer-by to shine his torch into the car. 'Are you looking for your All-Ireland medal?' inquired the Good Samaritan.

'Ah, no, sure I'll find that sometime but I've got a five naggin bottle of whiskey in here somewhere and I want to be certain it did not break in the crash.'

BACK DOOR

After Offaly lost the Leinster final in 1998 to Kilkenny, their manager, Babs Keating, met with the county board and decided to stay. However, the next morning he resigned because he was 'shocked' by an interview in a newspaper with Offaly's star midfielder, Johnny Pilkington, who had questioned his record with the county, stated that Babs had abandoned Offaly's tradition of ground hurling and queried the tactics against Kilkenny. Michael Bond replaced Babs and they went on to win the All-Ireland that year.

Broadcaster Peter Woods offers an interesting perspective on Offaly's revived fortunes under Michael Bond: 'You could lead them with a thread but you can't drive them with an iron bar.'

Hubert Rigney, the Offaly captain, in his victory speech after Offaly beat Kilkenny in the All-Ireland final, said: 'We might have come in the back door, but we're going out the front door.' Offaly came through the back door, having voted against it, and Offaly, true to form, voted against the back door the following year.

BUM-BASTIC

Memories from 1998 continue to linger in both counties. The film *Four Weddings and a Funeral* made Hugh Grant a star. It also spawned one of the biggest selling songs of all time from Wet Wet Wet with its intimately constructed lyrics 'Love is

All Around'. On Valentine's Day in 2014 love was all around again – well, almost. It was the day Ger Loughhane chose to write in his column in *The Star* that Offaly were the 'only team in the modern era with fat legs, bellies and ars*s'.

Twitter went into meltdown. Daithí Regan had a response that raised an intriguing biological question: 'Someone give Ger a replica Liam McCarthy Cup, stamp it 1998 "winners" and then he might crawl back up his ass.'

71

THE PLAYBOY OF THE SOUTHERN WORLD

Mick Mackey Reigns Supreme

Limerick's Mick Mackey was both an extraordinary hurler and a great character. He had an immense physical and social presence. Few people could match him for charisma.

Nicknames are not part of the culture in the GAA, unlike rugby. There is no question that this is a good thing. There have been a few exceptions, like former Antrim manager Liam Bradley, who is known as 'Baker' because back in the 1970s he always wore a white sports jacket.

One inter-county hurler was nicknamed 'Butter' – on the basis of the fact that butter is found in bread – and that his father married his first cousin.

What makes Mick Mackey unique amongst the giants of Gaelic games is that he had three nicknames. He was often described as 'The Laughing Cavalier', occasionally as 'The King of the Solo Run' but most often as 'The Playboy of the Southern World'. He always seemed to have a smile on his face – both on and off the field. He was one of those exceptional talents who made the crowd come alive because of his swashbuckling style. The higher the stakes, the better he performed, which is a sure sign of greatness.

FULL

On All-Ireland hurling final Sunday, 2018, as Limerick hurling fans braced themselves for what they hoped would be their first All-Ireland since 1973, two Shannonsiders were preparing to board the Luas in Ranelagh. As the Luas was already jammed to the roof, a Galway fan shouted at them: 'Hop on to the Calcutta Express.'

CLOSER TO HOME

In 1982 Kerry planned a holiday to Bali to celebrate what was expected to be their five-in-a-row. After sensationally losing the final to Offaly, the Kerry players were saying that the only Bali they would be going to was Ballybunion! Another said, 'It won't even be the Canaries this year. All we'll get is the Seagulls.'

72

A QUIET NIGHT IN

Sylvie Linnane Prepares for the All-Ireland

Mícheál Ó Muircheartaigh once said, 'Sylvie Linnane: the man who drives a JCB on a Monday and turns into one on a Sunday.'

Such was Linnane's toughness that one Galway fan claimed: 'Outer space exists because it's afraid to be on the same planet as Sylvie.'

Few hurlers generated the same drama on the pitch as Linnane. However, it is a little-known fact that Sylvie once created a drama off the pitch:

'We were in Dublin the night before an All-Ireland final and, as always, we were sent to bed early. The problem is that it is very hard to sleep the night before an All-Ireland. I was rooming with Steve Mahon and we heard a massive row going on in the street underneath. So I went to investigate and saw this fella beating up his wife or his girlfriend. I ran into the bathroom, got the waste-paper basket, filled it with water and ran over to the window and threw the water over the man. It did the trick: he stopped and the woman ran away.'

'A happy ending, or so I thought, until the man recovered from the shock and got really, really angry and started to climb up the drainpipe to pay back the person who threw the water on him. I didn't think the night before the All-Ireland was the best time to get involved in a brawl – especially as this guy looked like a pure psycho – and I decided discretion was the better part of valour. I turned off the light so he wouldn't know where to find me. I went quietly back to bed and listened attentively to see what would happen. What I hadn't known at the time was that the light immediately below my room was on! The room belonged to the former Galway great Inky Flaherty. Inky was not a man to mess with and a few minutes later I heard him forcefully eject the intruder out the window – which was not the typical way to prepare for an All-Ireland.'

NICE ONE CYRIL

In conversation with this scribe, Cyril Farrell revealed an enterprising side to Linnane's character: 'Sylvie loved a nice hurley. He always travelled to training with Seán Silke. Silke and Iggy Clarke used to get the hurls for us. Silke would usually have hurls in his boot. When Sylvie needed a hurl he would get out of the car, as Seán left him home after training, to get his gear and sneak off with the hurl he liked most. The next day Seán would ask him if he took the hurl. Sylvie would always deny it point-blank. Then a few weeks later he would casually stroll into training with the missing hurl!'

GOING BRAVELY WHERE NO ONE HAS GONE BEFORE

Noel Lane was another of the stars on the Galway team. One of the funniest memories from Lane's time with Galway is of a trip abroad:

'We went to America on the All-Star trip and brought a big contingent of Galway supporters with us. We visited Disneyland and a gang of us went on the Space Mountain train ride. I was sharing a carriage with Steve Mahon and some of the lads like Finbarr Gantley were behind us. Two of the most "mature" members of the group, John Connolly's dad, Pat, and Mick Sylver, were behind them. After we came down, we were all petrified and just glad to have got out of there alive. We went to a little bar nearby to catch our breath back. Just as we started to relax, who did we see in the queue to go back up Space Mountain but Pat and Mick!'

73

ARE WE THERE YET?

Ger Loughnane Hits the Road

Ger Loughnane is known for his capacity to talk. One evening, in the difficult year of 1998, he and Tony Considine were driving home late from a training session in Saint Flannans. As the road was very frosty, Considine was very careful with his driving. After he drove about ten miles, a garda pulled Considine over and said: 'Sir, do you realise your passenger fell out of the car five miles back?'

To which Considine replied: 'Thank God, I thought I had gone deaf.'

THE GOLDEN DAYS ARE OVER

When Loughnane became Galway coach in 2006, the Kilkenny fans told the story of the Clare hurling fan who was walking through the streets of Ennis when he saw a sale on at a video shop. When he stopped to look, he saw a video called *Clare Hurling: The Golden Years*. The guy entered the shop and asked how much the video cost. The shop owner replied, 'Three hundred euros.'

'What! I'm not paying three hundred euro just for a video,' the Clare fan replied.

'No don't be silly, the video is five euro; the Beta-Max video player is 295 euro.'

WHEN A MAN LOVES A WOMAN

Ger Loughnane offers a snapshot of the rivalry between Clare and their nearest neighbours:

'After we beat Tipperary in the replay in 1999, Tony Considine and I decided we'd walk into Cork City from Páirc Uí Chaoimh. It was about three quarters of an hour after the game. The crowd had dispersed. We were walking along and we saw this van up ahead of us with a Tipperary registration. When we were about twenty yards away from them, they spotted us and one of them jumped out of the van. I said to Tony, "Here's trouble."

'The man said, "Howya, Ger? Any chance of the autograph?"

'I was relieved that he wasn't going to attack me! I told him no problem and he handed me the programme to sign. He told me it was for his wife. I wrote, "To Marion. Best wishes. Ger Loughnane."

'He never looked up at me but turned to his friend and said, "Jesus, Johnny, she'll get some surprise when she goes home this evening. Christ, wait till she sees this."

'Then he turned to me and said, "You have no idea how much she hates you!"

'There was no other word. He got back into his van as happy as could be and off he went.'

74

DUNNE AND DUSTED

Mick Dunne Spends Big

A great champion of hurling was the late Mick Dunne, father of former newsreader Eileen. In 1949 Mick joined *The Irish Press* as junior librarian before quickly graduating to and becoming a Gaelic games correspondent and later Gaelic games editor of the Sports department.

He once sat in a hotel having his breakfast the morning after a Munster final and, two tables away, he could hear two men dissecting his report on the match. Their remarks were not very complimentary.

Later that morning he stopped for petrol at a small shop outside Thurles. As Tipperary had lost heavily the previous day the shopkeeper was still in foul humour. He asked Mick if he had been at the match. When Mick replied in the affirmative the shopkeeper went into a lengthy analysis of why Tipperary lost and then proceeded to ask Mick if he had seen 'what that f**king bast**d Mick Dunne had written in *The Irish Press*'.

When Mick politely replied that he was aware of the contents of the article, the shopkeeper launched into a vicious tirade about Mick's knowledge of hurling and cast a number of doubts on his parentage in the process.

Mick made no response until the very end, when the shop-keeper said, 'I bet that fella's getting a fortune for writing that rubbish. Tell you what, although I hate him, I wish I had his money.'

Mick calmly paid him for the petrol and said, 'Well, you've just got £5 of it.'

THE NUMBERS GAME

Mick was one of the journalists involved in selecting the team that would travel to New York to play in the Cardinal Cushing Games. It was almost the precursor of the All-Stars.

They tried in particular to pick some good players from the 'weaker counties'. The importance of picking players from the weaker countries led them to speak about the terms of reference in selection decisions.

One of their number blurted out immediately, 'Let's pick the team first and we'll sort out the terms of reference later!'

CALLED TO THE BAR

In 1971 Mick Bermingham was selected as right corner-forward in the inaugural All-Stars. Mick's career with Dublin spanned four decades. He first played senior inter-county hurling with Dublin as a sixteen-year-old in 1959 and his last game for Dublin in 1982 was at Intermediate level.

One of the impediments to Bermingham's hurling career was his work in the bar business, which caused him to constantly work anti-social hours. There was one memorable moment, though, when his job came back to haunt him on the hurling field. He played in the 1963 Leinster final against Kilkenny. It was a lovely sunny day and he was the free taker. Micheál O'Hehir had been praising him in his commentary. Then he got a free into the Canal End goal and Micheál said, 'The diminutive Mick Bermingham is about to take a free for Dublin and this will surely be a point.' When he was lifting the ball it tilted away from him and he put it wide. Mick ran back into the corner after the free where he was marking the young Fan Larkin. Then he heard a Dublin voice ringing out clearly among the 40,000 crowd saying, 'Ah sure, Bermingham, you can't score a point and what's worse you can't f**kin even pull a pint!'

75

THE MANAGERIAL MERRY-GO-ROUND

Joe Kernan Gives Advice

Galway footballers have changed managers with alarming regularity in the past.

After Joe Kernan retired as Galway manager, he subsequently met his successor, Alan Mulholland. He wished Mulholland the best of luck and ushered him aside: 'Just a little advice, as tradition goes, from one outgoing Galway manager to the next. Take these.'

He handed him three envelopes.

'If you fail to lead Galway to victory,' he said, 'open an envelope, and inside you will find some invaluable advice as to how to proceed.'

Mulholland got off to a flyer and Galway had a crushing victory away to Roscommon in the Connacht Championship in 2013. Then when Galway lost to Sligo things started to go badly wrong. Mulholland remembered Kernan's envelopes and, after that bad defeat, he opened the first envelope. 'Blame the referee,' it said.

He walked confidently into the informal press conference and said, 'Well, there wasn't much between the teams really. In a match like that, small mistakes can change the complexion of the game completely and, in that respect, I felt that the ref made some decisions that went against us which had a big bearing on the final outcome.'

The journalists nodded wisely. Kernan's advice was working well.

Another embarrassing defeat to Antrim quickly followed in the qualifiers. Bad news, Mulholland would have to use the second of the three envelopes.

'Blame the free taker,' it said.

Off Mulholland went to face the media. 'Well. I thought it was nip and tuck, we had them under pressure, but we tried a few different lads taking our frees, and unfortunately we didn't have the best of days with the old shooting boots and so the chances slipped away.'

Again, the journalists seemed satisfied with his response. Thank God for these get-out-of-jail-free envelopes, Mulholland reflected, though he still had failed to take Galway forward, which he knew was storing up trouble for himself.

In 2013 after Galway crashed out of the championship to Mayo, Mulholland was heartbroken and gutted by the scale of the humiliation. There was only one consolation: help was at hand. He walked into the dressing room, looking forward to some first-class advice from the third and last white envelope. He rummaged in his bag, pulled it out and tore it open. The advice was simple: 'Start writing out three new envelopes.'

DOCTOR KNOWS BEST

Pat Spillane was one of the many players who made trips to America to play in the New York Championship. It was an ideal opportunity to make a few dollars and have a holiday. Big name stars over from Ireland were always subject to 'robust' play on the field. On one occasion this necessitated Spillane visiting the medical room with blood pouring from his nose. An Italian doctor was on duty and was more interested in reading *The New York Times* than attending to Spillane. Without looking up from his paper he asked the footballer what was wrong. The Kerry star said, 'I think I've broken my nose.' With no concern in his voice, the doctor told him to go over to the mirror and clean off the blood. When this task was completed, the doctor inquired, 'Does it look different than it did this morning?'

Spillane replied, 'Yes, it's crooked.'

The doctor calmly replied, 'You probably broke your nose then.'

Thus ended the medical consultation.

WE'RE ALL GOING ON A SUMMER HOLIDAY

Exotic tours abroad were a feature of Spillane's life with the great Kerry teams of the 1970s and 1980s. In 1986 Mick O'Dwyer brought them on a holiday to the Canaries. It was mainly for rest and recreation but there was a small element of training. Every evening at 5 p.m. the players met for a run along the sand dunes of Playa del Inglés. Part of the beach was reserved for a nudist section. Spillane remarked that when the Kerry players reached that section of the beach, the pace dropped alarmingly!

Four years earlier, O'Dwyer brought the Kerry team for a run on a beach in San Francisco the day after they had given a horrendous performance against the All-Stars. The display was the legacy of a day-long drinking session by some of the squad at Fisherman's Wharf on the eve of the match. The most revealing evidence of the commitment of the Kerry players to the cause was that the first man home on the beach run was the former president of the GAA, Seán Kelly, then Chairman of the Kerry County Board.

76

SPAT SPILLANE

Pat Spillane's Grumpy Phase

Those of us who know him understand that this is not the case for Pat Spillane, but many fans think of him as a grumpy old man because of his performances on *The Sunday Game*.

Given his penchant for controversy, an RTÉ announcer made an interesting slip of the tongue when she introduced Pat as 'Spat Spillane' in 2009. True to form, Spillane took it in his stride and said: 'I've been called worse.'

Much, much worse.

AN EDDIE HOBBS MOMENT

Pat's passion for the game is still as strong today as in his playing days. I saw this at first hand watching him filling in a credit card application form. When it came to the question that asked: 'What is your position in the company?' he answered: 'Left half-forward.'

SUNNY SIDE UP

Spillane was invited by RTÉ to compete in their inaugural *The Superstars* to be recorded early in 1979. He joined Limerick hurler Pat Hartigan, soccer legend Dave O'Leary, swimmer David Cummins, Formula One driver Derek Daly, athlete Noel Carroll, Dublin footballer Jimmy Keaveney, boxer Mick Dowling and Cork's Jimmy Barry-Murphy. To give a light touch to the proceedings, the sports personalities were divided into teams each made up of two 'super athletes': one female athlete, one personality and one politician. Personalities who agreed to take part included Fr Michael Cleary, Frank Kelly and Dickie Rock. After Spillane won the competition, he took part in the *World Superstars* competition in the Bahamas. He did not know much about protecting himself from the sun and, as a result of his pink visage and body, a new phrase entered popular currency: 'Pat Spillane tan'!

ARE YOU BEING SERVED?

In 1981, after completing the historic four-in-a row of All-Ireland titles, the Kerry team went on the holiday of a lifetime to America, Hawaii and Australia. They were booked into a hotel in Adelaide in Australia after a long overnight flight. Shortly after, an irate member of the Kerry delegation rang down to complain about the lack of air conditioning in his room. He threatened to pull the entire Kerry party out of the hotel if the problem was not fixed immediately. A member of staff arrived up to the room and took a quick glance before looking the man with the complaint in the eye and coolly saying, 'Why not try and plug it in, buddy?'

TIPSTER

On that tour, Pat Spillane was reputed to have taken a taxi with a few of the other players after a drinking session one evening back to the team hotel. The taxi driver was 'hygienically chal-lenged', with a less than enticing aroma emanating from his body. In addition, he recounted a tale of woe about his lack of success with the opposite sex. After the Kerry lads paid their fare the taxi driver said, 'How about a tip?'

Before anyone could even think of reaching to their pockets for a second time, Spillane is said to have interjected, 'Certainly. Start using a deodorant and you might have some chance with the women.'

WHEN PAT NEARLY MET CHARLIE

Collegiality was a feature of that Kerry team as Spillane acknowledges:

'I was great friends with Páidí O Sé. I marvelled at the way he could make friends with people like Charlie Haughey. They had a lot in common. Neither was short on self-confidence. Charlie presented himself as a great statesman on the world stage. Mind you, Páidí himself did not believe that you should hide your light under a bushel. A visitor to his pub observed that only a North Korean dictator had as many photos of themselves as Páidí did. The local taxi man, when he took tourists from America to Páidí's, always told them that the church beside the pub was built as a shrine to O Sé. When they saw all the photos in the pub, they believed him.

'Páidí captained Kerry to the All-Ireland in 1984. The following morning, Páidí brought my brother, Tom, and a few of the other lads out to meet Charlie in Kinsealy. Sadly, though, I missed out on my own meeting with Charlie Haughey. I came very close. I was in the Skellig Hotel the morning after the Dingle Regatta and Charlie and his entourage were coiffing champagne. They were loud and boisterous, and I heard one of them say: "There's Pat Spillane over there."

'Charlie swanned over to the table beside me and tapped the man on the shoulder and said: "Pat Spillane, I presume."

'The astonished guy replied: "I wish."

'Charlie turned on his heels and walked back to his party as if nothing happened. So much for his great knowledge of Kerry football.'

77

THE THREE MACS

Cork Win 1966 All-Ireland

One of Jimmy Magee's favourite stories relates to the three Macs: Gerald, Justin and Charlie McCarthy. The night before an All-Ireland final, they were supposed to be tucked up in their beds for a night. The three young men decided to take a trip into the city centre to sample the atmosphere. The problem was that it was much harder for them to get a taxi back to the team hotel. Two of the team mentors, Jim 'Tough' Barry and Donie Keane, were patrolling the corridor. The three lads knew they would be read the riot act, so they hid until the coast was clear and they raced up the stairs and into their beds. Within moments there was a rap on the door. The three amigos pretended they were fast asleep. Then came a louder rap they could not possibly ignore and the question: 'What were ye lads up to?'

'We're in bed.'

'Open the door.'

Charlie McCarthy nonchalantly walked to the door, pretending to rub the sleep from his eyes as he let the two mentors in: 'What's the problem, Jim? We were fast asleep.'

Jim looked at him with steely eyes. 'Is that so? Jaysus, Charlie, you're the only man I know to wear a collar and tie in bed.'

BEAUTY SLEEP

In 1966 Kilkenny lost the All-Ireland to Cork, although they were red-hot favourites. Cork won by 3–9 to 1–10. The papers the next day were full of talk about 'the year of the sleeping pill'. It was the first year that players had taken them before an All-Ireland final. There were a lot of smart comments afterwards that the Kilkenny players took them too late because they hadn't fully woken up until after the match!

After they lost the All-Ireland, the Kilkenny team came home from Dublin on the train. At the station the great Kilkenny goalkeeper, Ollie Walsh, got on board the luggage car and started driving it around the platform. Most of his teammates were amazed he was not arrested.

DUNNE IN

In 1979, after Kilkenny beat Galway in the All-Ireland hurling final, Fan Larkin rushed off the field into the dressing room to tog in. A clearly startled Mick Dunne went into the Kilkenny room just minutes after the match to prepare later for a live interview only to see Fan already fully clothed. Clearly Fan had missed the presentation. Dunne asked him why he was in the dressing room so quickly?

'I have to go to Mass, Mick,' replied Fan in a matter-of-fact voice.

78

LORD OF THE RINGS

Christy Ring Switches Codes

Despite his interest in other sports, Gaelic games were Jimmy Magee's first love. It was while listening to the wireless commentary of the famous 1947 All-Ireland final between Kerry and Cavan in New York, the only one ever to be played outside Ireland, that the twelve-year-old boy first dreamed of becoming a commentator. One of his great heroes was Christy Ring, a friendship cemented during their involvement in the Jimmy Magee All-Stars, which raised over six million euro for various charities down through the years.

Ring was not above putting Jimmy in his place. During one match for the All-Stars, when Magee was not showing much mobility, Ring barked at him from the sideline, 'Did you find it yet, Jimmy?'

'What's that, Christy?'

'The thing you're looking for. You're running around the same spot, Jimmy. You haven't moved out of it.'

RINGMASTER

On one occasion, the motley crew of Magee All-Stars played a match in New York. Before playing, the team were watching a softball game. They were asked to try out this strange game and it was decided that Ring should be the team's representative. The Cork legend, though, feigned ignorance to his hosts. 'Give me that there what-do-you-call-it. Is that a bat or a stick, or what do you call it?'

After he was told it was a bat, he inquired with a puzzled tone, 'Now, do you hold it like this or like that?'

After he'd been shown how to hold the bat, he asked them to provide their best pitcher. When an athletic young man appeared, he gave a mighty effort but Ring struck it into the stratosphere and out of the stadium.

All the softball players looked at him in shock and awe. Ring nonchalantly said, 'That's a home run now, isn't it?'

79

ON THE DOUBLE

Cork's Year of Glory

Kerry were hammered by old rivals Cork 2–23 to 1–11 in the 1990 Munster football final. To misquote George Michael, time can never mend the careless whispers of rival fans. The rivalry was accentuated on the border despite Niall Tóbín's observation: 'Those from West Cork are just Kerry people with shoes.'

It was a stunning reversal of Cork's fortunes. The Kerry fans were in a state of shock. They started streaming out of Páirc Uí Chaoimh in their droves long before the game was over. One Leeside wit, the late John 'Bozo' Corcoran, a huge Cork fan in every sense of the term, was prompted to shout out: 'Shut the bloody gates and make them f**king watch.'

POETRY

Before the All-Ireland final a Cork fan said:

'Roses are red, the Cork jersey is too.

Cork's just beaten Galway and they'll beat Meath too.'

WALKING IN MEMPHIS

The Cork hurling team that won the first leg of Cork's double in 1990 were a fascinating mix of personalities. There was the quiet Tony O'Sullivan, 'the Baby Jesus', who did his talking on the pitch.

Then there was the more flamboyant John Fitzgibbon. He was awarded RTÉ's prestigious Goal of the Year award that season. When the late Mick Dunne presented him with his award, the RTÉ personality asked, 'Well John, what was the highlight of the year?'

There was a pregnant pause, which grew into an uncomfortable silence on national television. Finally, Fitzgibbon replied as only he could: 'Seeing Elvis's home in Memphis.'

AN AUDIENCE WITH CHARLIE

John's sharp wit was also in evidence when he was presented with an All-Star by the then Taoiseach Charlie Haughey. A puzzled Charlie asked him as he presented the award, 'And who are you?'

The forward responded, 'I'm John Fitzgibbon from Cork. And who are you?'

80

THE KEANE EDGE

Kerry Win the Munster Final

The entire Irish nation went into mourning in 2010 with news of the death of Moss Keane. Few sports personalities were more loved.

Moss had originally made an impact as a Gaelic footballer. However, he was not known for being 'fleet of foot'. According to folklore, after a less than resoundingly successful career as a Gaelic footballer, his conversion to rugby came when he overheard a friend saying in a pub that, 'A farmer could make a tidy living on the space of ground it takes Moss to turn.'

Stories about Moss are more common than showers in April – though few are printable in our politically correct times. Some are even true! Moss had a nice line in self-depreciating humour:

'After I left university, I found I had no talent for anything, so I joined the civil service! I won fifty-two caps – a lot of them just because they couldn't find anybody else.'

Moss is one of the all-time greatest characters in Irish rugby and is often associated with his teammate, the late Willie

Duggan, for the way they played on the pitch and the way they celebrated off it. In victory or defeat, Moss and Willie knew how to party after a game.

CHIPPY

On Moss's first cap in Paris, Willie John McBride, sensing that his huge frame needed extra nourishment, took him out for a bag of chips the night before the game. They were coming back to the team hotel via a rough area and one of the locals decided to do the unthinkable and steal the chips from Moss. The Keane edge surfaced immediately and Moss floored him with a right hook. His friends, though, all ganged up on the two Irish players and a brawl broke out. Before long, there was a trail of bodies on the ground – all of them French. Within minutes, four gendarmes arrived. Moss explained the situation: 'They started it. They stole my chips.' One of the officers responded, 'Messieurs, we didn't come to arrest you. We came to save the mob.'

Hence the joke: 'The Dead Sea was still alive until Moss swam in it.'

UP THE ASS

Moss made his debut in the Irish scrum in the cauldron of Parc des Princes in 1974. He was stamped on and was feeling very miserable. Consolation came in the form of his colleague, Stewart McKinney: 'Cheer up, Moss, it could have been a lot worse. You would have suffered brain damage if you'd been kicked in the arse.'

HEY MR POSTMAN

Moss also spoke about driving from Dublin for a match in Tralee with Dick Spring. The two boys always shortened the journey by doing the crossword from *The Irish Times*. Moss proudly held the record for getting the crossword done before they got to Kildare. On this day, though, Spring was on fire and answering every question. Spring was driving that day and Moss noticed that he was not pushing his foot on the pedal as hard as they approached Kildare, with a new record in sight. Moss called out a clue: 'Postman loses mail.'

Spring scratched his head and observed: 'That should be easy to do.' He repeated the clue a number of times. Finally, he asked: 'How many letters?'

Moss gleefully replied, 'Every f**king one of them!'

THE SWEETEST FEELING

Folklore about Moss grows with every day and distinguishing fact from fiction is not easy. Moss was playing for the Wolf-hounds, and in the side was Charlie Kent, the big blond English centre. Charlie is a diabetic and, at half-time, this rather puffed-up ambulance man arrived in the players' huddle and tapped Moss on the shoulder. The man asked Moss if he was the man who wanted a sugar lump. Moss said, 'Arra Jaysus, who do you think I am, Shergar?'

DO THE MATHS

Internationally, Moss too was a much-loved figure, as Welsh legend Ray Gravell told me:

'Willie Duggan was an awesome player and a great man to knock back a pint! I would probably say the same thing about Moss Keane. These guys were legends on the pitch and legends in the bar! Sometimes too much drink is not enough! It only took one drink to get them drunk. The problem was they could never remember was it the twenty-fourth or the twenty-fifth!'

HIGH FLYERS

Like Willie Duggan, Moss had a fear of flying and generally the only way they got on a plane was with the benefit of a lot of Dutch courage. As he drove to the airport for the Lions tour in 1977, Moss was so nervous about the flight that he crashed his car. The story is told that he rang his mother just before he took off and said, 'The car is in the airport. It is wrecked. See you in four months.'

Moss was once asked, 'Are you afraid of flying, Mossie?'

He replied, 'Afraid of flying? No. Afraid of crashing? Yes.'

Moss habitually had to sit on the back seat whenever he took the plane. Asked by Ciaran Fitzgerald why he always took the back seat, he replied, 'I've never seen a plane back into a mountain yet.'

LEAP OF FAITH

The definitive verdict on Moss came from Mick Doyle: 'For the first half, Moss would push in the lineouts, and in the second, he'd jump in the scrums. That would always confuse the English.'

RUDOLF IS MISSING?

Keane and Willie Duggan were flying to New Zealand on the Lions tour in 1977. It was a thirty-hour journey and Moss woke up Willie and said, 'Willie, we're over the North Pole.'

Duggan replied, 'Well, if we are, I can't see any f**king reindeer,' and promptly went back to sleep.

FEELING SHEEPISH

Moss had pulled a hamstring on the plane over and was unable to train for days and days. Eventually, the frustrated tour manager went to the Lions captain, Phil Bennett, and said: 'If

Moss Keane doesn't train tomorrow, I'm sending him home.'
Benny spoke to Moss, and the Irish legend agreed to train the
following day. Not surprisingly it was lashing rain and freezing
for the training session and Moss showed up in his shorts, a
T-shirt and sneakers. Just before he left the hotel, he told the
waiter: 'Can you please have some hot coffee and a rasher sand-
wich ready for me when I come back?' When Moss returned,
the waiter handed him a mug of steaming coffee but apologised:
'You won't believe it – we are out of bacon.' Moss looked aghast
and stared at him in disbelief: 'Three million sheep in New
Zealand – how can you be out of bacon?'

REGULAR HABITS

On that Lions tour in 1977, Moss roomed with Peter Wheeler
on the first night. Wheeler was woken up prematurely by Moss
turning on his bedside lamp, lighting a cigarette and opening a
can of beer. Wheeler exclaimed indignantly: 'It's five o'clock in
the morning and we're on a Lions tour to New Zealand.'

Moss answered: 'It's five o'clock in the evening back home in
Ireland and I always have a pint at this time.'

THE ROAD NOT TAKEN

I once asked Moss if he ever considered getting involved in
politics. He shook his head dismissively: 'Not a chance. Politics
is just show business for ugly people.'

MATCH OF THE DAY

When Moss went on his first tour to New Zealand with the
Lions, he was the only player in the first seven weeks whom the
BBC had not interviewed because they didn't think his strong
Kerry brogue would work well with a British audience. Eventu-
ally, the Lions players said they would refuse to do any more

interviews for the BBC until Nigel Starmer-Smith interviewed Moss. Nigel reluctantly agreed to this demand and asked on live television in a plummy BBC accent, 'Well, Moss, you've been here now for two months and you've played in your first Lions test, met the Māoris, what's been the best moment of the trip for you?'

In his thickest Kerry accent Moss replied, 'When I heard that Kerry beat Cork in the Munster final.'

81

MAROONED

Páidí Ó Sé Manages Westmeath

When Páidí Ó Sé became manager of Westmeath in 2004, apart from his strong language, some of the players found his stories a little baffling. One was about the seaman who met a pirate and noticed that he had a peg leg, a hook, and an eye patch.

'So how did you end up with a peg leg?' the seaman asked.

'I was swept overboard and a shark bit my leg off,' the pirate replied.

'What about your hook?' asked the seaman.

'Well, we were boarding an enemy ship and one of the enemy cut my hand off,' the pirate said.

'So how did you get the eye patch?' the seaman finally asked.

'I got something in my eye,' replied the pirate.

When the sailor looked confused, the pirate continued: 'It was my first day with the hook.'

To this day, the Westmeath players are still trying to figure out what point he was trying to make with the story.

THOSE MAGNIFICENT MEN IN THEIR FLYING MACHINES

Páidí was supposed to be getting a helicopter to fly him from Kerry to Westmeath for training sessions. During his days on the Kerry team, Páidí had an amazing fear of flying. Paudie Lynch shared that fear and, when they were travelling on trips abroad, the way the two of them coped was to get totally inebriated beforehand.

One day, when they got to Dublin airport, someone said, 'Look here, Páidí, if it's your day to go, it's your day to go.'

Páidí turned around to him and said, 'But if it's the f**king pilot's day to go, he's going to bring me down with him!'

GET SMART

Páidí was known for his keen intelligence. This trait was evident from an early age if a story heard in Kerry is to be believed. When he was a young man he entered the confessional box and said, 'Bless me, Father, for I have sinned. I have been with a loose woman.'

The priest asked, 'Is that you, Páidí?'

'Yes, Father, it is.'

'And who was the woman you were with?'

'Sure and I can't be telling you, Father. I don't want to ruin her reputation.'

'Well, Páidí, I'm sure to find out sooner or later, so you may as well tell me now. Was it Mary?'

'I cannot say.'

'Was it Monica?'

'I'll never tell.'

'Was it Lizzie?'

'I'm sorry, but I'll not name her.'

'Was it Patsy?'

'My lips are sealed.'

'Was it Fiona, then?'

'Please, Father, I cannot tell you.'

The priest sighed in frustration.

'You're a steadfast lad, Páidí, and I admire that. But you've sinned, and you must atone. Be off with you now.'

Páidí walked back to his pew. Pat Spillane slid over and whispered, 'What you get?'

'Five good leads,' said Páidí.

82

WE NEED TO TALK ABOUT KEVIN

Kevin McStay Wins an All-Ireland

Mayo manager Kevin McStay will always hold a unique place in the history of Roscommon football as the first man to manage a club from Roscommon (Saint Brigid's) to an All-Ireland title. He then went to guide Roscommon to a Connacht title and a National League title. After his time with the Rossies was over in 2019, McStay returned to *The Sunday Game* as a panelist and began a new career as a columnist with *The Irish Times*. As a former army officer, McStay brought a lot of conviction to the role:

'You need to call a spade a spade and not an agricultural implement. Accordingly, to explain the duty of the GAA analyst, I think of the parable of the donkey and the bridge.

'A man and his son were bringing their donkey to the fair. The man was walking with the donkey and his son was up on the animal's back. A passer-by said: "Isn't it a disgrace to see that poor man walking and the young fella up on the donkey having an easy time. He should walk and let his poor father have a rest."

'So the boy dismounted and the father took his place. A mile later they met another man who said: "Isn't it a disgrace to see that man sitting up on the donkey's back and his poor son walking. He should let his son get up on the donkey with him." When the man heard this, he instructed his son to get up on the donkey's back with him. After they travelled another mile, they met a woman. She said: "Isn't it a disgrace to see those two heavy men up on that poor little donkey's back. They should get down off him and carry the donkey for a change." The father and son dismounted, got a pole from the side of the road and tied the donkey to it and they carried him across their shoulders. Then disaster struck. Tragically the donkey fell as they walked over the bridge into the river and drowned.

'The moral of the story is that if you are an analyst and you are trying to please everyone, you might as well kiss your ass goodbye.'

THE PRICE OF FAME

McStay plays down the glamour of TV work: 'Gaelic football is drama's first cousin. It is theatre without the script. So I know I was very lucky to have had that wonderful job. But it is not as glamorous or as lucrative as people think, especially those who persist in comparing pundits to Statler and Waldorf, the two old men from *The Muppet Show*.'

PAST AND PRESENT

McStay also recalls: 'The biggest change is that I get recognised way more now than I ever did as a player. After the All-Ireland I played in, when I walked down Grafton Street, only one or two people recognised me. Now a lot of people recognise me. They may not all know my name but they know my face. Sometimes I am asked: "Are you the fella on the television?" Less flattering is: "Are you somebody?" The most sickening was: "Didn't you used to be Kevin McStay?"

SEX SYMBOL

With a big smile, McStay states: 'There is an amusing website which has a diary of a football pundit. According to this, the only reason why I spend any time in RTÉ is to try and catch the eye of Sharon Ní Bheoláin. That's so untrue. Those of us fortunate enough to work in RTÉ Sport have no need to be drooling over Sharon. We have our very own sex symbol – Marty Morrissey!'

THE WINDOWS

Kevin provides a revealing insight into his family life: 'Every rose has its thorns. Being away from home every weekend is not conducive to domestic bliss. All marriages are happy. It's the living together afterwards that causes all the trouble. My wife accused me of loving Gaelic football more than her. "Yeah, but I love you more than hurling or rugby," I replied.

'In fairness she did pay me a great compliment a few years ago. She told me that I brought "a little ray of sunshine" into her life. I was chuffed and asked her how. She took the wind out of my sails when she answered: "When you came home last night from working on *The Sunday Game*, foaming at the mouth and muttering something about Gaelic football, you slammed the door so hard that the venetian blind fell off the window."'

CLAIM TO FAME

A prominent official of the Connacht Council is in Los Angeles, and from the moment he arrives he is struck by the importance of the star system in the city. A major catastrophe ensues when he tries to check into his hotel and discovers that his booking details are wrong. When it looks like he is not going to be checked in to the hotel, his exasperated wife digs him in the ribs and whispers, 'Tell them you're from the Connacht Council!'

83

THE BATTLE OF THE BULGE

Nicky English Discovers the Perils of Management

Some Irish sports stars have struggled with their weight. Former Irish out-half Barry McGann always had a bit of a problem with the battle of the bulge. The Wales great Ray Gravell recalled his experiences of Barry for me:

'With Ollie Campbell, another superb kicking out-half I came across for Ireland was Barry McGann. Barry was the fastest out-half I've ever seen over five yards. The problem is that he was completely f**ked after five yards!'

The nice thing about McGann is that he can talk about being 'calorifically-challenged' with a smile on his face:

'The rugby scene was very different in my time. I missed out on the beauty contest! I do recall, though, that at one stage the Ladies Column in the *Evening Press* referred to me as "our chubby hero". My own mother was delighted with the final line in the feature: "Every mother should have one." Now, because of Sky Sports and so on, rugby stars are treated almost the same way as Kylie Minogue or Kim Kardashian!'

'What I most remember is the slagging I used to get whenever I went back to play in Cork. One time we were playing Cork Celtic. As I ran on to the pitch, I heard a voice saying on the terraces: "Who's that fella?"

"That's McGann the rugby player."

"Oh, wouldn't you know it by his stomach"!'

When Nicky English became manager of Tipperary, he was determined that he would leave no stone unturned until he got his team to be ready to claim the All-Ireland they won in 2001. Part of this punishing regime was the introduction of a Spartan diet. The results were immediate and spectacular throughout the squad, but there was one exception – Eugene O'Neill – whose weight remained unchanged. The Tipp management were baffled and summoned O'Neill for an interview. If O'Neill was hoping for a friendly chat, he was shocked to discover that it was more in the style of the Spanish Inquisition before English and his entire management team. After a stubborn resistance initially, O'Neill finally caved in and blurted out the one word that said so little but so much: 'Sausages.'

English was puzzled. 'What do you mean, sausages?'

O'Neill replied, 'Well, as you know, Nicky, I'm in college and when I get up in the morning, the boys have sausages for me for breakfast. When I'm home during the day, they stick on the pan and we have some more and then we have more in the evening. They're f**king killing me!'

THE FRIDAY FAST

Like Liam Griffin, Justin McCarthy is one of the great evangelists of the game:

'Hurling identifies my Irishness. I'm not an Irish speaker, so the game portrays my national identity.'

THE BATTLE OF THE BULGE

The late RTÉ GAA Correspondent Mick Dunne was an admirer of McCarthy's:

'He was very committed to everything he did and left nothing to chance. It was a very different time during his playing days. In 1966 he deservedly won the Texaco hurler of the year award. The morning after the reception, when he was presented with his award, Justin celebrated in style – by having a massive fry-up for breakfast. The problem was that in those times, Catholics were not allowed to eat meat on Fridays, with the result that fish was on the menu in most Irish homes on Fridays. When Justin realised the terrible sin he had committed, he went to his priest for absolution!'

JACK THE LAD

Irish sport has produced many great characters. Long after his retirement as a player, Karl Mullen was involved in one of the most famous incidents in Irish rugby. During a match he was attending, one of the great folk heroes of Irish rugby, Phil O'Callaghan, was in the thick of the action.

Philo is famed in story for his experiences playing for Dolphin. One goes back to a match played on a bitterly cold November day. He was lifting one of his forwards, Eoghan Moriarty, in the line-out. The big man shouted down at him: 'Philo let me down. My hands are frozen.'

After Philo put out his shoulder, Karl Mullen was to experience his tongue at first hand when he ran on the pitch to give him medical care. Dr Mullen said: 'I'll put it back but I warn you it will be painful.' He did and it was. According to the story, Philo was screaming his head off with the pain. The doctor turned to him and said: 'You should be ashamed of yourself. I was with a sixteen-year-old girl this morning in the Rotunda as she gave birth and there was not even a word of complaint from her.'

Philo replied: 'I wonder what she bloody well would have said if you tried putting the f**king thing back in.'

A FEW GOOD MEN

Armagh finally reached the Promised Land in 2002 when they won their first Sam Maguire Cup. One of their great personalities was their goalie, Benny Tierney. In 2003 Benny went to San Diego with the All-Stars. As part of the trip some of the tourists went to see an NBA basketball match. Among the attendance was legendary actor Jack Nicholson. At one point in the game there was a controversial call and Jack was incensed. He rose to his feet and started screaming at the officials. When the torrent of abuse died down, Benny stood and reprised one of Nicholson's most famous roles, in *A Few Good Men*, when he shouted: 'You want the truth? You can't handle the truth!'

COME DINE WITH ME

Armagh's pre-match breakfast menu provided Benny with another classic quote: 'It used to be a good old Ulster fry before matches, but we've changed that now to muesli – which tastes a wee bit like what you'd find at the bottom of a budgie's cage.'

84

YOU ONLY LIVE TWICE

Ger Loughnane Rises from the Dead

Even though the many controversies of 1998 brought their own pressures, Ger Loughnane's zest for the dramas of the hurling field was undiminished. The vicissitudes, induced by the media, inseparable from the manager's lot, were never likely to grind down someone whose long playing career had been overloaded with disappointments.

When Clare won their historic All-Ireland in 1995 it was such a big story that *The Irish Times* devoted an editorial to it. Loughnane believes, though, that the real enemy was not Offaly but closer to home:

'When I think back to some of the officials on the county board it's not a question of why did Clare not win anything but how could Clare possibly have won anything? They had a vice-like grip on everything and a total lack of respect for the players.

'I experienced it as a player. When we were in Dublin, Johnny Callinan and myself would have to pay our train fare home and then try to get it back from the county board. That was a really tough battle. We learned to wait 'til the treasurer had five or six pints in him to ask him for the money! It was absolutely terrible. They wanted you down to play but they didn't want to pay for it!'

PARTY CENTRAL

Bureaucracy has never been much of a contender for Loughnane's enthusiasm. As a player, even on All-Star trips, he never ceased to be amazed by the heavy-handedness of officialdom:

'I went on two All-Star tours. The first was in 1975. It was my first time in America. It was a dream come true. Seamus Durack, "the Duke", collected me to drive me to the airport. He was so excited, he came very early and I wasn't ready. As a result, I left in a hurry and we were five miles down the road when I realised that I had forgotten my hurleys! Seamus wasn't going to turn back. He told me he'd give me the loan of one of his.

'The Dublin footballers were on the tour with us. When we were staying in Los Angeles, we were having a party around a swimming pool at one stage, and one of the Dublin players was pushed into the pool. Within five minutes all the players had been pushed into the pool fully clothed, much to the consternation of the officials.

'When we were in Boston, we were given a free day but we were told that we absolutely had to be back for a function at 7 p.m. As the day was very drizzly, there wasn't much we could do, so a few of us spent most of the day in the pub. The main character in the group was P.J. Molloy of Galway. We forgot about the time until we suddenly realised that we were going to be late for our function. We rushed off to the venue. When we got there, we went through what we thought was the main door but in fact was the door to the stage and we found ourselves at the back of the stage as the President of the GAA was giving a speech. He was talking about how the GAA would never forget the GAA in Boston.

'At the time, Mike Murphy had a show on RTÉ radio every morning. One of the features of the programme was that he played what he called a "rotten record" every day and when it was over he said, "Yowsa, Yowsa, Yowsa." The president was going on and on with a most boring speech when P.J. Molloy shouted, "Yowsa, Yowsa, Yowsa." The whole place erupted with laughter! Afterwards P.J. got the most ferocious bollocking from the officials and didn't play in any other match on tour.'

A GRAVE MATTER

A number of years ago a national newspaper reported that Loughnane had died while he was undergoing treatment for a serious illness. His neighbour in Feakle was distraught when he read it and, although it was in the early morning, he woke up his son. They two of them drank the two bottles of wine they had been saving for a special occasion. When they woke up at noon the next day with massive hangovers, they found out that the reports of Ger's demise were greatly exaggerated. Rather than celebrating, to Ger's amusement, the father said with real feeling: 'F**k you, Loughnane, you ruined my two best bottles of wine.'

85

JEEPERS KEEPERS

The One That Got Away from Donegal

Packie Bonner was perhaps the greatest Gaelic footballer Donegal never had. As a teenager, he played midfield for the county before finding fame as a goalkeeper with Celtic in the 1980s and 1990s. He will always be a national icon in Ireland because of that famous penalty save in Italia '90.

Packie had the prayers of the fans backing him. One woman took it to extremes. She lit a candle and put it over the place on the television set that Packie occupied. Then she changed it in the second half when Packie changed positions to ensure that it would be burning over his head.

JIMMY'S WINNING MATCHES

Before Jim McGuinness became their manager, there was something of a drinking culture among some of the Donegal squad. After the 2007 Inter-Provincial tournament that Ulster won in Croke Park, they were staying at Donegal legend Brian McEniff's Skylon Hotel in Drumcondra. Late in the night one of the Ulster squad asked where all the Donegal players had gone too. He was puzzled when he was told they were gone to the airport: 'Off to the airport. Why?'

"Cos the bar at the airport doesn't close.'

FAMOUS SEAMUS

In 1979 Monaghan qualified for the Ulster final against Donegal. The match is best remembered for an infamous incident. The referee threw in the ball. Donegal's Seamus Bonner won possession, sent in the ball to the forwards and one of the forwards popped it over the bar. The only problem was that the band was still on the far side of the pitch and they were playing the National Anthem! The referee had to re-start the game and the Donegal point was disallowed.

SUDDEN STOP

Over his lengthy career Seamus Bonner was himself involved in some bizarre events. He was playing against Monaghan one day in a league match in Ballybofey and was soloing in with the ball twenty yards out from the goal with the defence beaten. He had a goal on his mind but he had his mouth open and a fly flew into his mouth; he swallowed it and nearly choked. He was clean through and came to a sudden staggering stop with nobody near him. He let the ball fall out of his hands and lost it. The Donegal fans did not know what had happened. Bonner was not sure what they were thinking about him, but he was sure it wasn't complimentary. He believed that the moral of the story is when you're on a football field you should keep your mouth shut!

86

MEN IN BLACK

Referees Rock

Ulster championship matches are renowned for their toughness. In 2002 former Monaghan manager Seán McCague, in his role of President of the GAA, expressed his unhappiness at the violence in the first International Rules test between Ireland and Australia. Reporting on McCague's disaffection on *Morning Ireland*, Des Cahill observed, 'He said he wasn't going to support the series' continuance.' Quick as a flash, Cathal Mac Coille quipped, 'Do you think the Ulster championship is in danger?'

NO LOVE ACTUALLY

Tough matches bring the role of the referees into sharp focus. They are not always loved. A man is flying in a hot air balloon and realises he is lost. He reduces height and spots a man down below. He lowers the balloon further and shouts: 'Excuse me, can you tell me where I am?'

Ciarán Whelan below says: 'Yes, you're in a hot air balloon, hovering thirty feet above this field.'

'You must be a GAA pundit,' says the balloonist.

'I am,' replies Ciarán. 'How did you know?'

'Well,' says the balloonist, 'everything you have told me is technically correct, but it's no use to anyone.'

Whelan says, 'You must be a GAA referee.'

'I am,' replies the balloonist, 'But how did you know?'

'Well,' says Ciarán, 'you don't know where you are, or where you're going, and you're in the same position you were before we met, but now it's my fault.'

CELEBRITY SPAT

Micheál Kearins's place in the lore of Gaelic football is made additionally secure by his phenomenal scoring feats. He was the country's leading marksman in competitive games in four different years in 1966, 1968, 1972 and 1973. In the drawn 1971 Connacht final he scored a record fourteen points for Sligo: five from play and nine from placed balls, including two 45s and one sideline kick. He won two Railway Cup medals in a thirteen-year career with Connacht, in 1967 and 1969. Two years later year he scored twelve points for Connacht against the Combined Universities in the Railway Cup, all from placed balls. With the Combined Universities leading by 3–9 to 0–17, Connacht got a line ball forty-five yards out in the dying seconds and Kearins calmly slotted it over the bar to earn Connacht a replay.

After his retirement from playing, he became a referee. His career with the whistle is probably best remembered for the time he sent off Colm O'Rourke:

'It was an incident after half-time and he got a heavy enough shoulder while in possession. It knocked the ball out of his hands but he didn't try to retrieve it but came after me. The play moved down the field and he followed me the whole way down sharing "pleasantries" with me! I had no option but to send him off.'

DISCREET MEASURES

Club football in Wicklow is not for the faint-hearted, especially for faint-hearted referees. One of the most famous incidents in its history was when a group of disaffected fans, after losing a club match, locked a referee in the boot of his car. In the return fixture, the nervous referee brought the two teams together and pointed to his whistle and said, 'Do ye see this yoke, lads? I'm going to blow it now and blow it again at the finish and whatever happens in between ye can sort out yerselves.'

87

FRANKIE GOES TO HOLLYWOOD

Roscommon Win the 2001 Connacht Final

In 2011, when Fergal O'Donnell stepped down as Roscommon county manager, Joe Brolly referred back to the county's former indignities: 'Fergal O'Donnell's resignation as county manager left the people of Roscommon in shock. The big man did an excellent job. When he began his tenure, Roscommon were a laughing stock – some of their past antics made the English rugby team's dwarf-throwing look like a quiet night in over a hot cup of cocoa.'

MATRIMONY

Former Roscommon star and Saint Brigid's manager Frankie Dolan is a cult figure. Like his brother Garvin, Frankie had a turbulent relationship with referees and umpires. When Frankie got married at Christmas 2010, some of the guests were surprised to see so many referees invited. One referee was told in no uncertain terms, 'You were lucky to get an invite.' The official coolly replied, 'I know, especially as I booked Garvin for the way he walked out of the church.'

The father of the bride had been a GAA umpire and brought the house down at the speeches during the reception when he recalled his first encounter with Frankie when he was umpiring a match and Dolan had sent a shot inches wide. After signalling the ball wide, his future son-in-law raced in to tell him in the most emphatic terms that he was a 'f**king b***ix'. Just as he was regaining his composure he was accosted from behind by Dolan's father, Frankie senior, who also told him that he was a 'f**king b***ix'.

Not to be outdone, the best man also had a big hit with the crowd when in his speech he said: 'Frankie has brought unique distinction to his club, his county and his province whenever he represented them' – dramatic pause – 'in a bar or nightclub.'

THEATRICS

In the Connacht final in 2001, Frankie Dolan was perceived by some Mayo fans as engaging in 'theatricals' which 'caused' a Mayo player to be sent off. They gave him a new nickname, 'Frankie Goes to Hollywood'.

WEIGHTY MATTERS

Frankie's waistline may no longer be of inter-county requirements but playing for Saint Brigid's he could do what most forwards cannot do and score points. After starring for Brigid's in their third consecutive Connacht club title in 2012, Pat Spillane was moved to write: 'The GAA needs more Frankie Dolans and less Freddie Fredericks.'

SHINE ON

In 1974 the most famous piece of music journalism was written. A reviewer went to a concert given by a guy nobody ever heard of and wrote: 'I've seen the future of rock and roll and its name is Bruce Springsteen.' In 2006, having seen a new star tear into the opposition with the same relish that Tiny Tim tucked into the family's Christmas ham, I sent a text to Dermot Earley which stated: 'I've seen the future of Roscommon football and his name is Donie Shine.'

If there's ever a DVD made of the history of Roscommon, Donie's winning point in the 2010 Connacht final will be one of the iconic moments.

Like Earley before him, Shine wears his fame slightly and both became ambassadors for Roscommon as much for their characters off the pitch as their brilliance on it. The difference is that Donie had a much higher female fan base than Dermot ever had.

According to rumour, Take That wrote their number one song 'Let it Shine' about him. I've been unable to confirm the veracity of the story with Gary Barlow.

MAKING A MARK

Donie has seen his share of uncomfortable moments in the county jersey: 'In the 2006 All-Ireland minor final we were playing Kerry when our goalie Mark Miley made a rare error which cost us a point. The game ended in a draw and, as I walked into the tunnel, I could see Mark was disconsolate but I wasn't sure what to say to him. When I got into the dressing room, Mark was there with his head in his hands. Everybody felt very awkward. Then Conor Devaney came in and said immediately: "Mark, for Jaysus sake, what the hell were you at?" Everybody laughed. It broke the tension and we all moved on. It seemed the worst possible thing he could have said but, actually, it was the best possible thing. Of course, in the replay Mark went on to keep his record of not conceding a goal in the Championship intact.'

IN THE NAME OF THE FATHER

Donie is called after his late father who both played for and managed Roscommon. Donie senior witnessed some unusual motivational speeches:

'A club team from Roscommon travelled 200 miles to a tournament game in Cork. At half-time they trailed by 7–2 to 0–5. A crisis meeting was held in the middle of the pitch. Recriminations were flying until the captain called for silence and an end to the bickering and a hush descended. One player said, "We need some positive encouragement."

'After a short delay, the manager-cum-trainer-cum-club secretary-cum groundskeeper said, "Come on now, lads. Let's go out there and show them up. It's plain to be seen. They can't score points!"'

88

THERE IS NO SHOW LIKE A JOE SHOW

Joe Brolly Takes Evasive Action

Some players like to use brawn. An indication of Leinster and Ireland rugby star James Lowe's personality came before Leinster's match with Wasps in October 2018. Somebody tried to break into his car. To the amusement of the gardai when he reported the incident Lowe asked if when they found the culprit, he could be left alone with him for ten minutes!

NO ORDINARY JOE

Mick Lyons said of his Meath team, 'We were like gunslingers. If you got shot, wheel him away.' Other players favour using their brain. In the 1990s Derry football produced one of the great characters in the history of the game, Joe Brolly. In recent times, though, he has become something of the nation's sweetheart since he decided to donate his kidney to Shane Finnegan, a man he barely knew.

SEALED WITH A KISS

In 1993 Brolly was at the heart of Derry's most famous day when they won their only All-Ireland. Joe never really surrendered to managers and was never short of self-confidence. This did not always endear him to his managers. One of them was heard to say, 'He's down there now letting people know how good he is playing.'

The Derry manager, Eamon Coleman, was away after they won their only All-Ireland in 1993 and his deputy, Harry Cribbin, was in charge and he didn't select Joe to start. He thought Brolly was too big for his boots. By his own admission, Joe would have been 'as cocky as anything'. There was a massive crowd because it was such a big deal for an Ulster team back then to have won an All-Ireland.

With fifteen minutes to go, Derry were struggling and Brolly was brought on. The first ball he got he put over the bar. The second ball he put over the bar. The score was tied and a high ball came in over the top. The Down defender thought he could get it and was back-peddling but he missed it. Brolly caught it and the Down goalie came out to him and he lobbed the ball in the far corner. The crowd was really animated. Brolly ran down the length of the field blowing kisses as a way of saying, 'Harry, you dirty bas***d for not picking me.' One of the subs told Brolly that Harry Gribbin said, 'Oh that wee bas***d's trying to sicken me.' It was the talk of the place and everyone really enjoyed it.

Down's heads went down after the celebration and Brolly could see after that it became a sort of psychological weapon. It became a thing that if he scored a goal in the Ulster Championship, it had a demoralising effect on the opposition. Fergal Logan told him that he had said to the Tyrone team when he was captain: 'The key thing is to stop that f**ker from scoring a goal.' Ten minutes into the second half, Brolly scored a goal. It deflated Tyrone.

The 1998 Ulster final between Derry and Donegal was, to put it at its kindest, something less than a classic. However, it produced one of the most dramatic finales ever when Brolly rounded Tony Blake in injury time to strike the decisive goal for Derry. He celebrated by blowing kisses to the terraces. That night the team returned to Henry Downey's bar and celebrated, in the words of Geoffrey McGonigle, 'until the birds were singing'.

SICK BAY

For his part, Pat Spillane's most famous feat of punditry came in 2003 when he described Tyrone's performance in their All-Ireland triumph over Kerry as 'puke football'. His remark provoked a tidal wave of indignation, particularly in Tyrone. Happily, there were a few gems among all the vitriol: 'Spillane's comment about puke football should be interpreted as Pure Unadulterated Kerry Embarrassment.'

89

BREAKING BALLS

Tyrone Tops

A week after the 2003 All-Ireland semi-final which saw a spectacular Kerry defeat, a Tyrone and a Kerry bloke were being executed together. The executioner said to them both: 'I'll grant you one last wish before I hang you.' The Tyrone fella said: 'I'm from Tyrone. We beat Kerry in the All-Ireland semi-final a few days ago and I'd like to go to my death after watching those magic moments once again.' The guard said, 'No problem. We'll wheel out a big screen and you can watch the game again.'

Then he turned to the Kerry man and asked him what was his last wish.

The Kerry man replied, 'Hang me first.'

A STRANGER ON A TRAIN

Pat Spillane was furious after the match. It was not unusual. Spillane's comments about the inadequacies of the Mayo forwards were not appreciated in Mayo, to such an extent that the mere mention of Spillane's name in Mayo was as welcome as a nun in a brothel.

One of the most memorable train journeys this writer ever experienced was shortly after Spillane's criticism of Mayo when they lost to Roscommon in the Connacht Championship in 2019. I found myself sitting beside a man of mature years, who was puffing away on his pipe. Given his disposition, I thought, at first, he might be a parish priest. The conversation quickly turned to football and he gave an incisive critique of the problems of Connacht football. Then he turned to the media reportage of teams from the West. Immediately, he had a transformation of Dr Jekyll and Mr Hyde proportions. He reeled off a litany of names of journalists and pundits, and what he proposed to do with them cannot be reprinted on the grounds of public order and morality. After his vicious tirade, he paused for a deep breath. Then he said, more in sorrow than in anger, 'F**k them all bar Spillane.'

I nearly fell off my seat. I heard myself ask incredulously, 'Why do you say bar Spillane?'

'Ah sure, young fella, Spillane is f**ked already.'

WRONG PLACE

Spillane, though, was not the renowned Kerry footballer of yesteryear who famously was the guest speaker at a dinner of a major club in Mayo. Páidí Ó Sé launched into a passionate speech as to why the club he named was one of the top clubs in the country. A few minutes into his speech, he knew that the audience reaction was much less warm than he anticipated. He discovered that he was talking about the wrong club! He excused himself and said he had to go the toilet. He never returned.

JEEPERS KEEPERS

In July 2002 the *Sunday World* asked Pat Spillane to do player-profiles of everyone due to play in the All-Ireland quarter-finals.

With eight teams involved, they wanted him to write pen-pictures of 120 players. That is a pretty difficult exercise. When you have to write about sixteen corner-backs, it is very hard to find sixteen different ways of saying 'tight-marker' and 'tenacious'.

His problems began, though, with the goalkeepers. There are not too many things you can say about a goalie other than he is a 'good shot-stopper', 'has great reflexes' and 'has a good kick-out'. Generally, the only variable is whether you can use 'very agile'. By the time he got to the last goalkeeper on the list, Armagh's Benny Tierney, Spillane was getting very bored with repeating himself, so he described him as 'fat and overweight'. Benny came up with a great retort. He said: 'Spillane is right. Yes, I am fat and overweight now, but he will always be ugly.'

Spillane took the insult in good spirit: 'I salute Benny for keeping a bit of humour in the game and I just wish there were a few more like him up north.'

DONEGAL CATCH

In 2011 Spillane was in the firing line with his repeated criticism of Donegal's negative tactics. One habit that football fans in Donegal have had since then is slagging Spillane off. Typical of this was a Ballybofey fan's summation of his football career: 'Pat Spillane had the speed of a racehorse, the strength of a plough-horse and the brains of a rocking horse.'

90

GOING DUTCH

Clare v Wexford

In 1981 Clare went to Holland to play in an exhibition game against Wexford. Ger Loughnane remembers it with affection:

'There was a hockey team there called "The Hurling Club" even though they had nothing to do with hurling! They were celebrating their centenary. The organisers made a serious mistake at the start because the first place they brought us to was the Heineken brewery in Amsterdam! We started lashing into the samples pretty fast. Next thing a sing-song started so the only way they could get us all out was by promising to take us to a barbecue. We were starving at this stage, so we had everything devoured in a few minutes!

'The Dutch tourist board had probably never targeted such clientele before. It is a reasonable assumption that they will not do so again.

'Our hosts gave us a really great weekend. We were determined to enjoy every minute of it and we certainly did. The trip produced some bizarre moments such as the sight of a Clare selector urinating into a canal in Amsterdam at three in the morning!'

BAG OF TRICKS

Although they were in a different country, all Loughnane's old feelings about the Clare County Board surfaced again:

'We played a match on the Sunday, on manicured lawns. We got on great with the Wexford lads and, thirty years on, when we meet any of them that were on the trip, we have a great laugh about it. We had arranged to swap jerseys with the Wexford team after the game but the Clare County chairman said in the dressing room afterwards that our Clare jerseys had to be handed back. He said, "I'm going to give you five minutes to hand them back." He went out and the quiet lads and the young players, who we knew they were going to pick on, gave their jerseys to the established players. I had three jerseys in my bag. When the officials came back all the jerseys had disappeared. They said, "We're going to search the bags." Predictably, they searched the bags of subs but the rest of us walked out past them.'

COMPASS POINTS

Yet it is the good times he chooses to remember:

'My abiding memory is of being in a pub in the seediest part of the red-light district in Amsterdam on the Saturday night. We had a great character on the team and I saw him walking out of the pub. I went out after him because I knew he didn't know where he was going. He was going into this dark street which was really dangerous. So I brought him back and as we were walking into the pub he asked, "Is this f**king O'Connell Street?" He thought he was in Ennis!'

BUSHWHACKED

Loughnane had a stormy relationship with officials, including those in Clare. Among their number was Brendan Vaughan, the former chairman of the County Board. Both were teachers and, once, at a schoolboy match between their two schools, they nearly came to blows. There were two coats down as goal-posts. There was no crossbar. Vaughan was umpire at one side. Loughnane was umpire at the other. A head-high ball came in at one stage. Vaughan said it was a goal. Loughnane said it was a point. After a full and frank exchange of views, Vaughan looked at Loughnane disdainfully and uttered the immortal words, 'Get away, you bushman from Feakle!'

RUNNING ON EMPTY

Clare began training for the 1995 Munster Championship the previous September. Clare trained all the way through the League. Luxurious conditions were not conducive to good winter training, so they trained in Crusheen. Mike McNamara was excellent for putting the players through that hard physical slog. The players will never forget their introduction to Mike's training methods and personality. On his very first night, standing on the pitch in Crusheen, he said, 'Okay, ladies. Let's go for a jog.'

91

RADIO DAZE

Pat Spillane Becomes a Radio Presenter

An elderly farmer in a remote part of Leitrim finally decided to buy a television. The shopkeeper assured him that he would install the antenna and TV the next day. The next evening, the farmer turned on his new TV and found only the pundits on *The Sunday Game* on every channel. The next morning, he turned on the TV and found only *The Sunday Game* no matter what channel he put on. The next day, the same again, so he called the shop to complain. The owner said it was impossible for every channel to only have the GAA pundits talking but agreed to send the repairman to check the TV. When the TV repairman turned on the set, he was stunned to find the farmer was right. After looking at the set for a while, he went outside to check the antenna. In a few minutes he returned and told the farmer he had found the problem. The antenna had been installed on top of the windmill and grounded to the manure spreader.

The repairman sagely remarked, 'GAA pundits are like nappies. They need to be changed often and for the same reason.'

DOYLER

Pat Spillane's media career was shaped most by a former Irish rugby coach and fellow Kerryman: 'The biggest influence on my style as a pundit was the late Mick Doyle. Mick was a great friend of mine. Doyler and his wife, Mandy, were at my wedding and it was probably Doyler more than anyone else who encouraged me to become a sports pundit. Mick used to come to Kerry on holidays and bought a house there and we became good friends. Unconsciously, I suppose I imitated Doyle's style on the telly as I have a lot of Doyler's traits in me.

'I was at the game in March 2004 when Ireland beat Scotland to win the Triple Crown. What I remember most forcefully from the game was listening to 'Ireland's Call' before the match. It would not psych up a person to go into battle.'

The night before the game, Mick Doyle was asked what it was he most disliked about rugby today. He replied: 'I'm not sure whether it's Brian O'Driscoll's hair or "Ireland's Call".'

MASS MISSER

'Doyler had a wicked sense of humour. He was taking the Irish team for a Sunday-morning training session. His prop forward, Jim McCoy, was not moving as swiftly as Doyler would have liked. Big Jim was an RUC officer and brought up in the Protestant tradition. Doyler shouted at him: "Hurry up, McCoy, or you'll be late for Mass!"'

SURE THING

'I had no doubts before Kerry played Galway a few years ago that the Westerners in the Super 8s were going nowhere. They beat us. I'm always like that. I may often be wrong, but I never have any doubts!

'Getting predictions wrong does not faze me unduly. I always get my predictions wrong and a few times a week I will meet people who will say something like, "Spillane, you're only a chancer. You know nothing about football. You were wrong again last Sunday."

'On such occasions, I always quote the lines of the Declan Nerney song: "If I knew then what I knew now ... I'd be a wiser man."

'The great thing is that RTÉ paid me for thirty years to come and tell the nation what I thought would happen. Then, when I made a dog's dinner of it and got it badly wrong, the *Sunday World* paid me the following Sunday to explain why I got it so wrong!

'I suppose what I took most from Mick Doyle was a desire to marry analysis with entertainment. There are, though, a number of pitfalls facing a television pundit. The golden rule is to be careful what you say – not something I am noted for!'

RADIO GAGA

In 2002 Pat Spillane presented *Sportscall* for much of the summer. His preparation beforehand was not what he expected:

'When I was invited to present the *Sportscall* programme on RTÉ radio, I went up early in the morning. I was certain I was going to be well trained before the programme started on studio control and on how to use all the gadgetry and technology and voice projection and all that.

'My preparation for prime-time radio involved the following:

'With ten minutes to go to air I am sitting on a studio chair not knowing what is going on.

'With eight minutes to air a woman walks into the studio. She looks at the computer. It is not on. She hits it and eventually something comes up on the screen.

'With five minutes to air a sound man comes in and says: "Press that button and shout into it." I pressed the button and said a few sentences. I now know that's what's known in the business as a soundcheck.

'With three minutes to go on air the producer comes in and tells me that there are no phone calls in yet but that I should keep talking and eventually something will come up on the screen.

'That was my introduction to *Sportscall*, a prime-time programme on national radio.'

92

KNOCK, KNOCK, KNOCKIN' ON HEAVEN'S DOOR

Meath v Dublin

Referees sometimes get a bad press. A Scottish referee, who will remain nameless, was making his international debut in Twickenham in an England-Ireland Five Nations Fixture in the 1970s. Irish rugby legend Willie Duggan was having a fag in the Irish dressing room. The time had come to run onto the pitch, but Duggan had nowhere to put out his cigarette. He knew that if he ran out in the tunnel with the fag in his mouth the cameras would zoom in on him straight away. When the referee came in to tell the teams it was time to leave, the Irish number eight went over to him and said, 'Would you hold that for a second please?' The obliging referee said yes but Duggan promptly ran out on the pitch – leaving the ref with no option but to put out the fag. He went out to face the glare of the cameras and the first sight the television audience had of him was holding a cigarette! Asked about the incident afterwards, the referee said, 'I've had a wonderful day – but this wasn't it!'

The referee did have the last word, though, at the post-match dinner when Duggan asked him if he minded his smoking. He said, 'I don't mind your smoking, if you don't mind my being sick all over you.'

Duggan sometimes got into trouble with referees. He was always phlegmatic about it: 'I don't consider I was sent off. The referee invited me to leave the pitch and I accepted the invitation.'

TWICE BLESSED

Some incredible stories have just the faintest touches of credibility and therefore enter the canon of GAA legend. A case in point was the story of a match in 1957 when a new pitch was being opened in St Brendan's Hospital. As reigning All-Ireland football champions, Galway were invited to play the home team and duly were awarded a penalty in the game. A Galway player, Mick Ford, who once scored a goal in a club hurling match in Dublin directly from a puck-out, is said to have hit the ball so hard that the lace of the ball came undone and the leather part went over the bar and the bladder went into the net. As a result, the referee is said to have awarded a goal and a point!

SPIN CITY

In the build-up to Donegal's 2013 All-Ireland quarter-final, Jim McGuinness spoke at length about his concern for his player's welfare in the light of the physicality of the tackles on them. Most pundits saw it as a thinly veiled attempt to influence referees. David Brady's verdict was: 'Jimmy's spinning matches.'

93

FOOTBALL FROLICS

More Than Words

One of the most endearing features of the GAA is the perennial humour of many of its characters. Witness this collection of Freudian slips, true confessions and double entendres which demonstrates that GAA foot-in-mouth disease is far more rampant than mad cow disease.

I know some fellas who were brilliant footballers but who were quiet and introspective and couldn't handle criticism. You have to handle these fellas differently than some lad who was a messer and who you knew needed to get a good kick up the hole every now and then.
Shane Curran

I imagine ninety-nine per cent of the Irish population haven't a clue whether Eavan Boland is a type of biscuit or an Irish poet.
Pat Spillane

He's just a contrary, cantankerous hoor.
Shane Curran on Frankie Dolan.

King Midas was asked to judge a musical competition between two Gods: Pan (pipes) and Apollo (harp). He agreed, which turned out to be the worst decision since Paddy Russell blew up 'God' for picking the ball off the ground in the 1995 final.
Joe Brolly. (God, in this case, is Peter Canavan.)

I've never seen a stout guy move so quick.
Pádraig Harrington on marking Dessie Farrell as a schoolboy.

There was more movement in a confessional box.
Willie Hegarty on the malfunctioning Roscommon forward line.

I'm not bleedin' Dumbledore . . . I can't wave a magic wand and produce a footballer out of nothing.
Johnny Magee reacts to criticism of Wicklow's league campaign in April 2015.

It's not a police state . . . this is not North Korea.
Joe Brolly argues against a Tyrone player being banned for the hair-ruffling incident which saw Monaghan's Darren Hughes sent off in the 2015 All-Ireland quarter-final.

If I get all these accusations against me and I win an All-Ireland, I don't give a sh*t to be honest.
Philly McMahon

I don't want to say Pat Spillane went down easily – but watching him in the 1980 All-Ireland final, I threw a paper napkin at him on the telly and he fell over.
Roscommon fan

I'm not saying it was really cold but I did hear a fan observing: 'There's a wind out there that would blow an elephant off his Missus.'
Down fan

It's a cage where twenty-five or thirty men are stripped down to their bare bollocks while rattling inside with fear and anxiety and insecurity.
Shane Curran on the dressing room.

Jamie Clarke is the Messi of Ulster football.
Pat Spillane

We had to work very hard for this – it took 119 years for us to get it.
Tyrone boss Mickey Harte after winning the 2003 All-Ireland.

Did you ever hear 'One day at a time, sweet Jesus?' Before yesterday there were no All-Irelands in Tyrone, now there's one.
Mickey Harte when asked about the possibility of two-in-a-row.

While there are many claims that managers are being paid under the table, the GAA couldn't even find the tables.
Former GAA president Peter Quinn

They said we were like the British Army, that we lose our power when we cross the border, but we've proved we have power today.
Peter Canavan as he lifted the Sam Maguire Cup in 2003.

It's not a North-South thing, sure we're all the same – it's six of one and twenty-six of the others.
Tyrone comic Kevin McAleer on the 2003 All-Ireland final.

The midfield area was like New York City, going down Time Square, crazy.
Seamus Moynihan after Kerry lost to Tyrone in 2003.

How would you know a Cork footballer? He's the one who thinks that oral sex is just talking about it.
John B. Keane

Somebody should check his birth cert because I don't think he was born, I think he's a creation of God.
Colm O'Rourke on the apparently divine Colm 'Gooch' Cooper.

The first time I got the ball I passed it to a teammate and raced on to take the return pass but instead he booted the ball two miles in the air.
Iggy Jones on his Tyrone debut.

Those guys are going to be bleeding all over us.
Cork player responds to the sight of a very heavily bandaged Willie Joe Padden in the 1989 All-Ireland final.

Don't be so modest, (Pádraic) Joyce. You're not that great.
Westmeath fan during Westmeath's shock defeat of Galway in 2006.

Jaysus, if Lee Harvey Oswald was from Mayo, JFK would still be alive.
Mayo fan

Even Iarnród Éireann don't carry as many passengers as we saw today.
Colm O'Rourke's verdict on the Dublin and Offaly forwards in the 2007 Leinster semi-final.

If Dublin win, it's over-hyped; if Dublin lose, it's over-hyped.
Ciarán Whelan

I used to think it was great being a wee nippy corner-forward, but it's better now being a big, burly one.
Former Meath All-Star Ollie Murphy

Keep your high balls low into the wind.
Advice to a young John B. Keane.

He'll regret this to his dying day, if he lives that long.
Dubs fan after Charlie Redmond missed a penalty in the 1994 All-Ireland final.

Referees are like wives: you can never tell how they're going to turn out.
John B. Keane

He simply wished us well for the second half and hoped the awful weather would improve.
Denis Allen's edited version of what Mickey Kearins said to him and Dublin captain Gerry Hargan when he pulled the captains aside before the start of the second half and instructed them to warn their players about their behaviour in the 1989 All-Ireland semi-final after a very physical first half.

Now listen, lads, I'm not happy with our tackling. We're hurting them but they keep getting up.
John B. Keane ventures into coaching.

Football and sex are so utterly different. One involves sensuality, passion, emotion, commitment, selflessness, the speechless admiration of sheer heart-stopping beauty, rushes of breath-taking, ecstatic excitement, followed by shattering, toe-curling, orgasmic pleasure. And the other is sex.
Joe O'Connor

Last guys don't finish nice.
Frustrated Leitrim fan

Mayo always had a big problem coping with being favourites and never lost it.
Former Mayo star Willie McGee

Why did they not take off their pyjamas?
A young boy to his father in 1960 watching Down became the first inter-county team to wear tracksuits.

Kerry would have won if Meath hadn't turned up.
A Kerry fan reflects on the All-Ireland semi-final defeat in 2001.

Behind every Galway player there is another Galway player.
Meath fan at the 2001 All-Ireland final.

When Joe Brolly is winning, he's objectionable. When he's blowing kisses, he's highly objectionable.
Cavan fan

Joe Brolly always talked a great game. The problem was that he didn't always play a great one.
Colm O'Rourke responds to a Joe Brolly after-dinner speech, which had a few digs at the Meath team O'Rourke starred on.

He (the referee) wouldn't see a foul in a henhouse.
Frustrated Sligo fan

There are two things in Ireland that would drive you to drink. GAA referees would drive you to drink and the price of drink would drive you to drink.
Another Sligo fan at the same match.

You get more contact in an old-time waltz at an old folks' home than in a National League final.
Pat Spillane

They (Cavan) have a forward line that couldn't punch holes in a paper bag.
Pat Spillane

The first half was even, the second half was even worse.
Pat Spillane reflects on an Ulster Championship clash.

Meath players like to get their retaliation in first.
Cork fan in 1988.

Meath make football a colourful game – you get all black and blue.
Another Cork fan at the same match.

Karl O'Dwyer will go down in history as the rat who joined the sinking ship.
Kerry fan after O'Dwyer switched from Kerry to Kildare.

Anxious corner-forward before club match in Sligo: Do you think I need gloves?
Mentor: For all the ball you'll get, it's not going to matter.

That's the first time I've seen anybody limping off with a sore finger.
Armagh's Gene Morgan to 'injured' teammate Pat Campbell.

We're taking you off but we're not bothering to put on a sub. Just having you off will improve our situation.
Mentor to club player in Derry.

FOOTBALL FROLICS

The fire happened on a Saturday night and when the fire brigade came, one of the firemen jumped off and asked me, 'Is the ball safe?' As I was watching my business go up in smoke, the ball wasn't my main priority.
Jimmy Murray after his pub-cum-grocery, which was home to the football from the 1944 All-Ireland final, was destroyed in a fire.

He was a man mountain – he would catch airplanes if it helped Kerry.
John B. Keane on Mick O'Connell

I warned the boys they couldn't go through the league unbeaten, and, unfortunately, they appear to have listened to me.
Tyrone's Art McRory after his side's defeat by Donegal.

In terms of the Richter scale, this defeat was a force 8 gale.
Meath fan after the 2001 All-Ireland final.

The grub in the hotel was the only good thing about the day.
Nemo Rangers fan after the 2002 All-Ireland club final.

I'm going to tape *The Angelus* over this.
Meath fan on receiving the video recording of the 2001 All-Ireland final.

John O'Mahony has given up football. He's just become Kildare manager.
Waspish Galway fan

Poor Mayo, with no real method up front, resembled a fire engine hurrying to the wrong fire.
Spectator at the infamous 1993 All-Ireland semi-final against Cork.

Lovely piece of wholehearted fielding. Mick O'Connell stretched like Nureyev for a one-handed catch.
Micheál O'Hehir

The rules of Meath football are basically simple – if it moves, kick it; if it doesn't move, kick it until it does.
Tyrone fan after the controversial 1996 All-Ireland semi-final.

Whenever a team loses there's always a row at half-time but when they win it's an inspirational speech.
John O'Mahony

Gaelic football is like a love affair: if you don't take it seriously, it's no fun; if you do take it seriously, it breaks your heart.
Patrick Kavanagh

What they say about Cork footballers being ignorant is rubbish. I spoke to a couple yesterday and they were quite intelligent.
Brendan Kennelly

A Kerry footballer with an inferiority complex is one who thinks he's just as good as everybody else.
John B. Keane

Life isn't all beer and football: some of us haven't touched a football in months.
A Kerry player during the league campaign in the early 1980s.

It gives a whole new meaning to powder your nose.
Fan's reaction to a rumour that a player was reacting to pressure by taking cocaine.

FOOTBALL FROLICS

My dad told me you were the man that lost the All-Ireland for Tyrone.
Young fan to Iggy Jones

Journalist: How's the leg, Kevin?
Kevin Moran: It's very fuc . . . it's very sore.
After the 1978 All-Ireland final.

Gravedigger pointing to the graves of all the famous Kerry footballers in 1994: It's a very impressive collection, isn't it?
Jack Bootham: 'Tis indeed, but the way things are going at the moment you'll have to dig them all up again if Kerry are ever going to win anything.

He (Colin Corkery) is as useless as a back pocket in a vest.
Kerry fan

Colin Corkery is deceptive. He's slower than he looks.
Kerry fan

He (Mícheál Ó Muircheartaigh) can take the ball from one end of the field to the other with just the players' occupations.
Jack O'Shea

Pádraic Joyce sold more dummies than Mothercare.
Willie Hegarty

The current Galway under-21s team has more bite than Luis Suárez.
Willie Hegarty in the wake of Galway under-21s' victory over Cork in the All-Ireland final and Luis Suárez's bite on Branislav Ivanović in 2013.

I think Mickey Whelan believes tactics are a new kind of piles on your bum.
Disgruntled Dubs fan

And here comes Nudie Hughes for Nudie reason.
Micheál O'Hehir

Every year we had a different trainer. In fact, we had more trainers than Sheikh Mohammed.
Kildare's Pat Mangan

Fermanagh has such a small playing base. Half is made up of water and half of the remaining half are Protestants.
Fermanagh fan bemoans the paucity of talent.

The only acceptable recipients of money from the GAA are administrators, coaches, security, bar and catering staff, hawkers, programme sellers, pirates, general scavengers, some managers . . . but no players. Stalin or Fidel Castro would love the way the GAA has and is being run. Even if something is wrong, nobody questions it.
Colm O'Rourke

There are quite a few black and white pictures up there (in the clubhouse), it will be nice to move them down the wall now.
Mossie Quinn after St Vincent's first All-Ireland club title in thirty-two years.

I find it hard to see how my northern cousins could get so worked up about counties created by British imperialists.
Colm O'Rourke

Any word of the (Clogherhead) Dreadnoughts, Seán? Will they ever take on the Man-O-War?
Seán Óg Ó Ceallacháin on the way people reacted to his radio results show.

The difference between winning a club and a county All-Ireland is when you get a slap on the back after the match, you actually know the person when you turn around.
Thomas Meehan

The International Rules series was a bit like the Vietnam War. Nobody at home cared about it, but everyone involved sure did.
Australian coach Leigh Matthews

Pádí Ó Sé is buttoned up like the most devout girl in the Amish community when it came to the pre-final interview.
Anon

I don't want to be biased, but what was the referee at there?
Sean Walsh, Galway Bay FM

Biddy Early now rests happily in heaven with Biddy Mulligan.
Ger Canning after Dublin won the 1995 All-Ireland a few weeks after Clare broke the curse of Biddy Early.

94

MISSING THE BUS

Galway Greats

According to legend, after Galway won the All-Ireland in 1956, Seán Purcell was waiting in Galway for the bus to Tuam, not realising that the last bus had gone. A driver was on his way back to the garage with an empty bus when he spotted 'the Master' and, although it was against all regulations, he stopped and asked him where he was going. When Purcell told him Tuam, the driver said, 'Hop in.' Four miles out from Tuam, the poor man nearly had a stroke when he saw an inspector standing in the middle of the road waving him down. The inspector was a seething mass of anger and demanded an explanation. 'I have the Master here,' answered the driver meekly.

'The Master. You can't be serious!' said the driver, boarding the bus to verify the fact. When he saw the evidence with his own eyes, he turned angrily to the driver again.

'How could you be so stupid? Turn around and get back to the garage straight away. How could you drive the Master in just a single decker bus. Get him a double decker straight away so that he can go upstairs if he fancies a cigarette.'

THE COMEBACK KID

During the late 1970s the All-Star team were managed by Seán Purcell. Seán called out the team before the first game and announced that he was playing centre half-forward. That got a great laugh, but Seán turned on them and said in all earnestness, 'What's so funny, lads?'

JACK THE LAD

Misunderstandings sometimes happen in Irish sport. Former Irish rugby international Eric Miller witnessed some strange sights with the Irish team:

'As the tour of South Africa in 2004 was coming to an end we organised John Hayes's stag party. We dressed John up in a gym-slip. The sight of a twenty-stone man in a gym-slip is one that I never want to see again! Colin Farrell was filming there at the time and he came to join us for the party. He was a very sound guy and certainly knew how to have a good time! We gathered around in a circle with John in the middle and everyone got to ask Colin a question. Everything was going to plan until Donncha O'Callaghan, as only Donncha can, asked, "What was it like to be the star of *Titanic*?" The whole place cracked up and we nearly fell off our seats laughing.'

One of Seán Purcell's teammates was Jack Mahon. Jack once bumped into a young fella in Galway and was a bit disappointed to hear that the youngster had never heard of him. He hoped he might impress his new acquaintance when he told him that he played at centre half-back on the Galway team that beat Cork in the 1956 All-Ireland final.

'Gosh that's shocking,' said the youngster.

'Why?' asked a bemused Jack.

'Because I've just discovered my dad's a liar. He's always said that when Galway won that All-Ireland, they never had a centre-back!'

NO JOHNNY COME LATELY

One of the stars of the Galway team in the 1970s was two-time All-Star Johnny Hughes. Although he does not have the All-Ireland medal his great talent deserved, he has many happy memories from his time with Galway and some hair-raising experiences. When the Galway team were training in Tuam, there would always be players looking for shampoo afterwards. Johnny always had shampoo, but Tomás Tierney and Tommy Joe Gilmore were always swiping some off him. Johnny was working for a chemical company at the time who manufactured a light oil which looked like Clinic shampoo. He poured some of it into an empty bottle of shampoo which he left outside his shower in the dressing room. He hid a bottle of shampoo in his bag and he went into the shower with some of it in his hand. A few seconds later, he saw Tierney's foot coming over and taking the bottle of shampoo, but Hughes didn't let on to see him. Tierney rubbed it into his hair and passed it on to Tommy Joe. A few minutes later, all hell broke loose. The incident stopped them from stealing Johnny's shampoo for a long time after that.

SALMON LEAP

In the early 1990s, Connacht footballers were invariably free in August and September and many took the route of weekend tourist for trans-Atlantic games.

Before their glory days of 1998, Galway were knocked out early in the Championship one year and a famous man in the GAA in New York, Jackie Salmon, rang Val Daly and asked him to travel over to line out for Connemara Gaels the following Sunday and to bring a couple of other good players with him. Daly rang around and persuaded former Galway full-forward Brian O'Donnell to travel with him. Brian had never played in a match in New York. The two lads flew out on the Friday evening and, on the plane, Daly briefed his colleague on how to get through the weekend. He said, 'Now, Brian, they do things differently over there. It's not like at home, so just enjoy the weekend, play the match and don't mind what anyone says. Whatever you do, say nothing.'

The Tribesmen enjoyed the first part of the weekend but the match went less well. At half-time the Connemara Gaels were seven points down. Jackie Salmon gave a team-talk and said, 'Ye're the most disgraceful shower I ever saw. Ye're a disgrace to the Connemara Gaels jersey. As for the big shots from over in Ireland, I'm sorry I brought ye out at all. Daly, you were hopeless and O'Donnell, you were even worse. You didn't even catch one ball.'

O'Donnell forgot Daly's advice and retorted, 'Sure, how could ye play football out there? There wasn't a single blade of grass on the pitch.'

Salmon turned around to him and asked, 'Did you come out here to play football or to graze?'

AT DEATH'S DOOR

A Gaeltacht club in Galway called Míchaél Breathnach had a junior manager and he was trying to round a team for a match. He rang one seventeen-year-old and asked, 'There is a match on Saturday, are you able to play with us?'

The young fella replied, 'No, I am going to Oxegen on Saturday.'

The manager had no idea that Oxegen was Ireland's premier music festival at the time and thought the young lad was going to hospital for some respiratory problem. He said, 'I'm so sorry, look after yourself.'

He rang three or four young lads in the local area and they all told him they were off to Oxegen. He thought there was some epidemic around the local area. Later that night, he was down in the pub giving out yards about the fella who gave him the phone numbers of the young lads and he said, 'Your man gave me a number of lads on their deathbeds.'

DYING WISH

The Longford-Westmeath rivalry is innovative, infectious and addictive for both sets of fans and is one of the most keenly contested in football, as was apparent in the 2007 Leinster Championship. An old Longford fan was dying and when it was obvious that he had very little time left, the local priest, a Westmeath man, was sent for. After the priest administered the last rites, he asked the old man if he had any last wish. He was astounded when the man asked if he could join the Westmeath supporters club. The priest, though, duly pulled out a membership card for the man and helped him to sign his name for the last time. When the priest left, the man's seven stunned sons crowded around the bed and asked their father why he had made this extraordinary request. With practically his dying breath, he said: 'Isn't it better for one of them to die than one of our lads.'

JUST SAY NO

For their part, the Westmeath fans have an assured composition of their own: 'The Longford forward line couldn't strike a match.'

Even more damningly, swelling with emotion and critical reflection, they add: 'Avoid excitement, watch Longford.'

These are just the nice things both sets of fans say about the other.

95

HEFFO'S ARMY

Dublin v Kilkenny

Humility is a virtue in the GAA. If you do not have it naturally, it will be delivered to you.

In the 1970s, when the great Dublin football team travelled down to Kilkenny, they expected it to be a meaningless feature against the county side. When they got to the ground, they were very gratified to see a huge crowd was in attendance to see what was spoken of as the greatest team of all time. The warm-up match was a club minor hurling championship fixture.

When the mighty Heffo's army took the field, their pride took a mighty dent. The ground was virtually empty because the majority of the crowd had gone home as soon as the hurling match was over.

SOMETHING'S COOKING IN CROKE PARK

After Seamus Darby's sensational last-minute winner for Offaly against Kerry in 1982, Mikey Sheehy's goal in 1978 is the most famous ever scored in an All-Ireland final. Paddy Cullen's

359

frantic effort to keep the ball out was memorably described afterwards by the legendary Con Houlihan, who wrote that it was 'like a woman who smells a cake burning'.

WHEN REVENGE IS NOT SWEET

From his days playing for Galway, Kevin Walsh has memories of the tables being turned:

'We were away on a team holiday and Seán O'Domhnaill was messing and pulled down the togs of, let's say, a prominent county board official in full view of everyone. Needless to say, the man in question was not too happy. Later when Seán was sunbathing on the beach the official sneaked up and took the wallet which was lying beside him. When he figured out what was happening, Seán ran after him down the beach. They were not a physical match and Seán was catching up with him, so your man threw the wallet into the ocean. He couldn't understand when Seán started laughing. The wallet belonged to Ja Fallon's wife, and she had asked Seán to mind it while she went for a swim!'

LAST WILL AND TESTAMENT

Bishop Willie Walsh has got to know many fascinating people through his love of hurling, particularly Paddy Duggan, 'the Duggie'. Duggie's whole life was hurling. He was a mentor to a host of teams in Clare. When he became ill, Bishop Walsh went to see him in hospital and Duggan had got the news that day that he only had a short time to live. He said to the bishop, 'I'd like you to do the funeral Mass and make all the arrangements.' The bishop agreed. Then the Duggie said, 'That's fine, Willie. I still believe that we'd have won the county final last year if they'd listened to me at half-time.' As soon as the funeral was arranged, he was straight back to the most important thing in life – hurling!

IT COULD HAPPEN TO A BISHOP

The Duggie was not above misrepresenting Willie Walsh in his days when he was a humble priest. Both were mentors for a juvenile team in Ennis and, in a club match, Willie was stunned when all of a sudden he saw a young lad, Tomás Fogarty, being introduced as a sub on their team. He ran up the sideline to ask the secretary who had given the order to bring him on and he answered, 'Was it not you? The Duggie came up to me and said, "Father Willie wants him in"!'

THE MAN FROM CLARE

As a Clare minor, Ger Loughnane's first introduction to inter-county hurling was under 'the Duggie'. Duggan gave a most amazing speech in the dressing room in Limerick. While whacking a hurley off a table, and as his false teeth did three laps of his mouth, he called on the team to kill and maim the opposition before saying an 'Our Father' and three 'Hail Marys'.

96

THE THREESOME

The Sunday Game

RTÉ has a history of threesomes.

For years its rugby coverage was dominated by the triumvirate of Tom McGurk, George Hook and Brent Pope. What made the dynamic between them so intriguing was that the viewer was never too clear as to whether Tom and George liked each other.

In 2018, as he prepared to present his very last All-Ireland final, Michael Lyster had a final confession: 'I am actually responsible for Joe (Brolly) and Pat (Spillane) ending up being pundits on *The Sunday Game*, so I would like to take this opportunity to apologise to the nation for all the grief and suffering over the last twenty years.'

Pat Spillane also presented *The Sunday Game* nighttime programme. His tenure was not without its bumps:

'My first night in the presenter's chair does not go smoothly. The centrepiece of the programme was the coverage of the National League hurling final. In a new departure, RTÉ were spending a lot of money sending a camera crew out to the venues. After Galway's victory, Marty Morrissey interviewed Eugene Cloonan, Derek Hardiman and Conor Hayes live in Gort. The three Galway men were very subdued and the small crowd behind them were very muted. Marty ended his piece by saying, "The party will continue into the small hours."

'I had the misfortune to say, "What party? I have seen livelier wakes."

'It didn't go down well in Galway. Cyril Farrell texted our panellist, Tomás Mulcahy, to say that the joke went down like a lead balloon. The championship was only a week old and already I had landed myself in trouble. Plus ça change . . .'

YOU DON'T BRING ME FLOWERS

While he was presenter of *The Sunday Game*, Des Cahill enjoyed a big fan base. His wife, though, is not always happy with him. On Valentine's Day she complained that he was lazy because he had not marked the occasion for her. She texted him from work: 'Three of the girls in the office got flowers. They are absolutely gorgeous.'

Unfazed, Des replied: 'That's probably why they got the flowers so.'

SCHOOL REUNION

Des Cahill went to visit his old school. He asked the students if anyone could give him an example of a 'tragedy'. One boy stood up and offered the suggestion that, 'If my best friend who lives next door was playing in the street when a car came along and killed him, that would be a tragedy.'

'No,' Des said. 'That would be an ACCIDENT.'

Another boy raised his hand. 'If a school bus carrying fifty children drove off a cliff, killing everybody involved . . . that would be a tragedy.'

'I'm afraid not,' explained Des. 'That is what we would call a GREAT LOSS.'

The room was silent; none of the other children volunteered.

'What?' asked Des. 'Is there no one here who can give me an example of a tragedy?'

Finally, a boy in the back raised his hand. In a timid voice, he spoke: 'If an airplane carrying you and *The Sunday Game* team were blown up by a bomb, that would be a tragedy.'

'Wonderful.' Des beamed. 'Marvellous. And can you tell me why that would be a tragedy?'

'Well,' said the boy, 'because it wouldn't be an accident, and it certainly would be no great loss.'

THE LONG WALK TO FREEDOM

In 1990 Nelson Mandela was freed from his years in captivity. The first thing he allegedly said after he was released was, 'Have Kildare found a decent forward since I was thrown into that bloody place?'

WRONG CALL

Mick O'Dwyer brought the glory days back to Kildare, taking them to a Leinster title after a forty-two-year-gap. The 2000 Leinster final is seared in Pat Spillane's memory:

'One of the games I got into most serious trouble for as an analyst came in 2000. It was the day of the Leinster senior football replay. Dublin led by 0–11 to 0–5 at half-time and had swept aside the Kildare challenge in the second quarter, scoring seven points without reply, playing some thrilling football. Kildare brought on two subs at half-time, two of their "imports", Karl O'Dwyer and Brian Murphy. I was in jocose mood and said Karl couldn't get on the Kerry team and Brian wouldn't have got on the Cork junior team. Within ninety seconds of the re-start, the picture had changed dramatically as Kildare got a two-goal blitz and Dublin collapsed and only scored a single point in the second half. Yet again, I was left looking silly and fully expected to eat humble pie but there was much more in store.

'All hell broke loose. To my mind, it was completely over the top. I was making just a few tongue-in-cheek observations, as is my wont, and had not intended to be taken too seriously, but it seemed to be the end of the world to people in Kildare. There was a huge sign outside Monasterevin to the effect that I was a goat. I was driving through Kildare for the next few weeks on wet Monday mornings with sunglasses on in case anyone recognised me. It was just ridiculous.

'The most sinister reaction was apparent when I was shown a letter in RTÉ from one of the most influential GAA officials in Kildare demanding that an apology would be issued and that I would be dropped as an analyst by RTÉ. If not, he would ensure that the GAA would not renew their contract with RTÉ. As the contract negotiations for the right to the GAA games were imminent, the powers that be in RTÉ were genuinely very worried about this threat.

'When all the vitriol had been finished, I thought of Brendan Behan's dictum, "All publicity is good, except an obituary notice."'

BLIND DATE

The most popular joke in Kildare at the time was that when Spillane was a young man, his friend, Joe, set him up on a blind date with a young lady-friend of his. But Spillane was a little worried about going out with someone he had never seen before. 'What do I do if she's really unattractive? I'll be stuck with her all night.'

'Don't worry,' Joe said, 'just go up to her and meet her first. If you like what you see, then everything goes as planned. If you don't just shout "Aaaaaauuuuuuggggghhhh!" and fake an asthma attack.'

So that night, Spillane knocked at the girl's door and when she came out, he was awestruck at how attractive and sexy she was. He was about to speak when the girl suddenly shouts, 'Aaaaaaauuuuuuggggghhh!'

SCROOGE-D

While he worked on *The Sunday Game*, some of the crew thought Pat Spillane was a little stingy. At his last Christmas party Spillane was determined to prove them wrong. He stood up and announced boldly to the entire group: 'I'm going to buy you a beer.'

Turns out they wanted one each.

97

FLOAT LIKE A BUTTERFLY, STING LIKE A BEE

Ali Lights up Croke Park

Of course, one of Ireland's biggest ever sporting occasions was held in GAA Headquarters. On 19 July 1972 it took Muhammad Ali eleven rounds to defeat an ex-convict from Detroit, Al 'Blue' Lewis, at Croke Park. The fight itself was unremarkable but it was a wonderful occasion, particularly after Ali announced that his maternal great-grandfather, Abe Grady, had emigrated from County Clare over a century before.

ALL RIGHT JACK

As part of the build-up to the fight, Ali met the Taoiseach, Jack Lynch, who informed the pugilist that despite his busy schedule he hoped to make it to the fight the following Wednesday. Ali replied, 'Since you're a busy man, I guess I'll get it over with quickly.'

'Ah sure, that would spoil it.'

'Well, in that case, I'll let Lewis stay in the ring for more than one round.'

'I might get in there for a few rounds myself and keep things going,' said Jack.

TALES OF THE UNEXPECTED

For Ali, his Irish adventure was a bit of a culture shock. On his second day in the country, he rang his publicist, Harold Conrad: 'Hey, Hal?' said Ali. 'Where are all the black people in this country?'

'Ali,' replied Conrad, 'there aren't any.'

THEOLOGICALLY SPEAKING

Ali's press conferences before the fight were never less than memorable. At one point he caught the journalists on the hop when out of the blue he asked, 'What were the last words the Lord uttered at the Last Supper?'

There was silence, as the hacks present were not known for their theological expertise. Ali answered his own question: 'Let every man pick up his own cheque.'

REBRANDING

Although the fight itself did not live up to the frenzied anticipation it created, one fan was heard to remark, 'After this performance, all we can do is rename the place Muhammad Alley.'

98

NO PAT ON THE BACK

Pat Delaney Leaves His Mark

In his playing days, Ger Loughnane witnessed a scene where a fire-and-brimstone speech produced a more robust response than had been envisaged:

'I went on an All-Star trip to America in 1978. We were hammered by about fourteen points by Cork in the opening match in Boston. The Cork half-back line was absolutely outstanding. After the match, we were told by the management that we were a "disgrace" and unless we upped our performance in the next match in San Francisco, there would be "severe repercussions".

'Pat Hartigan was team captain and he gave a speech in the dressing room before the second game. He threw his jersey on the floor in the middle of the dressing room and said, "Anyone not prepared to die for the jersey, throw it in there and get out of here now."

'One of our players was, shall we say, a little "impetuous". He was marking Denis Coughlan. The first ball that came into

369

him, Pat let fly and struck Coughlan on the side of the head and split it open.

'He then moved into the centre and the next ball that came his way he let fly, aiming for Johnny Crowley. He missed Crowley and struck his own man, Tony Doran. The game was only five minutes old, and he had sent two men to hospital!

'There was an immediate cry: "Get that mad man off." He was substituted immediately. He was very disappointed afterwards but not in the way you might expect.

'He said, "What harm but if they had just left me on another minute or two it would have been great. I was just going to move on Dermot McCurtin."

'He had taken it on himself to take out the entire Cork half-back line!'

SURFING USA

On the All-Star trips, romance often flourished as Irish GAA stars were highly pursued by misty-eyed Irish Americans hoping their 'cailín' would get married to one of the sport heroes from the old sod. However, two of the less-worldly All-Stars on the quest for a holiday romance got one hell of a shock when they discovered that they had arranged a double date with two crossdressers!

To compound their embarrassment, the two lads had been heard using very suggestive chat-up lines to their dates. The first had said, 'You know what, I'd look good on you.'

The second was even more expansive: 'Your eyes are like spanners. Every time you look at me, my nuts tighten.'

Perhaps these tactics were a response to their failure the previous night doing the rounds of a nightclub when they had struck a blank using the line, 'Tog out. You're selected.'

RISING TEMPERATURES

Fame can be a mixed blessing. One of the inevitable products of success is that there is increased interest in celebrities' private lives. GAA players are not insulated from this trend and, from time to time, suffer the slings and arrows of the rumour mill. Generally, the bigger the name, the more outrageous the rumour.

After their second All-Ireland in 1997, a few of the Clare players became the subject of salacious gossip. Even before the rumour-monger's paradise that is social media, they were by no means the first or last GAA players to suffer in this way and, as Ger Loughnane acknowledges, things came to a head when Clare played Waterford in the 1998 Munster final:

'When the players came back into the dressing room, I had never seen them so agitated and I asked what was wrong. They were fuming.

'One of the rumours doing the rounds at the time was that one of our players was beating his wife. Anyone who knows anything about his character would have known immediately how scurrilous and far off the mark it was and wouldn't have entertained it for a second. One of the Waterford players had shouted at the player in question, across the pitch, that he was a wife-beater. A lot of our players heard it. The player himself said nothing but it was the other players who were incensed. If anything triggered our players' huge response the following day it was that.'

If the entire Clare squad were galvanised by the wife-beating comments, Loughnane was livid with the poor showing of his team. Understanding the ambushes of the mind his team had capitulated to, he was determined to reverse the pattern in the replay. His eyes drove through his players like two steel nails.

'On the bus back all I was thinking of was our performance – which was brutal. At training on Tuesday night, the riot act was read! Mike O'Halloran was missing that night and when he came back the next evening he said, "I hear the paint was falling off the goalposts!"'

PUNCH OFF

For those of us of a certain age, the defining image of the Cork-Kerry rivalry saw Páidí Ó Sé knocking Dinny Allen on to the seat of his pants in the 1975 Munster final after Allen had thrown the first punch. Then came a moment of classic comedy when the referee, running in to admonish the two bold boys, slipped on the wet ground. To add to the sense of incredulity, neither player was sent off.

99

RIDDLE ME THIS

The Top GAA Riddles

Q. How many Cavan footballers does it take to change a lightbulb?

A. Are you paying with Visa or American Express?
   Monaghan fan

Q. What do Kerry footballers use for contraception?

A. Their personalities.
   Cork fan

Q: What's the difference between Paddy Cullen and a turnstile?

A: A turnstile only lets in one at a time.
   Kerry fan after Cullen conceded five goals in the 1978 All-Ireland final.

Q. What's the difference between Paddy Cullen and Cinderella?

A: At least Cinderella got to the ball.

Q: What's the difference between Philly McMahon and Kylie Minogue?

A: Philly marked tighter than Kylie's famous hotpants.

Q: What do Mayo footballers have in common with a Wonderbra?

A: Lots of support but no cup.

Q: What do you say to a Laois man in Croke Park on All-Ireland final day?

A: Two packets of crisps, please.

Q. Why did Kevin McStay climb the Eiffel tower?

A. He was looking for forwards.

Q: Who were the last two Westmeath men to play midfield in the All-Ireland final?

A: Foster and Allen.

Q: How many intelligent Cork fans does it take to screw a lightbulb?

A: Both of them.

Q. What's the difference between God and Pat Spillane?

A. God doesn't think he's Pat Spillane.

Q: What was the signature tune of the Meath team of the late 1980s?

A: You will never walk again.

Q: When do you know a Meath player is feeling generous?

A: He wears iodine on his studs.

Q: What happened when David Clifford swallowed the Christmas decorations?

A: He got tinselitis.

Q: What's the difference between the Pope and Sam Maguire?

A: The Pope has come to Mayo more often than Sam Maguire since 1951.

Q: What's the difference between the Fermanagh team and a KitKat?

A: A KitKat has more silver.

Q: What is the difference between tennis players and the Tyrone hurlers?

A: Sometimes tennis players put the ball in the net.

Q: 'Mick, why didn't you close your curtains and turn off the light when you were making love to your wife, as all the neighbours were laughing at you last night?'

A: 'Well,' says Mick, 'the last laugh is on them because I wasn't even at home last night, I was training with Kerry.'

Q: Carlow fan: 'What's the biggest joke I know?'

A: The Kilkenny footballers.

Q: What's the nicest thing Monaghan fans say about Cavan football?

A: A Monaghan fan has never said a nice thing about Cavan football.

100

A STAR IS BORN

The Man With the Golden Voice

True glory consists in doing what deserves to be written,
In writing what deserves to be read,
And in living as to make the world happier
And better for our living it.

PLINY THE ELDER

This year we lost an icon in sports broadcasting with the passing of the BBC's John Motson. Motty and his famous sheepskin coat left a rich legacy of gems such as:

Brazil – they're so good it's like they are running around the pitch playing with themselves.

Middlesbrough are withdrawing Maccarone the Italian, Németh the Slovakian, and Stockdale . . . the right-back.

Northern Ireland are ten minutes away from their finest victory. There's fifteen minutes to go here.

The Czech Republic are coming from behind in more than one way now.

Gary Lineker has now scored thirty-seven goals. That is precisely twice as many as last year.

What a time to score . . . Twenty-seven minutes!

The game is balanced in Arsenal's favour.

The referee is wearing the same yellow-coloured top as the Slovakian goalkeeper. I'd have thought the UEFA official would have spotted that – but perhaps he's been deafened by the noise of this crowd.

I've lost count of how many chances Helsingborg have had. It's at least five.

And I suppose Spurs are nearer to being out of the FA Cup now than any other time since the first half of this season, when they weren't ever in it anyway.

It's so different from the scenes in 1872, at the Cup Final none of us can remember.

The goals made such a difference to the way this game went.

Oh, that's good running on the run.

The match has become quite unpredictable, but it still looks as though Arsenal will win the cup.

A NATIONAL TREASURE

Closer to home, Mícheál Ó Muircheartaigh carved out a unique place in the affections of Irish sport lovers over the last sixty years. The most mundane of matches came alive in his commentary. Everything he said into his microphone was informed by a passion that was as basic to him as breathing. His commentaries were famous for the richness of their texture, abounding with references that delight and surprise.

His story is the broadcasting equivalent of *Roy of the Rovers*. He was only eighteen, training to be a teacher, and still adjusting to life in Dublin, when a friend saw a notice on the college noticeboard for part-time Irish-speaking commentators. The auditions were at Croke Park, a club game was in progress, and each applicant was given a five-minute slot – an opportunity to sort out the real thing from the pretenders:

'A group of us went – we went with the idea that it would be great fun, we'd be in Croke Park, a place we revered, and, most importantly, we knew we would get in for free. It was an adventure.

'They had to pick somebody and they picked me. It is still a very vivid memory. Naturally, none of us knew any of the players, but I knew one who managed to go to school in Dingle, Teddy Hurley, and another player in midfield. I just talked away at random and people I knew featured very prominently, even though they were not on the scene of the action at all!

'I then moved into the big-money league and was offered a massive contract – all of £6! The important thing, though, is that I still enjoyed it as much at the end as I did then.'

In his broadcasting career Mícheál has found evidence that if horse racing is the sport of kings, greyhound racing is the sport of princes. One of his coups was to become the first person to interview a British Royal, Prince Edward, on RTÉ radio. As joint owner of Druid's Johnno, Prince Edward was celebrating his semi-final victory in the English Greyhound Derby at Wimbledon. Mícheál stepped up and asked in his velvety soft tones, as only he can, 'Now tell me, Prince . . .'

Few people have done more to promote the whirr of the flying sliotar and the thrilling sound of ash against ash than the voice from Dingle who makes GAA fans tingle, Mícheál. To shamelessly steal from Patrick Kavanagh: among his earthiest words the angels stray.

SIMPLY THE BLESSED

Mícheál has left an indelible mark on the GAA landscape with a series of classic comments. This is my top baker's dozen of his gems:

1. I see John O'Donnell dispensing water on the sideline. Tipperary, sponsored by a water company. Cork, sponsored by a tae company. I wonder will they meet later for afternoon tae?
2. He kicks the ball lan san aer, could've been a goal, could've been a point . . . it went wide.
3. Colin Corkery on the 45 lets go with the right boot. It's over the bar. This man shouldn't be playing football. He's made an almost Lazarus-like recovery. Lazarus was a great man, but he couldn't kick points like Colin Corkery.
4. Stephen Byrne with the puck-out for Offaly . . . Stephen, one of twelve . . . all but one are here today. The one that's missing is Mary, she's at home minding the house . . . and the ball is dropping I lar na bpairce . . .'
5. Pat Fox has it on his hurl and is motoring well now . . . but here comes Joe Rabbitte hot on his tail . . . I've seen it all now, a rabbit chasing a fox around Croke Park.

6. Pat Fox out to the 40 and grabs the sliotar . . . I bought a dog from his father last week, sprints for goal . . . the dog ran a great race last Tuesday in Limerick . . . Fox to the 21, fires a shot, goes wide and left . . . and the dog lost as well.

7. Danny 'The Yank' Culloty. He came down from the mountains and hasn't he done well?

8. Teddy looks at the ball, the ball looks at Teddy.

9. In the first half they played with the wind. In the second half they played with the ball.

10. 1–5 to 0–8 – well from Lapland to the Antarctic, that's level scores in any man's language.

11. I saw a few Sligo people at Mass in Gardiner Street this morning and the omens seem to be good for them. The priest was wearing the same colours as the Sligo jersey! Forty yards out on the Hogan stand side of the field, Ciarán Whelan goes on a rampage, it's a goal. So much for religion.

12. . . . and Brian Dooher is down injured. And while he is down, I'll tell ye a little story. I was in Times Square in New York last week, and I was missing the Championship back home and I said, 'I suppose ye wouldn't have *The Kerryman*, would ye?' To which the Egyptian behind the counter turned to me he said, 'Do you want the North Kerry edition or the South Kerry edition?' . . . He had both . . . so I bought both. Dooher is back on his feet.

13. David Beggy will be able to fly back to Scotland without an airplane, he'll be so high after this.

THE LAST WORD

To quote Mr Broccoli, as Marty Whelan calls him, better known as Andrea Bocelli, it is: time to say goodbye.

Remember one thing.

Those who laugh . . . LAST.

101

THE FAITHFUL DEPARTED

Canon O'Brien's First Funeral

Cork has given the GAA a number of national treasures like Christy Ring, Jack Lynch and Jimmy Barry-Murphy. In the world of religion it has given a national treasure in the person of Michael O'Brien.

The late Canon O'Brien remains a legend of Cork hurling. He led the county to All-Ireland titles in 1984 and again in 1990. He shared some brilliant stories with me about the great and the good of hurling with astonishing candour and in more colourful language than I had ever heard from a man of the cloth. Unfortunately, my solicitor tells me that I can't share any of them because of libel laws. The only story they cleared me to relate was this one – his account of attending his first funeral.

'The richly carpeted room was unlike anything I had ever seen. Beautiful antiques were placed all around it. In the centre was an ornately carved table and the walls were covered in murals, conspicuous among them one of Noah's Ark. It was strange that my first visit to the canon's parlour was the day of his funeral. I was almost overcome with grief not by the occasion but because I had been told my services weren't needed as an altar boy. A pound note gone down the drain.

'The canon's funeral Mass was an awesome, if chaotic, sight. The spectacle of a bishop and a multitude of priests, crammed together like bees in a hive behind the altar, made a lasting impression on the faithful. Never have so few stood in so little for so long. One of the priests had forgotten his vestments. As he was only five-feet-one, an old, frilly white alb was found for him. He looked like a cross between an altar boy and Tom Thumb.

'The first problem was caused by the microphone. It seemed to have taken on a life of its own, emitting various crackling sounds at the most solemn moments. Such was the disturbance that one of the priests turned it off. This brought a hazard of its own. The celebrants had to rely on vocal projection. While this was fine for the bishop, it was less so for Monsignor Rodgers who always spoke as if he was suffering from a bout of tonsillitis. Those priests whose vocal ranges were somewhere in between seemed to think that they were obliged to break the sound barrier by shouting, rather than reciting, their modest contribution to the liturgical celebration.

'The second problem was that everybody assumed that somebody else was organising the ceremony, so that nobody knew who was doing what or what was supposed to be happening. A priest would stand up to intone some prayer and just as abruptly sit down on discovering that at least one other colleague had beaten him to it. There were protracted pauses as everybody looked to the bishop to see what would happen.

'Of course there was the choir. For reasons best known to himself the late canon had taken a particular aversion to the choir, with the result that they were normally only to be heard on Midnight Mass and Christmas Day. In light of the musical talent which was evident on those occasions, the canon's decision to employ their services so sparingly looked more and more judicious. Neither the organ nor the organist were in the first flush of youth nor even in the second. The combination of two idiosyncratic performances made for interesting – if not elegant – listening. The choir predictably lived down to expectations. Even by their own standards they were abysmal. The problem was exacerbated by the fact that the assembled clergy seemed to have formed a rival choral group, apparently singing the same hymns at a different speed to a different arrangement and musical notation.

'The last straw was the prayers of the faithful, which Monsignor Rodgers had arranged beforehand. Gerry "The Hop" McCarthy, the canon's right-hand man in the parish, had been asked to say one of the prayers as a recognition of his loyal service and friendship to our late pastor. In a trembling voice he mumbled something indistinguishable – even to those in the front row. He gained confidence though with each word – only to make an embarrassing *faux pas* just when his voice was clearly audible – by praying for the canon's "immorality" rather than "immortality".'

ACKNOWLEDGEMENTS

My special thanks to the great Dermot Earley for writing the foreword.

I also wish to express my gratitude to Joe Brolly, Iggy Clarke, Shane Curran, Marty Morrissey, John Mullane, Katie Power and Donie Shine for their help.

My profound thanks to the many players, past and present, who generously shared their stories and thoughts with me and who made this book possible.

Thanks to Simon Hess, Campbell Brown, and all at Black & White Publishing for their help.

Gareth O'Callaghan lights up Saturday morning for me with his wonderful show. More importantly, he has helped me to discover that if you have one true friend you have more than your share.

Fr Brian Darcy has been a great supporter of my books. His positive manner reminds me to keep my face always toward the sunshine because in that way the shadows will fall behind me.

Dave O'Connell embodies the best of the West. I am deeply appreciative for his practical help in promoting my books.

My profound thanks to Shannonside's Kevin McDermott for his ongoing support.

I am grateful for the assistance of Midwest Radio's Michael D. McAndrew with my books.

My grateful thanks to Ireland's funniest man, Killian Sundermann, for his practical support.

Particular thanks to the acclaimed television actor Helmut Sundermann, Germany's answer to Tom Cruise, except he is much taller.